Students with Mild Disabilities in General Education Settings

A Guide for Special Educators

Ada L. Vallecorsa
University of North Carolina at Greensboro

Laurie U. deBettencourt
University of Virginia

Naomi Zigmond
University of Pittsburgh

Merrill
an imprint of Prentice Hall
Upper Saddle River, New Jersey   *Columbus, Ohio*

Library of Congress Cataloging-in-Publication Data
Vallecorsa, Ada
Students with mild disabilities in general education settings : a guide for special educators/Ada L. Vallecorsa, Laurie U. deBettencourt, Naomi Zigmond.
p. cm.
Includes bibliographical references (p.) and index.
ISBN 0-02-422371-9
1. Learning disabled children—Education—United States. 2. Problem children—Education—United States. 3. Handicapped children—Education—United States. 4. Mainstreaming in education—United States. I. DeBettencourt, Laurie Ungerleider. II. Zigmond, Naomi. III. Title
LC4705.V35 2000
371.92′6—dc21 98-33186
CIP

Cover art: Super Stock
Editor: Ann Castel Davis
Developmental Editor: Gianna M. Marsella
Production Editor: Sheryl Glicker Langner
Photo Coordinator: Nancy Ritz
Design Coordinator: Diane C. Lorenzo
Text Designer: Pagination
Cover Designer: Mark Shumaker
Production Manager: Laura Messerly
Electronic Text Management: Marilyn Wilson Phelps, Karen L. Bretz, Melanie King
Director of Marketing: Kevin Flanagan
Marketing Manager: Meghan McCauley
Marketing Coordinator: Krista Groshong

This book was set in Novarese and Humanist 521 by Prentice Hall Publishing and was printed and bound by R. R. Donnelley & Sons Company. The cover was printed by Phoenix Color Corp.

Photo credits: pp. 3, 6, 25, 30, 55, 72, 76, 80, 93, 119, 162, 172, 179, 193, 215, 247 by Anthony Magnacca/Merrill; p. 7 by The White House Photo Office; pp. 16, 36 by Scott Cunningham/Merrill; pp. 44, 97, 105, 122, 145, 156, 208, 212, 238 by Anne Vega/Merrill; pp. 138, 228 by Barbara Schwartz/Merrill; p. 223 by Todd Yarrington/Merrill; p. 249 by KD Studios/Merrill; p. 256 by David Napravik/Merrill.

Printed in the United States of America

10 9 8 7 6 5 4 3 2 1

ISBN: 0-02-422371-9

Prentice-Hall International (UK) Limited, *London*
Prentice-Hall of Australia Pty. Limited, *Sydney*
Prentice-Hall of Canada, Inc., *Toronto*
Prentice-Hall Hispanoamericana, S. A., *Mexico*
Prentice-Hall of India Private Limited, *New Delhi*
Prentice-Hall of Japan, Inc., *Tokyo*
Prentice-Hall (Singapore) Pte. Ltd., *Singapore*
Editora Prentice-Hall do Brasil, Ltda., *Rio de Janeiro*

To the earth angels who saved my life and helped me over the hump so I could finish this project—Rita Rice Ledford, Elena Nazario, and Drs. Helperin, Hopper, Grandfortuna, Burney, and Kinard. Thank you, thank you, thank you.

A.L.V.

To my family, Dan, Justin, and Megan, for understanding my absences, and to my parents, Art and Eleanor, for always believing in me.

L. U. deB.

To Michael, who's always there even when he's not.

N.Z.

PREFACE

This text is for teachers of students with mild disabilities, or prospective teachers of students with mild disabilities, who will be delivering special education in general education classrooms. In designing this text, we made several assumptions.

First, students with special educational needs, particularly those with mild disabilities, will increasingly receive part, and in many cases all, of their education in inclusive settings. It is not that interventions to address their individual needs will no longer be provided, but rather that the provision of such services in separate special education settings will decline.

Second, this shift creates a difficult situation for many special educators, because they are being asked to carry out their professional responsibilities in ways and in settings that are quite new for them and for which they may lack training and experience. For example, most special education preparation programs include methods courses that place considerable emphasis on academic, behavioral, and social skill interventions that are easily implemented and managed in small group or individual teaching contexts. Little attention, however, is typically placed in these courses on teaching prospective special educators how to manage these interventions in a large group setting such as a general education classroom. In short, prospective special education teachers need to learn how to do the "business of special education" in a new arena.

Third, because special educators cannot be in every general education classroom all day, every day, there is a pressing need for them to know how to teach others (particularly general education teachers) how to implement appropriate interventions for special students. That is, they need to learn how to work collaboratively with colleagues. While teacher preparation programs have been addressing this third concern in recent years, many training programs tend to focus heavily on processes and models of collaboration and consultation and place less emphasis on other important and practical concerns such as how to analyze another teacher's instructional environment, or how to determine the critical elements of a classroom and of instructional tasks that should be considered in designing appropriate interventions or accommodations, or finally, how to evaluate and alter another teacher's classroom organization and management strategies so that individualized instruction is supported in a group setting.

These issues and concerns are central to this text. It focuses on how special educators can offer direct and indirect services in mainstream environments to address the range of learning and behavioral problems that are typical of students with mild disabilities. It teaches special educators how to apply effective assessment, instructional, and evaluation strategies to that setting, and shows them how to develop and implement programs in collaboration with general education class teachers. Several features distinguish this text from others:

1. The content of the text is grounded in methods that have been validated by research but are presented in a style that can be understood by teachers.
2. Its noncategorical orientation emphasizes approaches that are effective with a wide range of students with learning and behavior problems.
3. It presents a wealth of teaching strategies that are effective for general education classrooms and that can be implemented by either the special education teacher or the general education teacher.
4. Attention is paid to helping special education teachers work in collaborative and consultative roles.
5. Attention is given to the unique needs of secondary school age students with mild disabilities.
6. Each chapter begins with a brief case study; questions related to that case study are woven throughout the chapter to help students apply the content. Each chapter also includes a set of objectives and a listing of key words; these key words appear in bold type in the text for easy access by the students. Each chapter ends with suggested follow-up activities.

ACKNOWLEDGMENTS

Preparation of a text can never be accomplished by the authors alone. In the case of what we used to call "our little book," there are many individuals, in each of our three institutions, who have inspired, supported, and assisted. Ada wishes to acknowledge the contributions of Dana Bishop, administrative assistant, and Kathy Kirkpatrick, doctoral student, both at the University of North Carolina, Greensboro; Laurie thanks all the students in her clinic who inspire her with their tenacity, and all the teachers she comes into contact with for sharing with her their trials and tribulations; Naomi is grateful to the preservice students in teacher education at the University of Pittsburgh whose eagerness to learn how to serve students with disabilities in general education classrooms provided a context for this work. All three authors gratefully acknowledge the support and encouragement we received from our editors at Prentice Hall: Ann Castel Davis, senior editor, who believed enough in this project to give us a contract; Gianna M. Marsella, developmental editor, without whose continued enthusiasm and persistent prodding this book might never have been completed; Sheryl Langner, production editor; and Key Metts, copy editor.

We also wish to thank the following reviewers for their valuable input and suggestions: Linda K. Elksnin, The Citadel (SC); Judith J. Ivarie, Eastern Illinois University; Linda D. McCrea, Grand Valley State University (MI); Mark P. Mostert, Moorhead State University; Robert W. Ortiz, New Mexico State University; Susan C. Stewart, University of West Florida; and Qaisar Sultana, Eastern Kentucky University.

CONTENTS

PART I
SPECIAL EDUCATION SERVICE DELIVERY OPTIONS 1

Chapter 1
HISTORICAL ROOTS 2

Chapter 2
CHARACTERISTICS AND VARIATIONS OF IN-CLASS MODELS 24

PART II
IMPLEMENTING EFFECTIVE IN-CLASS PROGRAMS 53

Chapter 3
APPROACHES TO COLLABORATION/CONSULTATION 54

Chapter 4
APPROACHES TO EFFECTIVE COLLABORATIVE TEACHING OR CO-TEACHING 84

Chapter 9
BEHAVIOR MANAGEMENT STRATEGIES 246

PART I

SPECIAL EDUCATION SERVICE DELIVERY OPTIONS

CHAPTER 1 HISTORICAL ROOTS

KEY WORDS

mild disabilities
Fourteenth Amendment
PL 94-142
zero reject
nondiscriminatory assessment
procedural due process
individualized educational program
least-restrictive environment
parental participation
IDEA
self-contained
continuum of service delivery options
resource rooms
regular education initiative

OBJECTIVES

After reading this chapter, the student should be able to:

1. describe the major federal legislation that governs the education of children with disabilities.
2. describe the continuum of service delivery options in special education for students with mild disabilities.
3. provide a rationale for educating students with disabilities in general education classrooms.
4. describe a rationale for a shared responsibility for education of students with disabilities among general and special education teachers.

Dot Hill is a career teacher who is looking forward to her retirement. She has seen much in her 30 years as a special education teacher. Her first classroom was in the old book room in the basement of the school. There were no windows and ventilation was nonexistent. She and her students were crammed elbow to elbow as she tried hard to educate them with the few materials she had been given. Ms. Hill was in charge of every aspect of her students' education from reading to Four Square. Many of her students were poor and many had trouble with the English language. They were perceived as different and were not allowed to attend any classes with the other students in school. Ms. Hill felt as isolated as her students. But as frustrating as her job was, she felt lucky to have a job at all. She lived in fear of her program being cut due to budget constraints.

Then changes began to take place. Parents sued the school system to make sure their children were treated fairly. Laws were enacted to ensure special children an education, and Ms. Hill began to feel some sense of job security. As more laws were enacted, she felt the effect on her class. Her classroom was moved from the basement book room to a real classroom on the first floor. The population of students she served changed also. But the biggest change came as her students were allowed to attend classes with non-disabled students. Ms. Hill began to see most of her students for only one or two periods each day; they spent the rest of their day in the general education classroom with their peers.

Now, as Ms. Hill prepares to retire, more changes are taking place. Her students are more likely to stay in the regular classroom all day while she helps their general educator teach. Oh, some children still come to her for a class or two, and some she only sees once or twice a week, but most of her students are being included with their peers. Inclusion has been a difficult adjustment, but Ms. Hill thinks that if she were not retiring, she would enjoy the process.

In the past decade, it has become increasingly commonplace for special and general education teachers to share responsibility for educating children with disabilities in general classroom settings. Through consultation, collaboration, and co-teaching, the special educator and the general educator work together to adapt the environment, the curriculum, the instructional materials, the teaching strategy, and/or the assessment procedures to accommodate the needs of both the student(s) with disabilities and all the other students in the class. How to do that is the subject of this book.

The purpose of this chapter is to provide some important background information. First we will recap, briefly, the history of public education for students with disabilities. Our focus in this history, and throughout this book, will be on students with **mild disabilities**. These include students who are labeled as learning disabled, emotionally/behaviorally disordered, and mildly mentally retarded; they constitute, by far, the majority of students served in special education. Then, we will review the continuum of service delivery options for students with mild disabilities. Finally, we will describe the social and political forces which have shaped the policy of educating students with mild disabilities in general education settings, the policy of inclusion.

ENSURING EDUCATIONAL SERVICES TO STUDENTS WITH DISABILITIES

THE EARLY YEARS

Children with disabilities have not always been welcome in public schools, let alone in general education classrooms. Until 1975, when Congress passed the Education of All Handicapped Children Act (PL 94-142), only a few states required that any educational services at all be provided to students with disabilities. In many school districts, students who did not meet "minimum standards" were simply turned away. Parents of children with severe mental retardation, mental illness, or physical disabilities had three choices: they could keep their children at home, place them in expensive, private residential facilities, or consign them to free, large, public, custodial institutions. None of these choices was satisfactory.

Of course, some public school systems did design special programs for students with mild to moderate disabilities who had been admitted to school. These programs had two purposes: The first was to relieve general education teachers of children who were a burden because their learning and behavior deviated significantly from that expected of students in the public schools. The second was to protect and nurture students who were vulnerable to failure in schoolwork and to ridicule from classmates. The predominant educational strategy was to organize special programs that were isolated from the general education classroom; students assigned to them spent the entire school day in separate classes, often in separate school buildings.

With the introduction of intelligence testing in the early 20th century, most of the children assigned to these special programs were labeled "mildly retarded" or educable mentally retarded (EMR). Some state legislatures (e.g., New Jersey, New York, Massachusetts) *required* school districts to provide educational services for EMR students although not for students with more severe disabilities. The majority of states, however, enacted only permissive legislation which allowed, but did not require, school districts to spend the extra money needed to provide a special education for students with even mild to moderate special needs.

Between 1925 and 1950, children labeled as slow or troublesome were assigned by school personnel to separate, self-contained, special education classrooms. Increasingly, these included children from minority groups, children whose first language was not English, and children of poverty, all of whom were labeled EMR and removed from the general education classroom. The curriculum in these special education classrooms was essentially nonacademic, focusing on social development and the skills needed for finding and holding routine, low-skill jobs. By the mid-1950s, special education classrooms were not only overcrowded, they were consigned to the least desirable spaces in school buildings: basements, storage rooms, and boiler rooms. Furthermore, they were rapidly becoming custodial centers that protected those with disabilities from society, and society from those with disabilities.

Not all students with learning and behavior problems were assigned to these special education centers. In schools where programs were full, or that did not have spe-

Inclusion of students with diverse backgrounds in public school classrooms has many benefits

cial education services, students with learning and behavior problems usually remained in the regular classroom and received no special treatment. If their deportment in class exceeded the teacher's tolerance for misbehavior, they were labeled "troublemakers" or "disciplinary problems" and eventually suspended or expelled from school. If they did not make satisfactory grades, they were termed "slow learners" or "failures," and after repeating several grades, were encouraged to drop out.

AN IMPETUS FOR CHANGE

A shift in philosophy about educating students with special needs can be traced to *Brown vs. Board of Education* (1954), which challenged the practice of segregating students according to race. In its ruling, the U.S. Supreme Court declared that education must be made available to all children on equal terms. Although the court did not mention students with disabilities, the Brown decision began a period of intense questioning and reappraisal among parents of children with disabilities who wondered why the same principle of equal access to education did not apply to their children, as well. Numerous court cases were initiated in the 1960s and 1970s by parents and advocacy groups dissatisfied with a public education system that denied some children with disabilities access to school and placed others in severely segregated educational settings. The arguments in these court cases were based on the **Fourteenth Amendment** to the Constitution, which provides that no state shall deny any person within its jurisdiction the equal protection of the law and that no state shall deprive any person of life, liberty, or property without due process of law. When successful, these court cases opened school doors to students with disabilities within specific jurisdictions, but these court actions did not fundamentally change the sense of obligation of state education agencies or school districts to provide appropriate educational opportunities for students with disabilities.

Then Congress stepped in. In 1966, Congressional hearings revealed that many children with disabilities were still being excluded from school or were sitting idly in regular classes until they were old enough to drop out. In response, Congress enacted legislation (*Elementary and Secondary Education Act*, amended by PL 89-750) that authorized direct grants to states for initiation, expansion, and improvement of special education programs. Things improved, but not by much.

In 1974, Congress passed amendments to the *Elementary and Secondary Education Act* (PL 93-380) that introduced requirements for stringent safeguards concerning the

Federal support of appropriately serving students with disabilities in public schools has expanded since 1974.

rights of children in special education, mandated assurances of due process procedures at the state and local levels, and suggested that educational services for students with disabilities be provided in the least-restricted environment (i.e., in environments that gave students with disabilities access to students who were not disabled). PL 93-380 also established the goal of providing full educational opportunities for children with disabilities within each state, although it allowed each state to set its own time line for implementing these provisions.

FROM GOAL TO REALITY

Rep. John Brademas (D-Ind.), chairman of the House Select Education Subcommittee, and Sen. Jennings Randolph (D-W. Va.), chairman of the Handicapped Subcommittee of the Senate, were still not satisfied. They believed in an even greater federal commitment to children with disabilities, and led the fight for the passage of federal legislation that would set a deadline for providing a public education for these children. Their efforts culminated, in 1975, with the signing into law of the *Education of All Handicapped Children Act*, **PL 94-142**. This landmark legislation authorized federal money for local school districts to provide special education services to students with disabilities. The law provided funds for *all* children with disabilities, ages 6 to 21, through a state grant program (Part B of the Act) and a formula that based federal payments on a percentage of average per-pupil expenditures. Congress promised to pay 5% of each school district's excess costs of educating students with disabilities in 1978, and to cover 40% of excess costs by 1982. It also authorized a $300-per-child incentive payment to states for every child with disabilities, age 3 to 5, enrolled in special education. The Act set 1980 as the deadline when a free, appropriate, public education must be available to all children with disabilities, no matter how severe the disability, if states wanted to continue receiving federal education funds of any kind.

PL-94-142 required six specific assurances from state education agencies:

1. **Zero reject**: A free, appropriate public education must be provided to *all* children with disabilities regardless of the nature or severity of the disability. Schools must enroll *every* child; no school-age child with a disability may be excluded from school.
2. **Nondiscriminatory assessment**: Each state must establish diagnostic and assessment procedures to eliminate racial or cultural bias in the identification systems; furthermore, no child may be classified as eligible for special education services based on only one test, or on the opinion of only one professional.
3. **Procedural due process**: Due process must be established in each state for children with disabilities and their families; safeguards to protect the rights of students with disabilities and their families must include not only due process procedures but also confidentiality of records.
4. **Individualized education program**: Each child receiving special education must have a written individualized education program (IEP) that includes assessment of current educational performance, annual goals and short-term instructional objectives, provision of educational services (date of initiation and anticipated length of service), and procedures for evaluating progress toward objectives.

5. **Least-restrictive environment**: Schools must provide a continuum of service delivery options for educating students with disabilities; settings that permit maximum access to peers without disabilities are the most desirable placement options and constitute the least-restrictive environment for students with disabilities.
6. **Parental participation**: Parents of children with disabilities are entitled to notice, consultation and hearings regarding their child's special education services. They must be given opportunities to participate in, and present complaints about, their child's identification, evaluation, placement, and IEP.

PL 94-142 revolutionized special education *and* general education. It changed the face of education in the United States. It affected every school in the country. It changed the roles and responsibilities of every special educator, school administrator, parent of students with disabilities, and other professionals involved in the education process.

REFLECTION BOX 1–1

Consider the changes that took place in Dot Hill's classroom over the years. What changes do you think occurred in terms of the types of students assigned to her class? What changes do you think she observed in the types of children who were referred for special education services?

EXPANDING THE SCOPE OF PL 94-142

In 1983, Congressional reauthorization of PL 94-142 broadened even further the federal support for students with disabilities. It introduced two discretionary programs aimed at ensuring students with disabilities access to an unbroken chain of services from birth to adulthood. One provided special funding for early education training, research, and demonstration programs. The second focused on the transitions youth with disabilities needed to make from school to vocational training, work, or postsecondary education.

The early education emphasis in the 1983 reauthorization bill did not, however, require services for preschool children with disabilities. By June 1986, only 7 states had mandated services from birth, 1 state from age 2, 13 states from age 3, 4 states from age 4, and 14 states from age 5. After a contentious battle led by Sen. Lowell Weiker (R-Conn.), Congress passed PL 99-457, *The Education of the Handicapped Act Amendments of 1986*, which affirmed a mandate of public education for children with disabilities ages 3 to 5 years, and added incentives to districts that provided early intervention services for infants and toddlers with disabilities (birth to age 2).

A third amendment to PL 94-142 was passed in 1990. It changed the name of the law to the *Individuals with Disabilities Education Act* (**IDEA**) and added two new categories of disability (autism and traumatic brain injury) to the list of 10 categories of disability through which a child may be eligible for special education services (learning disability, speech or language impairment, mental retardation, serious emotional disturbance, multiple disabilities, hearing impairments, orthopedic impairments, other health impairments, visual impairments, deaf-blindness). It *required* schools to provide transition services (a coordinated set of activities for students with disabilities designed to promote movement from school to post-school activities including post-secondary education, vocational training, or employment), beginning no later than age 16. But most important, it reaffirmed the commitment to the six basic principles of PL 94-142: (1) zero reject, (2) nondiscriminatory assessment, (3) due process, (4) individualized educational program, (5) least-restrictive environment, and (6) parental participation.

In the 1997 reauthorization of IDEA (PL 105-17), Congress sought to move beyond access to special services toward greater emphasis in the federal law on what is educationally best for students. Congress also wanted to reduce the emphasis on paper work; give professionals more influence and flexibility on the delivery of special education at lower costs; enhance even further parent input into decision-making; and clarify disciplinary procedures that can be applied to students with disabilities in attempts to make schools safer. The 1997 reauthorization again affirmed the six principles of the original law and Congress' preference for educating students with disabilities alongside nondisabled peers when an appropriate education can be achieved. The 1997 IDEA also required states to establish performance standards for students with disabilities, to develop assessment indicators by which to judge the educational progress of students with disabilities, and to include students with disabilities in statewide as well as local assessments.

THE CONTINUUM OF SERVICE DELIVERY OPTIONS

In the 1950s and 1960s, students with severe disabilities, if they attended school at all, were assigned to special day schools or residential institutions. But for students with mild disabilities (usually students labeled EMR), the most widely used public school setting was the **self-contained** class, in a regular school building, where they received all their educational experiences separate from nondisabled students. In the 1960s and 1970s, self-contained classes became commonplace for students classified as learning disabled, as well, and separate classes and schools for students labeled emotionally disturbed also began to appear.

These segregated placements were, however, only part of a **continuum of service delivery options** which could, theoretically, be chosen as appropriate for students with disabilities. This continuum of services is represented in Figure 1–1. "The tapered design indicates the considerable difference in numbers involved at the different levels and calls attention to the fact that the system serves as a diagnostic filter" (Deno, 1970, p. 235). Even before the passage of PL 94-142, Deno believed that a school system should make available whatever kind of setting is necessary to provide appropriate services to students with disabilities.

As Deno conceptualized the continuum of placement options, most students would attend regular classes, though their teachers might receive supportive consultation from a special education teacher. The next-largest group of students would

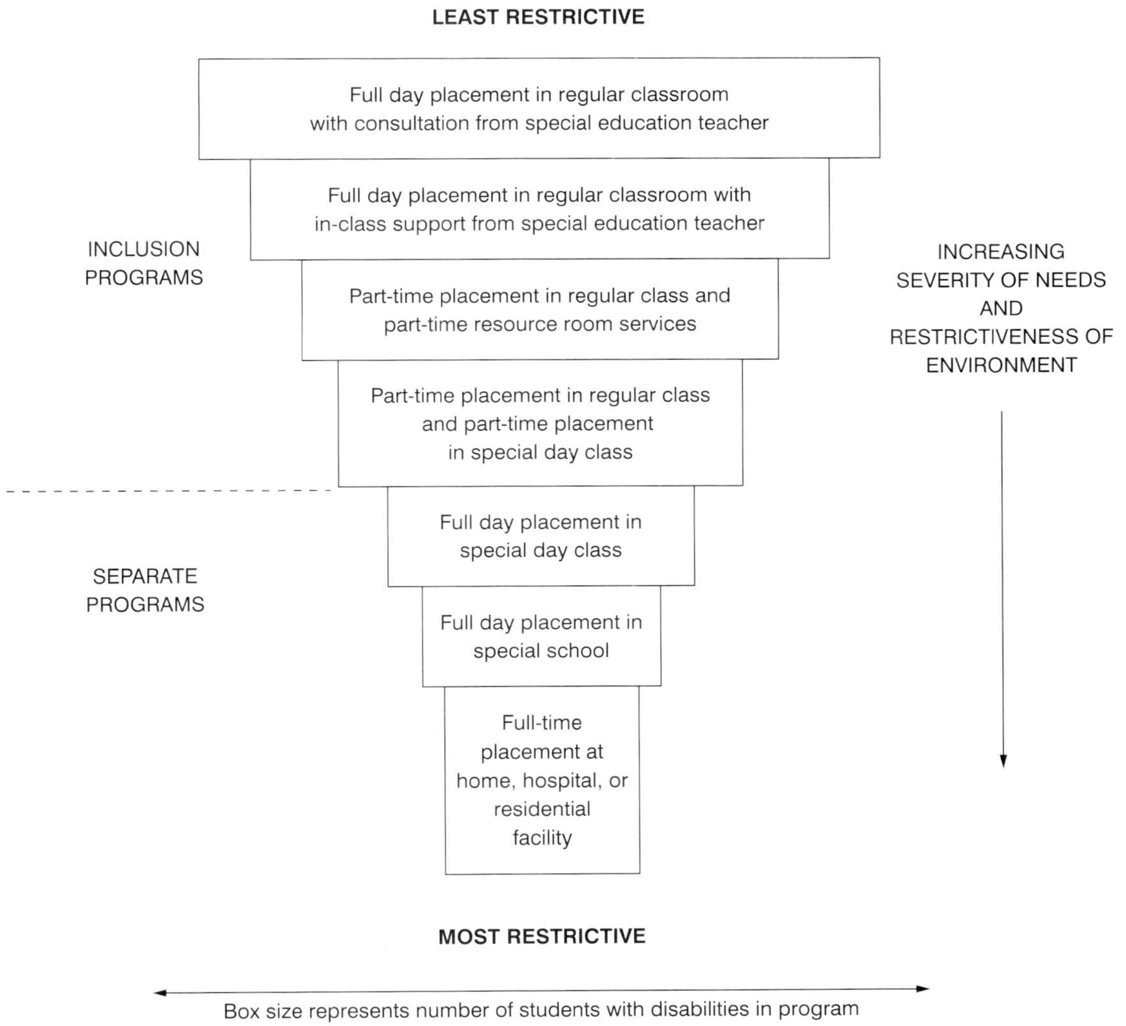

FIGURE 1–1 Continuum of Service Delivery Options
Note: *From "Special Education as Developmental Capital," by E. Deno, 1970,* Exceptional Children, 37, *pp. 229–237.*

attend regular classes but receive help from a special education teacher visiting these regular classrooms. At the next level, students would spend most of the school day in a regular classroom, but leave for part of the time to go to a special education **resource room**. Resource room students would receive specialized educational services from a specially trained teacher, individually or in small groups, outside the general education classroom for at least one period each day.

Further down the continuum of services pictured in Figure 1-1, even fewer students would attend special classes full time, and still fewer would attend special day schools controlled by the school district. Deno added a seventh level to the cascade to account for students with disabilities who did not attend public schools, but received special education and related services outside the school system, in a hospital, at home, or in a residential treatment or detention center. As Deno imagined it, students would be placed only as far down the continuum of services as was absolutely necessary, and would be moved up the continuum back towards the top level as rapidly as feasible.

Although Deno did not write about it until 1970, examples of this continuum in practice were evident in the special education literature as early as 1967. At the Fourth Annual Conference of the Association for Children with Learning Disabilities, Todd (1967) described a continuum of placement options for students assigned to the Ohio program for neurologically handicapped students. The target population for this program were students in the primary grades who were not successful at learning through the usual teaching methods and who were developing behavior problems probably as a result of school failure. These students today would have been classified as children with learning disabilities, but then were called "children of functionally average or better intelligence who are experiencing learning and/or behavior difficulties related to a neurological handicap" (Todd, 1967, p. 109). Todd described a three-tiered program for students with different levels of need:

> There are some children who can profit from adjustments which can be practically carried out in the regular classroom. There are some children who can profit from a program of organized supplemental instruction in addition to the regular classroom activities. [But] a large portion of these children need the benefits of a class specifically designed for learning and behavior disorders. (p. 110)

Todd was clearly describing the upper levels of Deno's continuum. Todd also anticipated Deno's ideas about students moving up the continuum as they were ready. "An attempt is made to manipulate the controls available in the special class structure to shape the child gradually back into a regular class situation" (Todd, 1967, p. 110).

The continuum of service delivery options was central to the mandate of PL 94-142 and was reflected in the least-restrictive environment provision. In writing this provision into the 1975 law, Congress recognized the value of educating students with disabilities alongside nondisabled peers, and recommended that it be done to the maximum extent appropriate. The regulations accompanying the law required that for students already placed in more restrictive settings (lower down on the continuum), the school district make every effort to move the child up the continuum (towards regular class placement) as soon as it is appropriate. For students being placed for the first time, the school district was to assign them to a special education setting as high up on the continuum of alternatives as appropriate. Bateman and Chard (1995) suggest that six regulatory provisions serve as guides for the placement decision. They also emphasize that the least-restrictive environment is a *decision*, not a *place*, which results from following this set of procedural requirements.

Three of these requirements are mandatory, absolute, binding, and without an "escape clause":

1. The district must make available a full continuum of alternative placements, including resource rooms, special classes, special schools, and so forth.
2. In placement decisions, consideration must be given to any potential harmful effect on the child or on the quality of services he or she needs.
3. Placement must be based on the IEP and be determined annually (p. 291).

Three other LRE provisions are "qualified," that is, they are preferences to be implemented to the extent indicated:

1. Children with disabilities must be educated with nondisabled children to the maximum extent appropriate.
2. They may be removed from the regular education environment only when the nature or severity of the disability is such that education in regular classes with the use of supplemental aids and services cannot be satisfactorily achieved.
3. Children should attend neighborhood schools unless the IEP requires otherwise, and the non-neighborhood school placement should be as close "as possible" to the child's home. (Bateman & Chard, 1995, pp. 291-292).

What constituted an appropriate educational placement for an individual child was, of course, a local matter, to be decided by parents and school personnel at an IEP meeting. The overriding rule was that the decision had to be made individually, rather than by categorizing the child as belonging to a particular group or carrying a particular label, and that all options be considered for every child to ensure an appropriate education. (For a more complete discussion of the legal and judicial constraints on the placement decision see Bateman & Chard, 1995, and Yell, 1998).

In the 1976–77 school year, the first year for which national data on placement rates are available, the majority of students with mild disabilities (students diagnosed as learning disabled, mentally retarded, or emotionally disturbed) were, indeed, spending at least part of each school day in a regular classroom (i.e., at the highest levels on the continuum of placement options); a comparatively small percentage of children with disabilities were being educated in separate school facilities or other educational environments (see Figure 1–2). There was considerable variation by disability label, however. Students with learning disabilities were most likely to be found spending at least some of their school time in the regular classroom, while students with mild mental retardation were more likely to be segregated into separate classrooms. Placement in a separate day school was rare for students with learning disabilities, but considerably less rare for students diagnosed as emotionally disturbed or mentally retarded (see Figure 1-3).

REFLECTION BOX 1–2

Dot Hill indicated that were she to continue teaching, it would take a considerable adjustment for her to get used to the way special education services were provided in schools today, even though she would enjoy the process. This suggests that Ms. Hill supports the shift in programming practices that has taken place over the years. What do you think she might see as some of the more positive aspects of the move toward a policy of increased inclusion? What might she see as the principal negative concerns or obstacles?

SHAPING A POLICY OF INCLUSION

FROM DIVIDED RESPONSIBILITY TO SHARED RESPONSIBILITY

Even before the passage of PL 94-142, schools had begun to integrate children with disabilities into the general education classroom when their teachers judged that they could profit, academically or socially, from such a placement. Education for these students was a *divided* responsibility. The special education teacher was responsible for

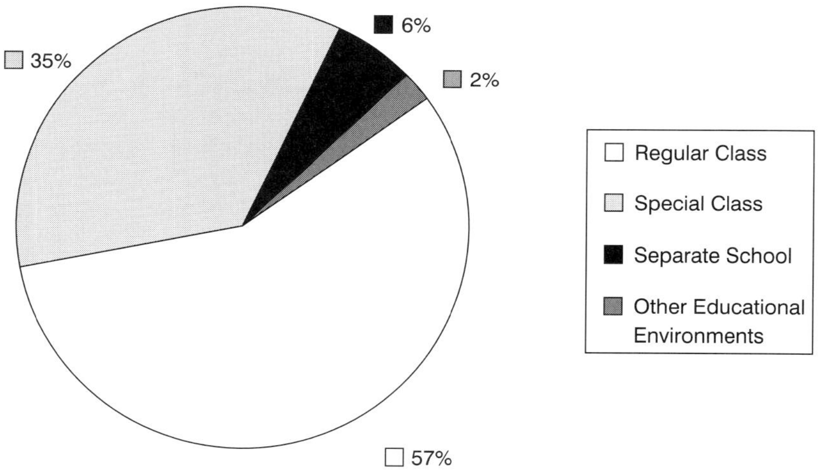

This figure indicates that the majority of students with mild disabilities (57%) were spending at least some of the school day in a regular classroom. Another 35% of students with mild disabilities were being educated in special day classes, and only 8% were in separate schools or other educational environments.

FIGURE 1–2 Placements of Students with Disabilities in 1976–77 School Year

Note: *From* A Report to Congress on the Implementation of Public Law 94–142: The Education of All Handicapped Children Act *(p. 169), by U.S. Department of Health, Education, and Welfare, 1979, Washington, DC: Government Printing Office.*

This figure indicates that students with learning disabilities were most likely to be found spending at least some part of their school day in the regular classroom, while students with mild mental retardation were more likely to be found in segregated separate classrooms. Placement in a separate day school was rare for students with learning disabilities, but considerably less rare for students diagnosed as emotionally disturbed or mentally retarded.

FIGURE 1–3 Placements of Students with Mild Disabilities in 1976–77 School Year

Note: *From* A Report to Congress on the Implementation of Public Law 94-142: The Education of All Handicapped Children Act *(pp. 170–171), by U.S. Department of Health, Education, and Welfare, 1979, Washington, DC: Government Printing Office.*

the portion of the school day during which students were pulled out of the general classroom; the general education teacher was responsible for the portion of the school day that students remained in the general classroom. The special education teacher taught an adapted or alternative curriculum, and was not bound to the district-adopted curriculum, textbook, or materials that were used with students without disabilities at the same grade level. The general education teacher taught the standard curriculum using district-adopted textbooks and materials, with minor adjustments and accommodations for the student with disabilities, as necessary. When there was time, the two teachers might confer, particularly if the student with disabilities was having difficulty in the general education classes and the teachers needed new ideas or suggestions for how to cope. If students had very mild disabilities, they were placed full time in the general education class, and conferring with the general education teacher was likely the responsibility of an itinerant special education teacher or special education consultant. Traveling from school to school, this special education professional might meet regularly with general education teachers and suggest modified instructional approaches or prepare modified materials or tests that could be used with children with disabilities in the course of instruction. Students who needed more help were usually assigned to a resource room for one to four periods each school day, where a special education teacher would provide remedial or supplemental instruction in core academic subjects. Students who could not cope with the general academic curriculum at all were placed in a self-contained special education class, and joined general education peers only for the nonacademic parts of the school day—art, music, and physical education.

The least-restrictive environment provision in PL 94-142 did not require that all students with disabilities, regardless of the nature and severity of their disability, be included in general education classes. In fact, while Congress clearly desired the integration of students with and without disabilities as a governing objective in placement decisions, there was no intention that every child with disabilities be placed in general education classrooms. Thus, the June 1975 Report of the House of Representatives on H.R. 7217 stated the following:

Shared responsibilities of students with disabilities in the least restrictive environment can be advantageous.

> An optimal situation, of course, would be one in which the child is placed in a regular classroom. The Committee recognizes that this is not always the most beneficial place of instruction. . . . When it is clear that because of the nature or severity of a child's handicap, the child must be educated in a setting other than the regular class, it is appropriate to implement such a placement. However, the least-restrictive environment provision is also designed as a rights provision to protect against indiscriminate placement of a child in a separate facility solely because the child is handicapped and not because special education is needed in that type of setting. (H. Rept. No. 94-332, p. 9).

Obviously, Congress imagined instances in which particular children should be placed in a setting other than the regular classrooms. However, there had to be good reasons for such placements, and these reasons had to be based on the nature or severity of the child's disability and the child's need for special education and related services.

The LRE provision did not come out of nowhere. In a serious critique of segregated, self-contained special education, Dunn (1968), from Peabody Teachers' College, called for the elimination of special classes and special schools for students with mild disabilities, grounding his recommendations in the evidence provided by Coleman (1966) and others that academically disadvantaged African American children in racially segregated schools made less progress than those of comparable ability in integrated schools. Other studies have since corroborated Dunn's impression of special classes being well-intentioned, but impoverished learning environments. In a detailed study of 10 elementary level, self-contained, special education classrooms, Leinhardt, Zigmond and Cooley (1981) found that students with mild disabilities spent only 10% of their school day actively engaged in reading orally or silently, only 2% of their school day composing written texts, and only 6% of their school day in instructional interactions with their teachers (Leinhardt, Zigmond, & Cooley, 1981; Silverman, Zigmond, Zimmerman, & Vallecorsa, 1981).

In two ethnographic studies of high school students with mild disabilities, Zigmond and her colleagues found that students in the special education classes received watered-down content instruction that was designed to help students achieve passing grades, but which was seriously limited in substance (Miller, Leinhardt, & Zigmond, 1988; Zigmond & Miller, 1992). Special classes were characterized by slower paced, more deliberate instruction, but also substantially lower cognitive demand (Partanen, 1993). As an alternative to special classes and special schools, Dunn (1968) had proposed more integrated service delivery models for students with mild disabilities in the form of part-time, pull-out, remedial resource rooms, staffed by special education teachers, as the way to provide a better education for children with learning problems (because these resource rooms are part-time placements, they are designated as "regular class" placements in Figures 1–2 and 1–3).

Resource rooms do appear to be more advantageous to students with learning disabilities and students with behavior disorders than either self-contained classes or full-time placement in general education classrooms. Resource room instruction can increase students achievement and on-task behavior (see, for example, O'Connor, Stuck, & Wyne, 1983). Resource room services do not seem to be associated with diminished self-concept (Prillaman, 1981) and may even enhance teacher and student perception of academic progress and personal social adjustment. As Madden and Slavin (1983) concluded, if increased academic achievement is the desired outcome, "the research favors placement in regular classes . . . *supplemented by well designed resource programs*" (p. 530, italics added).

But 10 years after the implementation of PL 94-142, and 18 years after Dunn (1968) recommended them, these very resource rooms, were subject to criticism. "Although well intentioned, this so-called 'pull out' approach to the educational difficulties of students with learning problems has failed in many instances to meet the educational needs of these students," wrote Madeline Will (1986, p. 413), then Assistant Secretary of Education and head of the Office of Special Education Programs. Will and others (e.g., Gartner & Lipsky, 1987, 1989; National Association of State Boards of Education, 1992) called for even more fully integrated educational experiences for children with learning problems to achieve "improved educational outcomes" (Will, 1986, p. 413), "academic growth" (Gartner & Lipsky, 1989, p. 21), and "better outcomes" (National Association of State Boards of Education, p. 4). They argued that pull-out special education services were expensive, and they questioned their economic feasibility (Special education costs, 1988). They complained that the diagnostic criteria used for placement of students into various categorical pull-out programs were unclear (Ysseldyke & Algozzine, 1983). They emphasized the purported social stigma attached to being segregated from the general education environment (Dunn, 1968; Foster, Ysseldyke, & Reese, 1975). In particular, they decried the *divided and fragmented* educational services being provided to students with mild disabilities assigned to pull-out special education services. They suggested that all students with mild disabilities be returned full time to general education classrooms and that any special education services that were needed be provided in that setting. Supporters of this **regular education initiative** (REI), as it came to be known, established their legal foundation for full inclusion of students with mild disabilities in general education classrooms in the least-restrictive environment (LRE) provision of PL 94-142 and IDEA which stipulated that removal of children with disabilities from the regular education environment should occur only when the nature or severity of a child's handicap is such that education in regular classes with the use of supplemental aids and services cannot be achieved satisfactorily (Turnbull, 1998, p. 134). For some (Lilly, 1986; Reynolds, Wang, & Walberg, 1987; Stainback and Stainback, 1984; Will, 1986) the REI became a rallying cry for a merger of special and general education, a return of special education students full time to the general education classroom (the highest two levels on the continuum of service delivery options in Figure 1–1), and a "joining of demonstrably effective practices from special, compensatory, and general education to establish a general education system that is more inclusive and better serves all students, particularly those who require greater-than-usual educational support" (Reynolds, Wang, & Walberg, 1987, p. 394). For them, REI was a civil-rights movement, a demand for equal access to an inclusive education for students with mild disabilities and a challenge to any kind of segregation.

For others, the REI was simply a catalyst for a reappraisal of the division of responsibility between general and special education for the education of students with mild disabilities. Those who were reluctant to abandon pull-out special education services entirely (Mesinger, 1985; Leiberman, 1985; Fuchs & Fuchs, 1995a; Zigmond & Baker, 1995) agreed, nevertheless, on the necessity to increase involvement of students with mild disabilities in general education classroom processes. They called for a better alignment of special education and general education programs to achieve better academic outcomes than had been achieved with more traditional, fragmented pull-out programs. This is the position we take in this book. We do not advocate abandoning the continuum of services. We do not believe there is sufficient evidence to conclude that all the needs of all children can be met in the general class. We do, however, believe that the "divided responsibility model" does not serve students with disabilities well.

The alternative for both those who advocate full inclusion and those who acknowledge the need to preserve a continuum of services is a model of service delivery built on a *shared* (rather than divided) responsibility between general and special education teachers in the education of students with disabilities who are now being served in larger numbers in general education classrooms and regular schools (Figure 1–4). The shared responsibility would be facilitated by consultation, collaboration, and co-teaching.

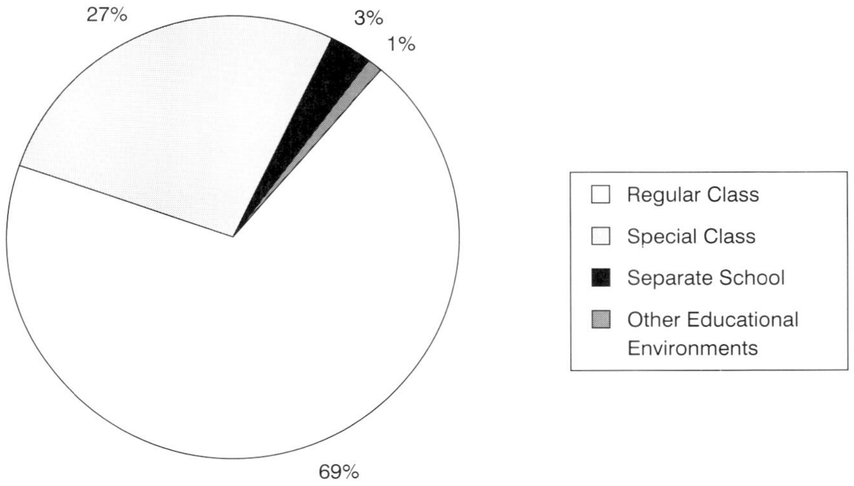

This figure shows an 12% increase in the number of students with mild disabilities spending some part of the school day in a general education classroom, an 8% decrease in the number of students with mild disabilities in separate day classes, and a 4% decrease in the number of students in separate schools and other educational environments.

FIGURE 1–4 Placements of Students with Mild Disabilities in 1994–95 School Year
Note: *From Nineteenth Annual Report of Congress, 1997, pp. A-51, A-55, A57)*, Washington, DC: Government Printing Office.

REFLECTION BOX 1–3

Changes in the way special education services are delivered have led to important changes in the roles and responsibilities that teachers must assume. What effect do you think these changes have had on Dot Hill and the general education teachers with whom she works? What are the implications of this shift for teacher preparation programs?

COUNTERVAILING FORCES

To become more involved in the education of students with disabilities was not high on the list of reform priorities of general education teachers, at least not initially. General education teachers were coming under increasing scrutiny and criticism. There were enormous pressures from school boards, legislators, and the public to reform U.S. education and raise standards. *Goals* 2000: *Educate America Act* (PL 103-227) passed by Congress in 1994 codified a set of proposals initially generated by the governors of all 50 states to reform virtually every aspect of general public education, including curriculum and textbooks, teaching practices, use of educational technology, evaluation and measurement of student progress, teacher training and inservice development, parent and community involvement, and school administration and management (for a listing of the *Goals* 2000, see Figure 1–5).

The reforms focused on improving student outcomes, by helping "all" students reach higher academic and occupational skills standards before leaving high school.

America's Education Goals

Goal 1	All children in America will start school ready to learn.
Goal 2	The high school graduation rate will increase to at least 90 percent.
Goal 3	American students will leave grades four, eight, and twelve having demonstrated competency over challenging subject matter, including English, mathematics, science, history and geography; and every school in America will ensure that all students learn to use their minds well, so they may be prepared for responsible citizenship, further learning, and productive employment in our modern economy.
Goal 4	U. S. students will be first in the world in science and mathematics achievement.
Goal 5	Every adult American will be literate and will possess the knowledge and skills necessary to compete in a global economy and exercise the right and responsibilities of citizenship.
Goal 6	Every school in the United States will be free of drugs and violence, and will offer a disciplined environment conducive to learning.

FIGURE 1–5 America's Education Goals

Note: *From* America 2000: An Educational Strategy *(p. 19), by U.S. Department of Education, n.d., Washington, DC: Author.*

Teachers could not avoid feeling pressure to increase the academic press of their classrooms, demand more of their students, hold students to higher standards of achievement, and grade more harshly. At the same time, special education colleagues in the schools were suggesting adding even more hard-to-teach students to the general education teachers' classroom mix. It is not surprising that surveys indicated that general education teachers did not feel prepared for any increase in their professional responsibilities towards students with disabilities, and were not enthusiastic about increasing the amount of time these students spent in general education classrooms (Coates, 1989; Semmel, Abernathy, Butera, & Lesar, 1991).

There is no question that the challenges facing the classroom teacher are great. General education classrooms are complex places and never have classroom groups been so diverse: children of affluence and children of poverty; children whose first language is English and children whose first language is not English; children of traditional families and children of divorce, blended, or nontraditional families; children who are able-bodied and children with disabilities. Teachers must organize and manage their classrooms so that the task of teaching the required curriculum to the required set of children is doable. Teaching and learning need to be orchestrated and structured. Time needs to be filled productively. Diversity needs to be accommodated. High standards need to be achieved. This requires careful planning and lots of decisions. When good decisions are made and good strategies are implemented, students are more likely to achieve. If general and special education teachers *share* responsibility for the decisions being made, particularly those that govern the time students with disabilities spend in general education classes, then both teacher time and student time are more likely to be productive.

There is no turning back the clock—not in the reform of the education of students with disabilities nor in the reform of general education. Children with disabilities will be present in general education classrooms. Whether they are spending full time in these classrooms and receiving supplemental aids and services in that setting, or are spending part of their time in general education classrooms and receiving educational services in both in-class and pull-out settings, shared decision-making and shared responsibility will make for a more coherent and successful program.

FOLLOW-UP ACTIVITIES

1. Interview a special education professional about how the field has changed during the past 10 years. Ask for this person's views concerning the most and least positive aspects of the changes that have taken place. Discuss this same issue with a general education teacher. How do their perspectives differ? Share your findings with others in your class to see if they are consistent. Do the teachers' perspectives differ depending on the grade level at which they teach?
2. Assume you have been asked to make a few remarks at the next school board meeting concerning your district's approach to providing special education ser-

vices. What would you say in support of the district's plan to increase its emphasis on inclusion and what important cautions might you offer? What concerns would you expect opponents of the plan to raise and how might you respond to them?

3. Prepare a chart that summarizes the major differences among PL 94-142, its reauthorization as the *Individuals with Disabilities Education Act* (IDEA), and the 1997 reauthorization of IDEA, PL 105-17. What additions or deletions in the most recent version of the law would you want Congress to make in its next reauthorization?
4. Interview special education students who are served in different settings. Get their reactions to self-contained, resource, and inclusion practices. Do the students feel different based on their grade level? Are your findings consistent with those of others in your class?
5. Speak with several parents of students who receive special education services. Get their reactions to the type of program model being used with their child. What do they view as strengths and weaknesses of the approach?

CHAPTER 2 CHARACTERISTICS AND VARIATIONS OF IN-CLASS MODELS

KEY WORDS

team teaching
station teaching
contingency contracting
co-teaching
peer-mediated strategies
token economy
parallel teaching strategies
intervention model
cooperative learning
school survival skills

OBJECTIVES

After reading this chapter the student should be able to:

1. discuss the rationale for using in-class models for service delivery for students with mild disabilities.
2. compare the characteristics of direct instruction methods and collaborative teaching procedures.
3. describe several strategies for co-teaching.
4. describe several organizational, training, funding, and instructional issues related to in-class models.

AMAZING SHARKS

Ms. Johnson, an eighth-grade social studies teacher, is working with a group of 20 students who are comparing population maps with topographic and agricultural maps and drawing conclusions about the demographics of different countries. Two of her students have been identified as having mild learning disabilities. On the other side of the room, Ms. Greer has a group of eight students, four of whom have learning disabilities; she is teaching them to interpret population maps using the map legend and the mileage scale. Fifteen minutes later, all the students are in one group discussing their map projects, which are due in a week. Both teachers are involved in reviewing the project directions, answering questions, and showing examples.

In a fourth-grade classroom, Mr. Clark is showing the entire group of students how to use a graphic organizer on cause and effect to make note-taking easier and more useful. After Mr. Clark demonstrates the graphic organizer, Ms. Denton delivers a minilecture on the causes of the American Civil War and the effect each cause had on the country. The students use the graphic organizer to take notes. Mr. Clark circulates in the room assisting students with their note-taking. After the lecture, Mr. Clark presents a completed graphic organizer so that the students can compare their notes with his.

Mr. Telfar and Ms. Holder are co-teaching a unit on the struggle different groups have had for civil rights in the United States. The class has been divided in half and each teacher is delivering a portion of the material. Mr. Telfar is discussing the civil rights movement of the 1960s and Ms. Holder is discussing the women's movement. Halfway through the class period the teachers switch groups and redeliver their lessons. At the end of the class, both groups convene together and a whole-group discussion takes place. Both teachers are involved in the discussion.

Mr. Mason is an eighth-grade science teacher. He follows the same overall teaching routine from week to week. On Mondays he introduces a new chapter to the whole class using a lecture format. Students read a portion of the chapter in class and are assigned a follow-up work assignment. Tuesdays and Wednesdays are used for additional large group work and include both lecture and discussion. A portion of class on each of these days is devoted to having students complete some form of small group activity. On Thursdays students participate in classroom experiments or projects, if appropriate, or they watch a video related to the current science topic. Mr. Mason typically ends the week with a chapter exam. While this approach works fairly well for most of his students, he has found it doesn't seem to be meeting the needs of Ashley, an extremely bright 14-year-old who rarely gets decent grades because he fails to complete much of his classwork or his homework. Ashley constantly blurts out in class, talks to anyone who is around him, and gets out of his seat several times each class period to sharpen his pencil or get a drink of water. Whenever he moves about the room, he disturbs other students by thumping them on the head, punching their arms, and pushing their books and papers onto the floor. In addition to this, Ashley gets into frequent arguments and fights. Fortunately, because Ashley has been identified as having a behavior disorder, he receives support from a special education teacher who meets regularly with Mr. Mason to discuss strategies for working with Ashley. Together the two teachers are trying to find ways of improving Ashley's classroom behavior and performance.

The purpose of this chapter is to describe in-class collaborative models of special education service delivery. First, several approaches to consultation and collaborative teaching in the general education classroom are characterized, including consultation only, consultation with special instruction, and collaborative teaching. Then, organizational, training, funding, and instructional issues are discussed. Follow-up activities are provided at the end of the chapter.

RATIONALE FOR IN-CLASS MODELS

"As the social fabric of society has changed, children and youth bring more challenges to teachers than ever before" (Pugach & Johnson, 1995, p. 8). The social, academic, and cultural constitution of classrooms has never been more complex or diverse (Kameenui, 1993). This increase in diversity is found in public schools all across the United States. Many believe that general education teachers will need support from each other and from other professionals to meet the complex challenges their general education students pose. Teachers will no longer be able to work in isolation; instead, they will have to work collaboratively to meet the needs of this diverse student body.

The diversity of the general education classroom has increased even more in recent years as a result of an educational policy to include greater numbers of students with disabilities in general education settings. Current estimates are that 73% of all special education students spend substantial amounts of school time in general education settings (U.S. Department of Education, 1996). This includes 43% who spend a majority of their school day in regular classes (U.S. Department of Education, 1996), often with special education services brought in, instead of the student being pulled out. This practice has increased the need for specific collaborations between special and general educators.

Having generalists and specialists working together in the same classroom is not easy. For one thing, general educators appear to define teaching quite differently from special educators. General educators see their job as teaching the whole group, and they feel keenly the public and professional pressure to cover the prescribed curriculum (Friend & Cook, 1996). Special educators view their job as teaching individuals; they are often more concerned about teaching their students coping skills and learning strategies than teaching them the prescribed curriculum. These differing views can make it difficult for the two to collaborate in educating students with disabilities. Yet despite these difficulties, collaboration is the only way to better serve students with disabilities who are placed in general education classrooms.

IN-CLASS APPROACHES

Recently, there has been a significant increase in the use of administrative arrangements in which students with disabilities are taught, full time, in general education classrooms. These in-class approaches take many forms:

1. *consultation*—all instruction done by the general education teacher with consultation provided by the special education teacher.
2. *consultation with direct instruction*—most of the instructional responsibilities assumed by the general education teacher with the special education teacher

providing not only consultation but also some specific in-class instruction to several students, not just the child (or children) with disabilities.

3. *co-teaching*—the special education and general education teachers share instructional responsibilities for all children for some portion of the school day.
4. *pull-aside special education*—the special education teacher teaches a separate curriculum to the student with disabilities in a separate section of the general education classroom.

The goal of each of these approaches is to provide an accommodating, personalized education for all students, including those with disabilities, within the general education classroom. In the following sections we discuss these in-class models.

CONSULTATION

For some students with mild disabilities, all their educational needs can be met by a general education teacher providing an accommodating and personalized education. In this model, special educators and general education teachers consult about modifications that can be made to assist students with disabilities in the general education classroom. Often this means helping general educators incorporate strategies and approaches that have been found to be successful with students with disabilities. Such approaches include teacher-directed instruction, peer-mediated strategies, cooperative learning, and explicit behavior management techniques. In consultation-only service delivery models, the student with disabilities receives no pull-out or pull-aside instruction from a special education teacher; instead, the special education teacher helps the general education teacher learn how to modify the general instruction to meet the student's special needs.

TEACHER-DIRECTED INSTRUCTION. One way to help students with special needs in the general education classroom is through the use of active teaching or teacher-directed instruction. Brophy and Good (1986) suggest that active teaching occurs when "the teacher carries the content to the student personally rather than depending on the curriculum materials to do so" (p. 361). In active teaching, the teacher directs the learning activities. Students spend most of their day being taught and supervised by the teacher rather than working independently or teaching each other. By contrast, in classrooms where teachers adopt a social constructivist teaching paradigm, students lead discussions, select their own objectives, and are responsible for their own learning; the teacher acts as a facilitator.

When teachers use direct instruction they demonstrate appropriate strategies for each task, allow for guided practice, and provide systematic and frequent feedback. Teachers introduce a task, model and demonstrate, check for understanding, maintain a brisk pace and a high success rate, and monitor seatwork and progress (Englert, Tarrant, & Mariage, 1992). The teacher is directly in charge of instruction and the students usually are not involved in the decision making. See Figure 2–1 for an example of teacher-directed instruction.

With teacher-directed instruction, selection of the learning task is a critical instructional decision. Then the task is described as precisely as possible. Teachers consider

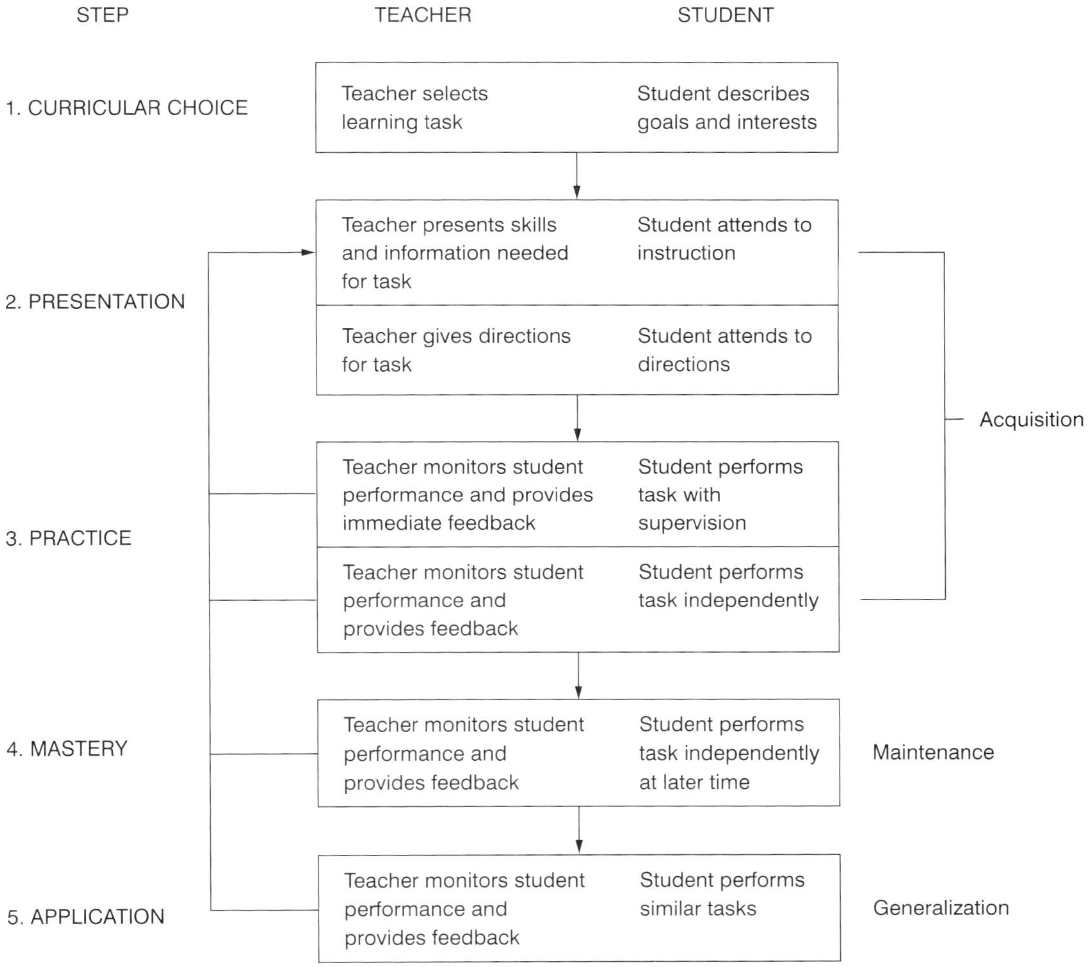

FIGURE 2–1 Teacher and Student Responsibilities in Teacher-Directed Instruction
Note: From Teaching special students in the mainstream (5th ed.), 1999, by R. B. Lewis & D. H. Doorlag. Reprinted by permission of Prentice Hall, Upper Saddle River, NJ.

the current performance level of the students and give the students practice activities on a level at which they can succeed. When using teacher-directed instruction, teachers break instructional tasks into several smaller tasks and present each in a systematic fashion. This means that the teacher provides a demonstration, then guided practice, and finally independent practice. If implemented correctly, teacher-directed instruction can be used to teach any curricular area.

Research shows that the more time students spend with the teacher, the more they learn (Rosenshine & Stevens, 1986). Teacher-directed instruction increases the time students spend with the teacher. Teacher-directed instruction can be used to teach a whole class, a small group, or in one-to-one teaching, although one-to-one is not the grouping arrangement of choice in general education classrooms. Teachers who use teacher-directed instruction effectively keep their students actively involved in learning experiences, and that promotes learning for all.

PEER-MEDIATED STRATEGIES. **Peer-mediated strategies** are another way that general education teachers can meet the needs of students with disabilities in the regular classroom. Peer-mediated strategies are instructional systems in which pairs or small groups of students assist one another and students learn by teaching (Jenkins & Jenkins, 1985). The tutor and tutee are often but not always peers from the same class. Sometimes their roles are fixed; often they reverse roles in the course of a peer tutoring session. Peer tutoring not only provides additional guided practice opportunities for students who have not yet mastered a particular skill, but also enhances social skill development and attitudes toward school for both the tutor and the tutee.

In successful peer-tutoring systems, the tutor is given a carefully scripted plan designed by the teacher, and the teacher supervises the tutoring sessions. "Tutoring programs should be well planned in advance, well supervised by competent adults, and used to reinforce previously taught material. They should not be used as a means of teaching new information" (Idol, Nevin, Paolucci-Whitman, 1994, p. 159).

Peabody Classwide Peer Tutoring (CWPT) is a peer-mediated strategy that gives general education teachers greater flexibility to accommodate diverse students needs in their classroom (Mathes, Fuchs, Fuchs, Henly, & Sanders, 1994). When using the Peabody CWPT system, the students in a class are paired, with each pair including a higher- and a lower-performing student. Pairs are assigned to a team and are awarded points for engaging in the instructional activities and for behaving appropriately. Each activity is about 10 min-

Peer tutoring systems provide general educators greater flexibility in accommodating students with diverse needs.

utes long and tutors are trained to identify and correct errors as they occur. The higher-performing student serves as a model, but within each pair, the roles of tutor and tutee are reciprocal. Classwide peer-tutoring programs have been used effectively for improving basic reading and math skills in the elementary grades (Cooke, Heron, & Heward, 1983), but can also be implemented across the curriculum and at all grade levels.

For classwide peer-tutoring programs to be most effective, Maheady, Sacca, and Harper (1987) suggest identifying an explicit presentation format that encourages active student responses, enforces contingent point-earning, institutes an error-correction strategy, and posts the results of student performance. Figure 2–2 summarizes the responsibilities of the tutor in a peer-tutoring program.

COOPERATIVE LEARNING. Like peer tutoring, **cooperative learning** involves students working together. Unlike peer tutoring, cooperative learning groups are usually larger than pairs. Cooperative learning has been used extensively and effectively with heterogeneous groupings, often groupings that include students with disabilities (see Tateyama-Sniezek, 1990, for a review).

1. The tutor shares the objective with the tutee.
   Example: The tutor says, "I'm going to work with you to teach you your multiplication facts so you won't have to use your fingers to multiply."
2. The tutor describes the steps in the lesson.
   Example: The tutor says, "First, I'll show you a fact on a flash card. Then, I'll ask you to tell me the answer. If you are correct, you keep the card. If you are wrong, I keep the card and we'll go over it again."
3. The tutor asks the tutee to repeat the directions.
   Example: The tutor says, "So, what are you going to do?"
4. The tutor presents the task.
   Example: The tutor holds up a flash card for a few seconds and asks for the answer.
5. The tutor gives feedback.
   Example: If the student is wrong, the tutor says, "No, the answer is 15." If the student is correct, the tutor says, "Good, you know these facts. Wow!"
6. On a recording form, the tutor monitors by marking each fact that the student knows with a plus and each fact that the student does not know with a minus.
7. The tutor goes over the missed facts by stating the correct answer and having the tutee repeat the answer.
   Example: The tutor says, "6 times 7 is 42. Your turn. Say the whole thing."
8. The tutor retests the student by showing the tutee the missed facts again and giving the student the card if the tutee is correct.
9. The tutor closes the session with a pleasant comment.

FIGURE 2–2 Peer Tutoring in Mathematics

Note: From Teaching children and adolescents with special needs (2nd ed., p. 306), 1996, by J. L. Olson & J. M. Platt. Reprinted by permission of Prentice Hall, Upper Saddle River, NJ.

In effective cooperative learning, the groups are small enough for each student to participate in a clearly assigned task. Students are directed to (a) each learn some of the information for which the entire group is responsible, then (b) ensure that all members of the group learn all of the information (Johnson & Johnson, 1986). Stevens and Slavin (1991) suggest that when cooperative learning includes individual accountability and group rewards, achievement changes are positive. For cooperative learning programs to succeed, students must learn the social skills necessary for working cooperatively with classmates. Figure 2–3 presents steps for teaching cooperative skills.

Many cooperative learning paradigms exist. The most common ones are the following: "(a) the jigsaw approach, (b) the group project, (c) the competitive team approach, and (d) team-accelerated instruction" (Olson & Platt, 1996, p. 312). In the *jigsaw approach*, each member of the group becomes knowledgeable about one aspect of the project and teaches that information to the others in the group. For example, one group (Billy, Justin, Megan, and Susan) was studying the Navajo. Each person within the group was assigned, or chose, one aspect of the Navajo. Billy chose to study their music, Justin, their housing, Megan, their food, and Susan, their geographic location and clothing. The students mastered their own topics, then shared the information

For cooperative learning programs to be successful, it is critical that students learn social skills to guide their interactions with classmates. These are some suggestions for effectively teaching cooperative skills to your class.

1. Identify the skills students need to learn, based on your observations and other assessments of their skills and needs.
2. Clarify for students why they are being asked to learn cooperative skills and explain how they should interact. For example, you might use a playground or hallway altercation as a nonexample of cooperative interactions, or stage spontaneous role-plays in which you model positive or negative responses.
3. Identify the skills to students. For example, label one skill "Encouraging."
4. Demonstrate the skill for students. For encouraging, use phrases such as "Keep trying," "That's a good response," and "You really did a good job on that." Use a few poor examples of poor encouraging ("I thought you could do better.") to teach students to discriminate between positive and negative examples.
5. Have student practice skills, first with a partner, then with a small group.
6. As students learn several skills, have them play an instructional game in the cooperative group; stressing practice on cooperative skills. Ask the groups to identify examples of positive skills used and examples of situations in which skills were not used well.
7. Praise examples of student skills that you observe. If a student consistently fails to use cooperative skills, talk with that student's group and, if necessary, work privately with the student.

FIGURE 2–3 Steps for Teaching Cooperative Skills

Note: From Including students with special needs, 1996, p. 472, by M. Friend & W. Bursuck. © 1996 by Allyn & Bacon. Reprinted/adapted by permission.

with the rest of the group. Finally, the group as a whole combined the individual information for the final project, which was a written report and a poster. Each person had a piece of information that was joined together to complete the entire puzzle (e.g., the topic of the Navajo). To implement the jigsaw cooperative learning arrangement successfully, Slavin (1988) suggests assigning two students instead of one to each subtopic to prevent absenteeism from causing difficulties.

In the *group project* approach, students pool their knowledge and skills to complete a project. Each person's individual part builds on another student's part to make the entire project successful. For example, one student may study the best structure of beams for the building of a tower of 30 feet. Another student might study the size of the beams needed, etc. The third may study how to purchase and transport the beams to the site. Without each student's information, the construction of the building could not be planned successfully.

In the *competitive teams* approach, competition is emphasized. Students study a topic throughout the week with their group members. On Friday, a quiz or a tournament game is scheduled with points awarded individually to be added toward a group total. For example, the topic for the week may be world geography with particular emphasis on the Middle East. On Friday, the teacher develops a Jeopardy-style game asking questions about Middle Eastern countries. Students in the group answer their questions independently, but the group with the highest total number of points wins.

The final approach, *team-accelerated instruction*, combines individual instruction and cooperative learning (Slavin, 1984). Teams of students work together on individual worksheets. Group members help each other and check each other's work. The teacher may then average individual scores to compute a team score at the end of the period.

When implementing cooperative learning activities in the classroom, teachers should do the following:

- Select the approach or model of cooperative learning to be used (*the teacher may want to use the jigsaw approach*).
- Specify both the academic and the collaborative objectives (*the teacher's goals include understanding of several Native American tribes and learning to work collaboratively*).
- Determine the size and makeup of the groups (*the teacher divides the class into five groups of four students with even gender distribution*).
- Explain the task activity guaranteeing individual accountability and participation (*the teacher explains the activity to the groups and has the students announce the topics they are choosing within their group*).
- Obtain all materials needed (*the teacher gathers the students' social studies books, a list of sources available in the school library, and sources available on the computer*).
- Monitor the effectiveness and the behaviors within the groups (*the teacher sets aside time each week during class to check on progress of groups outside of class*).
- Evaluate the process and the group product (*the teacher collects materials and has students give oral presentations to the entire class*).

Figure 2–4 provides a checklist of decisions teachers need to make before they use cooperative learning techniques.

1. Specify group objective.
   Academic:
   ____
   ____
   ____

   Motivated to attain by:
   _______ a. Points
   _______ b. Certificates
   _______ c. Free time
   _______ d. Praise
   _______ e. Homework pass
   _______ f. Other
2. Specify group objective.
   Collaborative:
   ____
   ____
   ____

   Motivated to attain by:
   _______ a. Points
   _______ b. Certificates
   _______ c. Free time
   _______ d. Praise
   _______ e. Homework pass
   _______ f. Other
3. Select model.
   _______ a. Jigsaw
   _______ b. Group project
   _______ c. competitive team
   _______ d. team accelerated instruction
4. Assign students.
   _______ a. Even number of girls/boys
   _______ b. Two high-level/two low-level
   _______ c. Special students divided
   _______ d. Students of various cultures/interests divided
   _______ e. Random
5. Decide team schedule.
   Time Frame: ______________
   _______ a. Number of weeks
   _______ b. Number of days
6. Arrange room materials.
   _______ a. Clear access for teacher
   _______ b. Storage for materials
7. Guarantee individual accountability.
   _______ a. Grade individual quizzes or projects
   _______ b. Assign roles
   _______ c. Select one student's project
   _______ d. Tokens
   _______ e. Other
8. Have students evaluate their own cooperative behaviors.
   _______ a. Complete student evaluation form
   _______ b. Answer questions
9. Evaluate students' work.
   Products:
   ____
   ____
   _______ a. Points
   _______ b. Grades
   _______ c. Other

   Process:
   ____
   ____
   _______ a. Points
   _______ b. Grades
   _______ c. Other
10. Recognize group effort.
    _______ a. Bulletin board
    _______ b. Newsletter
    _______ c. Other

FIGURE 2–4 Teacher Checklist for Implementing Cooperative Learning Strategies
Note: From Teaching children and adolescents with special needs (2nd ed., p. 320), 1996, by J. L. Olson & J. M. Platt. Reprinted by permission of Prentice Hall, Upper Saddle River, NJ.

BEHAVIOR MANAGEMENT STRATEGIES. Maintaining a well-managed instructional environment is an important way a teacher can help students with disabilities succeed in a general education class. In Chapters 8 and 9, we discuss how to assess and manage particularly troublesome behaviors in students with disabilities. In this chapter, we present general strategies that can be used classwide to achieve a better managed instructional environment. But before discussing classroom behavior management procedures, a few important terms need to be defined: (a) *reinforcer,* (b) *positive reinforcement*, (c) *punishment*, and (d) *extinction*.

A *reinforcer* is the stimulus or event that is delivered or taken away to increase the likelihood of a behavior occurring in the future. The most common categories of reinforcers and several examples of each are provided in Figure 2–5. Social reinforcers include hugs, verbal praise, or a positive phone call home. Activity reinforcers include helping a teacher in another class or participating in a group game. Tangible reinforcers include prizes or stickers, and primary reinforcers are food or snacks, such as candy.

Positive reinforcement is the contingent presentation of a stimulus that increases the future likelihood of a behavior. The stimulus that follows the behavior and that increases the likelihood that the behavior will be repeated is known as the positive reinforcer. For example, the teacher tells a student that after he finishes writing a page in his journal he may use the computer; the student completes the journal entry and is permitted to spend 5 minutes on the computer. Working on the computer is a positive reinforcer and is used to increase the likelihood of the student finishing his writing in the future. Of course, what might be a positive reinforcer for one student may not be for another. An important element in the use of positive reinforcement is the identification of stimuli or events that can be used as positive reinforcers for individual students.

Punishment is used to decrease the occurrence of a behavior by following it with an aversive event. Examples of aversive events or punishers are verbal reprimands, poor grades, or time-out. In time-out the student is removed from a situation that is reinforcing, or the possibility of getting a positive reinforcement is withdrawn for a specific period of time. Time-out should be carefully planned, implemented systematically, and the effects carefully evaluated. Punishment is not usually an effective means of controlling behavior because it does not teach the child a new behavior to substitute for the undesirable one. A teacher should choose punishment as a method to manage behavior only if more positive approaches are not feasible.

Extinction involves withholding positive reinforcement so that the behavior associated with it will decrease; in practical terms, it is the act of ignoring the behavior until the student stops performing it. This strategy is often appropriate when a student has a minor but annoying undesirable behavior, such as tapping a pencil. But teachers

FIGURE 2–5 Types of Reinforcers

Reinforcers	Examples
Edible	chocolate, candy, cookies, pizza
Tangible	puzzle, trinket, sticker
Exchangeable	token, star, checkmark
Activity	game, free time, field trip
Social	smiles, teacher attention, verbal praise, facial gestures

Allowing students to be teacher assistants is frequently a positive reinforcer.

must remember that before ignored behavior decreases, it usually increases. If the teacher will not be able to ignore a behavior while it increases (for example, if the behavior is harmful to someone), extinction is not the strategy to use.

Three classroom management strategies can be useful to the general education teacher who is trying to accommodate a variety of needs. First is the establishment and enforcement of *classroom rules*. There should be no more than five rules and each rule should be stated in clear, concise, and positive terms. For example, "work at your seat" is a better rule than "don't get out of your seat." Positively stated rules that are established at the beginning of the school year with input from the students are usually more successful in helping students control their behavior than several negative rules already posted by the teacher when the students arrive.

The second strategy for achieving a well-managed classroom is the use of ***contingency contracting.*** This is a group behavior management strategy that involves a written agreements between students and their teachers concerning the exchange of positive reinforcers. The contract outlines the target behaviors and the consequences of displaying those behaviors. The contract should include the following:

- a statement, in observable terms, of the behavior the students are to increase or decrease.

- a statement of the environmental conditions during which the strategy will be implemented.
- a listing of the type and amount of reinforcers that will be provided and who will provide them.
- a schedule of when the delivery of reinforcers will take place.
- a listing of the roles teacher and students can perform to increase the success of the system.
- a time frame for the length of the contract.
- signatures of the students and the teacher (Salend, 1998, pp. 437–438).

The third strategy for a well-managed class involves the use of ***a token economy.*** A token economy (Kazdin, 1975) creates a system in which students earn "tokens" that can be exchanged for rewards. Some tasks have more value than others, and some rewards have more cost. To set up a token economy:

- Identify the behaviors for which students will earn credit.
- Decide on the classroom "currency."
- Assign a value to each target behavior.
- Decide on the privileges or rewards students will earn.
- Assign purchase prices to the privileges and rewards.
- Explain the economy to students.
- Establish a systematic way for students to exchange their currency for privileges or rewards (Friend & Bursuck, 1996, pp. 416–417).

General educators and special educators can collaborate to create rules, contingency contracts, and token economies that are appropriate for a particular class and a particular teaching style. To work effectively, these systems need to be carefully planned, consistently implemented, and adjusted when needed. Consultation from the special education teacher can make this happen.

REFLECTION BOX 2–1

Consider the introductory vignette for Mr. Mason's class. How might a token economy be used to help improve Ashley's completion rate for homework and classwork?

CONSULTATION WITH DIRECT INSTRUCTION

For some students with disabilities, special education is provided when special educators come into general education classes to teach "strategies." This instruction by special educators supplements the guidance and consultative support they also give to the general educator who teaches the diverse class of students the rest of the school day. "Strategy instruction" may be presented to the entire class or taught to a small group of students including students with special needs. Several examples or models of such strategy instruction have been developed. The following have been especially useful in helping students with disabilities be more successful in general education classrooms.

COGNITIVE STRATEGIES. Recent approaches to teaching have increasingly conceptualized learning as an active process in which students construct meaning through thinking, use of prior knowledge and experience, and specific cognitive strategies to understand ideas (Jones, Palincsar, Ogle, & Carr, 1987). Cognitive strategies are especially useful for students with mild disabilities who are described as passive learners and who need guided instruction in how to be strategic in their learning. Once cognitive strategies have been learned, students are likely to be able to process information independent of adult direction.

By knowing "how to learn" through the application of cognitive strategies, students with mild disabilities have a much improved chance for individual task improvement and for surviving in the general education classroom (Graham & Harris, 1993). Students learn to understand the requirements of the learning process. Time is spent teaching the student how to assess the learning situation with respect to the variables of text, task, strategy, learner characteristics, and executive control. Several features of effective cognitive strategy instruction include the following:

- New information is taught by making it familiar.
- Teachers model the strategy.
- Strong emphasis is put on visual imagery.
- Students are encouraged to personalize their ways of coding information.
- Instruction includes overt or active steps to be taken by the students.
- Instructional cues or prompts are gradually faded.

Educators have developed a variety of cognitive strategies to help students learn to plan, check, monitor, and evaluate their own learning. For example, students are often asked to memorize information in general education classrooms and several mnemonic strategies can be used to facilitate students' recall (Ellis, Lenz, & Sabornie, 1987). One such strategy is the CAN-DO strategy. The letters stand for a step-by-step process:

C—Create a list of items to learn
A—Ask self if list is complete
N—Note details and main ideas
D—Describe components and their relationship
O—Overlearn main ideas followed by learning details (Hoover & Patton, 1997).

STRATEGIES INTERVENTION MODEL. The **Strategies Intervention Model** is a specific example of a cognitive strategies approach to teaching students "how to learn." It employs techniques that encourage students to think and act strategically to solve academic problems (Deshler, Ellis, & Lenz, 1996). The Strategies Intervention Model consists of three components: (a) a strategic curriculum (the strategies), (b) the strategic instruction (the procedures used to teach the strategies), and (c) a strategic environment (an environment that promotes the use of the strategies).

The *strategic curriculum* consists of four types of strategies:

1. learning strategies (e.g., reading, test-taking)
2. social skill strategies (e.g., getting along with others, conversational skills)
3. motivation strategies (e.g., establishing goals)
4. executive strategies (e.g., choosing appropriate strategies)

The curriculum is organized as a series of instructor's manuals with accompanying student activities, detailed lesson plans for teachers, and teaching materials.

Teachers proceed through eight stages in teaching the strategies to their students (Table 2–1). According to the developers of the Strategies Intervention Model, it is important to follow the stages during instruction if maximum results are to be obtained (Deshler et al., 1996). Strategy instruction also needs to be provided regu-

TABLE 2–1 Stages and Phases in the Acquisition and Generalization of Learning Strategies

Stage	Phase
1. Pretest and make commitments	1. Orientation and pretest 2. Awareness and commitment
2. Describe the strategy	1. Orientation and overview 2. Current strategy and remembering system
3. Model the strategy	1. Orientation 2. Presentation 3. Student enlistment
4. Verbal elaboration and rehearsal	1. Verbal elaboration 2. Verbal rehearsal
5. Controlled practice and feedback	1. Orientation and overview 2. Guided practice 3. Independent practice
6. Advanced practice and feedback	1. Orientation and overview 2. Guided practice 3. Independent practice
7. Confirm acquisition and make generalization commitments	1. Confirm and celebrate 2. Forecast and commit to generalization
8. Generalization	1. Orientation 2. Activation 3. Adaptation 4. Maintenance

Note: From "Perspectives on instruction and learning strategies," p. 38, by E. S. Ellis & B. K. Lenz, in Teaching adolescents with learning disabilities: Strategies and methods (2nd ed.) by D. D. Deschler, E. S. Ellis, & B. K. Lenz, 1996. Reprinted by permission of Love Publishing Co., Denver, CO.

larly and intensively. Teachers and students should set daily and weekly goals specifying the strategies they want to learn.

In a *strategic environment*, instruction is planned so that strategic learning is facilitated and enhanced. During initial strategy instruction, the teacher emphasizes learning the key aspects of the strategy rather than learning the content (Ellis & Lenz, 1996). When the strategy is learned, the instructional emphasis shifts to applying the strategy to tasks that naturally occur in the student's school life. As each strategy is mastered, the teacher's role in providing feedback lessens. The teacher deliberately and gradually passes to the student the responsibility to learn and perform.

The Strategies Intervention Model, when used effectively, provides students with support and guidance for learning how to learn. Special educators assist general educators in explicitly modeling and guiding students through the routines of learning that will help them learn the content material being taught in their general classes. Training in the Strategies Intervention Model is available nationwide by contacting Dr. Donald Deshler at the Center for Research on Learning at the University of Kansas.

SCHOOL SURVIVAL SKILLS. General education teachers rated student skills necessary for success in the regular classroom. Following are the four highest ratings: (a) following directions in class, (b) coming to class prepared (i.e., with needed materials), (c) using class time wisely, and (d) making up assignments and tests (Ellett, 1993). Such skills have been termed *survival skills* (Zigmond, 1978) because they are critical to school success. Some students with disabilities and some students without disabilities need explicit instruction to learn to perform these skills.

Zigmond and colleagues (see Silverman, Zigmond, & Sansone, 1981) developed a **school survival skills** curriculum for teaching such skills to students with learning disabilities. The curriculum has three strands: (a) behavior control, (b) teacher-pleasing behaviors, and (c) study skills/test-taking strategies.

Teaching *behavior control* relies heavily on simulation and role playing to help students learn to recognize what they and others do in school situations, the effect of one's behavior on other people, alternative ways of responding to specific situations, and the consequences of behaving one way or another (Silverman, Zigmond, & Sansone, 1981).

Teacher-pleasing behaviors focus on what students do to cope with the rules and demands within their classes. Teacher-pleasing behaviors include coming to school consistently and on time, completing assignments, being attentive, and displaying compliant behavior. In some cases, teaching students to monitor themselves on the performance of these teacher-pleasing behaviors increases their output of such behaviors.

The third set of survival skills focuses on *study skills* and *test-taking*. Many students with and without disabilities do poorly on tests because they lack study skills or take tests poorly. Students are taught how to prepare for tests, how to gather and retain information they need to complete assignments and fulfill requirements of content subject courses, and how to demonstrate what they have learned on tests. More information on the School Survival Skills Curriculum can be obtained by contacting Dr. Naomi Zigmond at the University of Pittsburgh.

ONGOING COLLABORATIVE TEACHING

REFLECTION BOX 2–2

The introductory vignettes include several examples of co-teaching or collaborative teaching. These examples show different ways that co-teaching can be used in a classroom. While the examples differ, a number of similarities cut across these methods with respect to what teachers must do to implement each approach effectively. What key features and procedures do you think need to be addressed when two teachers will be teaching collaboratively?

In **co-teaching** or collaborative teaching, the special education teacher is not responsible for teaching a separate curriculum. Instead, the general and special education teachers work simultaneously in the general education classroom and share responsibility for teaching the required instruction in that setting. Co-teaching uses the unique and specific skills of each professional as they teach together. Most general educators are knowledgeable about curriculum and curricular sequencing, especially in the traditional academic areas. In addition, they are skilled and experienced in managing large groups of students. Special educators traditionally have expertise in assessing areas of difficulty within the curriculum and analyzing and adapting instructional materials and strategies (Bauwens, Hourcade, & Friend, 1989). The two professionals working together bring an impressive combination of skills to a single classroom. Many believe that the instructional approaches developed by the two together will inevitably be superior to those developed by either of them alone. Co-teaching typically occurs for a set period of time either every day or on certain days of the week (for example, on Monday mornings). In a high school, co-teaching might occur in every fourth-period Algebra 1 class.

Successful co-teaching requires many meetings and much planning to define roles and expectations, but the extra work brings extra payoffs. Scott and Smith (1988) found that teachers who work in collaborative school environments report enhanced levels of enjoyment of work and also perceive themselves as more effective in the delivery of instruction. Those who co-teach collaborate to design and carry out educational programs that foster students' growth and prevent problems from developing (Pugach & Johnson, 1995). Co-teaching becomes the means by which teachers can challenge themselves and jointly take the risks needed to improve the quality of teaching and learning for their students (Pugach & Johnson, 1995). Co-teaching often also improves the working conditions for teachers by fostering more community spirit.

Pugach and Johnson (1995) suggest the following principles as the basis for implementing co-teaching:

- Teachers challenge themselves to improve their teaching.
- Teachers share responsibility for all students.
- Teachers share responsibility for instruction.

- Teachers communicate regularly about the progress of their work.
- Teachers support their partners (p. 179–186).

Many variations of co-teaching are described in the literature (Bauwens, Hourcade, & Friend, 1989). Friend and Cook (1996) suggest seven approaches to co-teaching (see Figure 2–6). We will discuss three of these here: parallel teaching; station teaching; and remedial teaching.

PARALLEL TEACHING. In **parallel teaching**, the special education teacher and the general education teacher are both teaching the same basic content in the same classroom, but the students are divided into two groups with each teacher responsible for only one group. One teacher may take the accelerated students and provide the same instructional material but add extra problem-solving tasks. The other teacher may work with the students with learning disabilities and other lower-achieving students and teach more slowly and more explicitly. In parallel teaching, the two teachers share responsibility for developing the curriculum units, implementing the activities, and evaluating student mastery of the content. Through co-teaching, each student receives instruction in a smaller group. By sharing their expertise, each teacher can help meet the needs of all the children in the class, especially those with special needs.

STATION TEACHING. In ***station teaching,*** teachers divide instructional content into two parts (e.g., vocabulary development and written-expression practice). Each teacher prepares a lesson on one of the parts and teaches that lesson to half the class. Then the teachers switch student groups and teach the same lesson to the other group. Every student gets both teachers and both lessons. The division of content may depend on the expertise the teachers bring to the classroom. For example, Mrs. Smith, the general education teacher, may develop a vocabulary lesson using words that will be used in the new literature book to be introduced next week. Mrs. Spencer, the special education teacher, develops a written-expression activity on the computer that will generate interest in the topic of the literature book that will be introduced. Each teacher works with half the class and then switches groups.

REMEDIAL TEACHING. When part of the classroom group has mastered a concept but part has not, a remedial teaching approach to co-teaching may be introduced. The group needing remedial assistance is taught by one teacher while the second teacher does an enrichment or extension activity with the remainder of the class. Note that it is not always the special education teacher who is assigned the remedial group. Once the remedial group has caught up, the teachers return to another mode of co-teaching. For example, the two teachers have just completed co-teaching a unit on fractions, but on the unit test it was clear that five students needed more practice before the entire class could move on to the next math unit. One teacher takes these five students and works on the concepts of fractions again with new materials. The second teacher takes the remainder of the class and introduces problem-solving activities that involve the use of fractions.

Co-teaching has several advantages: Both teachers are present and can monitor all learning activities going on in the classroom. It is a useful preventative strategy because many students, not just those with identified disabilities, at one time or another may need

1. **One teach, one observe**

   In this arrangement, one teacher has primary instructional responsibility while the other gathers observational information on students in the class. It is important to remember that either teacher could take on either role.

2. **One teach, one "drift"**

   This approach is an extension of the above. One teacher has primary instructional responsibility while the other assists students with their work, monitors behaviors, corrects assignments, and the like.

3. **Station teaching**

   To station teach, teachers divide instructional content into two parts (e.g., vocabulary and content; new concepts and review). Each teacher instructs half the class in one of the areas; they then switch student groups so that all students receive the same instruction.

4. **Parallel teaching**

   In this approach, each teacher instructs half the student group. The two teachers are addressing the same instructional material.

5. **Remedial teaching**

   Remedial teaching requires that one teacher instruct students who have mastered the material to be learned while the other takes students who have not mastered the material and reteaches it.

6. **Supplemental teaching**

   In this approach, one teacher presents the lesson in standard format. The other works with students who cannot master the material, simplifying it and otherwise adapting it to meet their needs.

7. **Team teaching**

   This co-teaching approach involves both teachers presenting the lesson to all students. It may include shared lecturing, a division of responsibilities for presenting the instruction, or what one teacher has affectionately called "tag team teaching," in which one teacher begins the lesson and the other takes over when it seems appropriate.

FIGURE 2–6 Seven Approaches to Having Two Teachers Co-Teach in a Single Classroom

Note: From Interactions: Collaboration skills for school professionals (2nd ed., pp. 47–50), 1996, by M. Friend & L. Cook. Copyright 1996 by Longman Publishers. Reprinted with permission.

remedial or supplementary instruction. Students benefit from the reduced teacher–student ratio. Teachers can group students along many different dimensions at different times. And finally, the teachers benefit greatly from planning instructional lessons jointly.

Effective collaborative teaching is characterized by positive relationships between partners. It offers teachers an approach to better serve the increasingly diverse and increasingly challenging student body that they are encountering. Yet, co-teaching is not without its challenges:

- Someone is always watching you teach.
- You no longer have your own room.

- You may have philosophical differences with a co–teacher.
- You lose some of the "autonomy" generally associated with teaching.
- You may find your co-workers have different levels of expertise (Pugach & Johnson, 1995).

An especially significant challenge is that co-teaching requires professionals in the schools to make significant changes in their well-established professional identities (Bauwens & Hourcade, 1995). Finding time to plan jointly for the collaborative instruction is also a significant demand of co-teachers. And yet, effective co-teaching is one of the most powerful manifestations of professional collaboration (Pugach & Johnson, 1995).

PULL-ASIDE SPECIAL EDUCATION

As classroom teachers are required to provide instruction to increasingly diverse student bodies, special educators are more frequently asked to provide direct instruction to a small subset of students within the general classroom. Classroom teachers are often torn between covering the full content of the curriculum and spending sufficient time on specific, individual components of that curriculum to ensure that the slower students learn what they are supposed to learn. Many students with mild disabilities need explicit instruction in content and skills already mastered by the other students in

Small-group instruction provides opportunities for students to ask questions.

the class. For these students, an adapted curriculum may be needed for some period of time. A special educator may be asked to teach that adapted curriculum to students with mild disabilities in a separate section of the general education classroom.

This pull-aside, one-to-one, or small-group instruction provides more opportunity for students to ask questions, participate freely in discussions, and respond to teacher's questions. Within this small group, the special education teacher can provide adaptations and accommodations with more ease than when working with these same students within the larger class.

One advantage of using a pull-aside model of special education (instead of the more typical pull-out to a resource room) is that the special and regular classroom teachers have more opportunities to co-plan. Because the special education instruction will be going on in the general education teacher's classroom, it makes sense for both teachers to plan for the students with and without special needs, outlining overall goals and outcomes for the entire class and for the specific students with mild disabilities who are being pulled aside. Planning can cover a single lesson, a unit of study, or a particular length of time (Bos & Vaughn, 1998). Figure 2–7 provides an example of a weekly co-planning form that could be used to facilitate the planning process. Several issues need to be discussed before using a pull-aside model:

Which teacher will give grades to students in the pull-aside group?
Which teacher will make classroom management decisions?
What space will be used for the pull-aside group?
When do both teachers engage in planning and coordinating?

Effective and efficient management and communication are the key aspects of good pull-aside models of instruction.

REFLECTION BOX 2–3

Each of the classrooms described in the introductory vignette demonstrates a different in-class approach to special education. Can you identify the model being used in each example? Consider the model of service delivery Mr. Mason is using to address Ashley's needs. Given that Ashley continues to experience considerable difficulty in the class it appears a new approach may be needed. What alternative strategy would you suggest in this situation?

CHALLENGES FACING IN-CLASS APPROACHES

In the next sections, we discuss organizational, training, funding, and instructional issues relevant to the adoption of in–class collaborative models of instruction.

Time Period: ____________		**Week of:** ____________
Content Area: ____________		
Goals:	**GE**	**SE**
	____________	____________
	____________	____________
Activities	**GE**	**SE**
Monday:	____________	____________
Tuesday:	____________	____________
Wednesday:	____________	____________
Thursday:	____________	____________
Friday:	____________	____________
Material(s)	**GE**	**SE**
Monday:	____________	____________
Tuesday:	____________	____________
Wednesday:	____________	____________
Thursday:	____________	____________
Friday:	____________	____________
Groups/Students	**GE**	**SE**
Monday:	____________	____________
Tuesday:	____________	____________
Wednesday:	____________	____________
Thursday:	____________	____________
Friday:	____________	____________
Evaluation		
____________		
____________		
Other:		
____________		
____________		

FIGURE 2–7 Weekly Planning Form for Co-Teaching

ORGANIZATIONAL ISSUES

One feature of the shift in thinking about the relationship between general and special education from one of *divided* responsibilities to one of *shared* responsibilities has been an increased awareness that existing physical and organizational structures of schools need to change (Baker & Zigmond, 1990). Services and resources for individuals with disabilities will no longer be provided someplace else by someone else. Instead, general and special education teachers would share responsibilities and resources for educating students with disabilities and all other children in general education classrooms. This requires an accompanying shift in the organizational system to a needs-driven, full-inclusion, service-delivery model rather than one tied to placement locations (Welch & Sheridan, 1995).

Pugach and Johnson (1995) have discussed three approaches to full-inclusion models of service delivery, each with a different degree of formal structure:

- one-to-one consultation between special education and classroom teachers
- small teams of teachers working together
- **team teaching**, or co-teaching, in which special education and classroom teachers or groups of classroom teachers form permanent teaching teams (p. 10).

Most would agree that such organizational changes work best when teachers participate in the decision to move in this direction (Friend & Cook, 1996). Such empowerment enables teachers to feel more respected (Maeroff, 1988).

However, changes in organization take time, space, and resources. When more than one person is involved in teaching a class, and more than one teaching philosophy must be reconciled, difficulties can arise. The key to success is the training of the personnel involved in the changes.

TRAINING ISSUES

Most general education teachers have been trained to function individually as expert problem solvers (Friend & Cook, 1990). Furthermore, "few preservice programs for special education teachers offer comprehensive training in collaborative consultation" (Heron & Harris, 1993, p. 31). Even inservice education on being a consultant or a consultee is virtually nonexistent. Although teachers' roles and responsibilities have increased and have become more complex and collaborative in nature, their training has not kept pace. Most teachers do not know how to work together effectively.

Idol and West (1987) suggest that special education teachers lack performance training in consultation skills. They found that although many teacher-training programs recognize the importance of training teachers in the use of the communicative/interactive process of consultation, only a few use performance criteria for evaluating the degree of competence in the trainee. More thorough training, including performance-based assessment of both general and special educators on how to work collaboratively in classrooms, needs to occur at both preservice and inservice levels.

FUNDING ISSUES

Many proponents of in-class, full-inclusion service-delivery models believe that such programs will cost less than the more traditional pull-out service delivery approaches to meeting the needs of students with disabilities. Certainly, in collaborative models resources may be reallocated, but the total cost of services is not likely to change

(Fuchs & Fuchs, 1995b); costs may even go up. When special education services are provided through consultation "resources traditionally used to test and place large numbers of students are redirected toward providing assistance for students and their teachers in the regular classroom, where the problems first arise" (Graden, Casey, & Christenson, 1985, p. 377). Funding in-class services requires a reconceptualization of how funding is allocated to a school system and to a particular school, classroom, or student. The historic legislative use of categories and labels for determining funding would no longer be applicable. IDEA 97—which allows the use of federal special education funds, appropriated for students with disabilities, to provide incidental benefit to classmates who do not have disabilities—established a funding mechanism that supports co-teaching models.

INSTRUCTIONAL ISSUES

In a traditional classroom, instruction is provided by the general educator and the focus of the instruction is on the needs of the entire class. Within the constraints of the district-adopted curriculum and materials, teachers are the only ones making the instructional decisions for their classes. In many traditional classrooms, the needs of individual students are balanced against the demands of the curriculum and what is best for the group as a whole. "Average students" tend to dictate the pace of the class, the design of assessments, and the style of instruction.

As more students with special needs are being served in general education classrooms and co-teaching/collaborative teaching becomes more common, the instructional issues are changing. General education teachers need to be able to not only accommodate students with disabilities in their classrooms, but also accommodate the presence of a second professional in the room. Instructional decisions within these classrooms increasingly will be made by two teachers, not just one (Pugach & Wesson, 1995).

Fundamental instructional changes in most general education classes must occur if students with special needs are to be successful (Baker & Zigmond, 1990). General educators will need to figure out how to integrate more effective instructional techniques for students with disabilities into their routines, and how to integrate a second professional into their room. Collaborative relationships among general and special educators are becoming more critical and are changing the nature of instruction itself. If these changes are to come about successfully, teachers, both general and special, will need to be trained in providing meaningful, challenging, and complex tasks and in planning for interactive group activities with other professionals. Both special and general educators need to work together to support each other as their instructional roles change.

CHOOSING A MODEL

In this chapter, we have described three models for providing special education within general education settings. It should be clear that these models vary considerably from one another with respect to several key features, namely the *extent* to which the special educator is directly involved in providing instruction, and the *duration* of that involvement. Given these differences, how should one approach the task of deciding which model to use in a given situation?

We suggest that selection be guided by several considerations. First of these is the *characteristics* of the students to be served in a particular classroom. Selection of a model must take into account not only the number of students with special needs to be served, but also the severity of their needs. It is also important to consider *curriculum issues* such as the amount of variation a classroom teacher will have to deal with and the number of students who will require unique curriculum objectives, both of which are obviously related to student characteristics. Finally, selection of a model should reflect consideration of *instructional issues* such as the extent to which students will require an alternative instructional approach and the amount of expertise required to provide it.

Figure 2–8 presents a checklist of questions, the answers to which can guide the selection of a model. A rule of thumb in using the checklist is that the greater the variation a general educator will have to deal with, the more extensive the on-going involvement of the special educator will have to be. We suggest that the special educator and the general class teacher complete the checklist together to identify the most appropriate approach for their particular setting. This strategy is especially useful because it engages both teachers in joint planning, establishing a collaborative

Student Characteristics

- How many students with special needs are in the class?
- How extensive are the special needs of these students?
- How much variation is there among special needs of students?
- Will it be difficult to group students with special needs together and with others?

Curriculum Issues

- How much variation in curriculum content will be required?
- How many students will require uniquely different curriculum content?
- To what extent will alternative curricular materials be needed?
- To what extent will curricular modifications be needed?
- How accessible are alternative materials?

Instructional Issues

- To what extent will alternative instructional methods be needed?
- To what extent will instruction require special expertise?
- How available are instructional aides and other support staff?
- How much variation in the pacing of instruction will be required?

FIGURE 2–8 Considerations for Selecting an In-Class Special Education Model professional relationship from the beginning. It also provides an opportunity to discuss the roles and responsibilities each teacher will assume and how those roles and responsibilities might change over time.

One final consideration in selecting an in-class special education model is to remember that *flexibility* is the key. No single approach to providing in-class services will be appropriate all the time and in all situations, given the range of needs typically found within a school. Instead, special educators must be prepared to move among models based on the needs and characteristics of each teacher, classroom, and group of students to be served. Indeed, it is likely that the model selected for a particular classroom will change many times over the course of a school year. Figure 2–9 illustrates this point. The top portion of the figure presents the four in-class models introduced at the beginning of the chapter. These have been placed along a continuum that reflects the special education teacher's level of responsibility for providing *instruc-*

MODEL	Consultation	Consultation with Direct Instruction	Collaborative or Co-Teaching	Pull-Aside
	• discuss strategies • plan modifications • develop materials	• expand consultation activities to include active involvement in teaching • short-term instructional involvement • fade direct instructional support over time	• expand role to include greater emphasis on teaching • longer-term instructional involvement • less fading of direct instructional time	• assume primary responsibility for providing special education instruction

WHEN TO USE	Limited Teaching Assistance Needed	Greater Teaching Assistance Needed	Separate Instruction Needed
	• limited curriculum variation required • limited instructional variation required • limited student variation (fewer students to accommodate, not greatly unlike others in class) • teacher experienced in making modifications, dealing with diversity	• modeling and demonstration required • provide help in establishing a routine or setting up a system • provide training for others (e.g., instructional aides) • special instructional expertise required • teacher less experienced in making modifications	• highly unique curriculum objectives • limited curriculum overlap with others • different instructional method required (e.g., much slower pacing, more frequent repetition and review, different mastery criteria, etc.)

FIGURE 2–9 Continuum of In-class Models of Special Education

tion. The bottom portion of the figure presents a second continuum which describes conditions under which each model might be useful.

We chose to use a continuum format in Figure 2–9 to show that although we presented the models as distinctly different entities, in practice there would be overlap and movement among them. A special educator might use the "consultation" model with a particular teacher, but periodically move towards "collaboration/consultation" when it would be helpful to provide short-term teaching assistance for the general education teacher. For instance, when Ms. Clark suggested to Mr. Cochran that he emphasize teacher-directed instruction with one of his algebra classes and set up cooperative learning groups in another, she participated in these classes for a number of sessions to demonstrate and help Mr. Cochran get started. Ms. Clark resumed her consultative role once Mr. Cochran was comfortable using the methods. Similarly a special educator might move away from "on-going collaborative teaching" to a more "collaboration/consultation" model, as Ms. Clark did in Ms. Robinson's social studies class. The two teachers had been using parallel teaching for several months. During that time, Ms. Robinson's instructional aide had been included in all of their planning activities and had been given a role in delivering instruction. As the aide became more skilled, she was given even greater instructional responsibilities, and Ms. Clark assumed a more supportive role.

SUMMARY

As we move into the 21st century, general education teachers will continue to demand more support from each other and from other professionals to meet the complex challenges their students pose. Teachers will no longer be able to work in isolation. General education classroom teachers and specialists will need to work collaboratively to meet the needs of their diverse student body. Collaboration will become a part of all educators' responsibilities. In addition, as more and more students with diverse and special needs are served in the regular classroom, application of in-class models of instruction, such as those discussed in this chapter, will be critical for all students to experience success. Teachers can resolve some of the challenges their diverse student body brings to the classroom by carefully selecting an in-class approach that enables them to form partnerships with other teachers so that all students' learning is optimized.

FOLLOW-UP ACTIVITIES

1. Identify a target classroom to serve as a context for a planning activity. Select one of the co-teaching models described in this chapter and outline the steps

you would use to implement that approach. Be prepared to discuss why you think the model you selected was a good choice for your target classroom.

2. Use resources such as workbooks and teacher guides to design a scripted peer-tutoring plan that can be used in teaching a student to correctly spell 10 new words. You may also wish to ask other teachers how they might structure such a plan. Your plan should incorporate the key features suggested by Maheady, Sacca, and Harper (1987), which were discussed in this chapter.
3. Write a one-page "defense" for your school principal outlining a rationale for allowing you and a fellow teacher to implement a co-teaching arrangement. Your response should include consideration of instructional, funding, and training issues.
4. Develop a token economy for a fifth-grade classroom. Choose any curriculum area. Be clear about what will be needed, how it will be presented to the class, and any key guidelines that should be taken into account in implementing the plan.
5. Work with several partners to learn more about the competitive teams cooperative learning model. Develop a short presentation for your class which shows how this approach is implemented in classrooms. Your presentation should focus on the procedural steps that should be followed to use this approach.

PART 2

IMPLEMENTING EFFECTIVE IN-CLASS PROGRAMS

CHAPTER 3 APPROACHES TO COLLABORATION/ CONSULTATION

KEY WORDS

collaboration
behavioral model
interpersonal communication
effective listening
needs assessment

OBJECTIVES

After reading this chapter the student will be able to:

1. define collaboration.
2. describe the similarities and differences among theoretical models of the consultation process.
3. describe the nine stages in collaboration.
4. describe questioning, listening, observing, and interpersonal communication skills needed for effective collaborative relationships.
5. list and discuss ways to manage time and energy, resistance and conflict, and consultative resources and records.

I can't take it anymore!" shouted Mr. Hernandez. *"Jeremy is driving me absolutely crazy! You have got to get him out of my classroom. I can't teach. The other kids can't learn and nobody wants to work with him. He shouldn't be allowed in my class. He needs to be in a special class with others like him. I want him out!"*

"Sounds as if you've had a rough day," said Ms. Hart. *"Why don't you tell me exactly what it is that Jeremy is doing? Maybe I can help."*

"He can't sit still. He's always tapping or banging on something. He never raises his hand. He jumps up without permission. He's forever hitting other kids. He can't read, and he won't even try the work. He's lazy. He disrupts every group I put him in by playing and talking."

"He can be a handful sometimes," Ms. Hart *agreed. "Why don't I come in and take some notes about what he's doing? That way I'll have a better idea about his behaviors. Then, if you like, we can sit down and come up with a plan of action to help you out. How does that sound?"*

"That would be great. I'm really at the end of my rope."

"I know what you mean. It can get frustrating at times. I think I can arrange to come to your class tomorrow to observe Jeremy. That will let me get a feel for the situation. Then we can try to connect later in the day or after school to discuss the problem and decide where to go next. I might be able to give you a suggestion or two that may help right away, but we'll probably also want to look at the problem over time. When we meet we can talk about a game plan for dealing with Jeremy."

"Yeah, okay," said Mr. Hernandez. *"I'm not sure there's much I can do with Jeremy, but I'm willing to give it a shot. See you tomorrow."*

The purpose of this chapter is to describe consultation and the collaborative process that it involves. Several theoretical models of the consultation process are presented. The stages of collaboration are reviewed, as are the specific skills needed for implementing collaborative approaches in schools and for managing the implementation process.

Historically, teachers have worked in their own environment (e.g., classroom), isolated from peers. They have each had singular responsibility for their group of students. More recently, however, this approach to teaching has given way to more collaborative approaches that involve two or more professionals taking responsibility for the same group of students. This approach has been particularly evident in serving students with disabilities. In the early 1990's, collaboration among general and special educators and among teachers, related services professionals, and parents gained momentum, in part because of the increasing number of students with special needs being served in general education settings. Today's teachers are expected to provide instruction that is individually appropriate, culturally sensitive, and universally effective to an increasingly diverse student body. To meet this challenge, educators are adopting more collaborative approaches to effective instruction (Berdine & Cegelka, 1995).

What is a collaborative approach? Bauwens and Hourcade (1995) suggest that "collaboration is an ongoing style of professional interaction in which people voluntarily engage in shared program planning, implementation, evaluation, and overall program accountability" (p. 6). Idol-Maestas (1983) suggests that collaboration occurs when special education support services are provided to general educators. Friend and Cook (1996) define collaboration as an interpersonal process, "a style for direct interaction between at least two co-equal parties voluntarily engaged in shared decision making as they work toward a common goal" (p. 6). We define collaboration in much the same way, as an interaction between two or more professionals who are working together to generate solutions to a shared concern. Figure 3–1 illustrates several defining characteristics of this collaboration.

A number of educators in the field of special education have sought to develop approaches to facilitate collaboration between general and special education teachers. In the following section, we discuss several of the theoretical models that have affected collaborative relationships in schools today.

MODELS OF THE CONSULTATION PROCESS

The various approaches or "models" of collaboration used in schools today prescribe the way collaborative participants relate to one another, the types of motivation selected, and the responsibilities of each of the collaborators to implement the interventions. Gallessich (1982) refers to six broad models: mental health, clinical, organizational, behavioral, program, and educational. Babcock and Pryzwansky (1983) differentiate among four models: collaborative, medical, mental health, and expert models. From all of these, we have selected four models we believe represent the theoretical orientations to collaborative interventions in schools today: mental health, behavioral, organizational, and clinical models (see Table 3–1).

MENTAL HEALTH MODEL

The mental health model is based primarily on the neocentered client theory of Rogers (1959), but it also takes into account interpersonal factors. In this model, the collaborator often serves as a facilitator or relationship builder. Proponents of the mental health model focus on improving the interpersonal skills of the teacher. The

FIGURE 3–1 Defining Characteristics of Collaboration

Note: *From* Interactions: Collaborations skills for school professionals *(2nd ed., pp. 6–9), by M. Friend and L. Cook, 1996, White Plains, NY: Longman. Reprinted with permission of Addison–Wesley Educational Publishers, Inc.*

- Collaboration is voluntary.
- Collaboration requires parity among participants.
- Collaboration is based on mutual goals.
- Collaboration depends on shared responsibility for participation and decision making.
- Individuals who collaborate share their resources.
- Individuals who collaborate share accountability for outcomes.

TABLE 3–1 Theoretical Models of the Consultation Process

Consultation Model	Theory for the Consultation Relationship	Knowledge Base for Problem Solving	Goals	Stages/Steps	Responsibilities
Mental Health (Caplan, 1970; Meyers et al., 1979)	Assumes that consultees have the capacity to solve most of their work problems and that consultants can help them increase their range of effectiveness (Gallessich, 1982). Theories that have been applied to how the consultant treats the consultee include neoclient-centered psychology (Rogers, 1959) and Adlerian psychology (Adler, 1964).	Psychodynamics; clinical skills; crisis concepts; specialized diagnostic and decision-making skills; theme interference reduction; one downmanship; avoidance of therapy; relationship building.	Consultant chooses one of four possibilities: client-centered, consultee-centered, program-centered, or administrative-centered. Success is measured by the degree to which the consultation expands the consultee's capacity to diagnose, cope with, and solve emotional or technical problems of the consultee or the client.	Consultant chooses type of consultation for the problem and primary target of interventions. Example 1. Consultant seeks information on nature and scope of work problem, consultee's capacity for problem solving, and ways the consultation might be useful. 2. Consultant "treats" the consultee by offering expert opinion or shared, straightforward problem solving.	Consultant is responsible for gathering information on the nature of the problem and for providing solutions to problems. The consultant/consultee relationship is egalitarian (Gallessich, 1982).
Behavioral (Bergan & Tombari, 1976; McNamara & Diehl, 1974)	Assumes that consultant's application of behavioral/social learning theory will help consultee solve problems.	Flexible knowledge of behavioral programming, principles of social learning theory, and applied behavior analysis.	To reduce the frequency of an undesirable client/consultee behavior; to increase the frequency of desirable client/consultee behavior.	1. Problem identification 2. Problem analysis 3. Plan implementation 4. Problem evaluation	Consultant serves as an expert; consultee is the recipient, although sometimes mutuality of problem solving is emphasized.

TABLE 3–1 *continued*

Consultation Model	Theory for the Consultation Relationship	Knowledge Base for Problem Solving	Goals	Stages/Steps	Responsibilities
Organizational A. Human Relations Model (Argyris, 1964; Lippitt, 1969)	Organizational theory: Problems of organizations must be solved in a manner that incorporates into the process all individuals in the organization because of the focus that each brings to bear upon the other (Lewin, 1951); the influence of the environment on personal growth (Rogers, 1942, 1951, 1959)	Communication skills; decision-making skills; force-field analysis; data collection and feedback; social/psychological, cognitive behavioral; ecological; psychodynamic systems; statistical models and methods; humanistic values and assumptions (Gallessich, 1982)	To bring about planned change by focusing on individuals and their attitudes, values and group processes in the organization; to increase organizational productivity and morale (Gallessich, 1982)	1. Orientation 2. Contract setting 3. Reconnaissance 4. Problem and opportunity development 5. Aspirations 6. Analysis 7. Experimentation 8. Results analysis 9. Program design 10. Implementation 11. Evaluation and feedback 12. Recycling	Consultant facilitates the group's progression through all stages
B. Organizational Thinking (Schmuck & Runkel, 1972)	Same as for the Human Relations Model	Group conflict, inter- and intra-group communication, decision making, methods of goal setting, defining roles	1. Working with subsystems of the organization to develop problem-solving skills 2. Developing communication skills 3. Developing training exercises that start with simulation and evolve to real issues of the school (Schmuck & Runkel, 1972).	1. Entry phase 2. Diagnosis of organization's functioning 3. Selection of a subsystem of the organization 4. Demonstration of the intervention 5. Organizational training	Consultant facilitates process, demonstrates interventions, and provides training

TABLE 3–1 *continued*

Consultation Model	Theory for the Consultation Relationship	Knowledge Base for Problem Solving	Goals	Stages/Steps	Responsibilities
C. Advocacy	Any practitioners of other models may use advocacy consultation; based on conflict theory (i.e. Chesler, Bryant, & Crowfoot, 1981)	Knowledge of law, organizing people, organizing events, media use, negotiation, parent partnership, persuasive writing and speaking, building support networks, tolerance for ambiguity and conflict; known for what they believe in, *not* by particular methodologies. Some advocacy consultants have both expert content knowledge and advocacy process knowledge (Conoley & Conoley, 1982).	To seek due process for various types of clients; to facilitate group process to help people work together; to organize events; to develop partnerships with parents of clients	None specified	Consultant facilitates effectiveness of others
Clinical (Doctor–Patient)	The general characteristic is that it is patterned after psychiatry and adapted for use when consulting with colleagues about clients' problems. *No specific theory.*	Specialized expertise concerning the client's problem; expert power; referent power based on specialized expertise	Expert diagnosis of a client's mental or emotional condition and an authoritative recommendation as to how consultees should treat the 'patient' (Gallessich, 1982); problems are conceived as patient's; goals are limited to the particular case; to increase consultee's coping effectiveness	1. Diagnosis 2. Prescription 3. Treatment	Consultant assumes responsibilities for the case, determines data to be gathered, how to gather them, directly examines client, treats or prescribes treatment; consultant/consultee relationship is hierarchical

Note: *From* The Educational Consultant: Helping Professional, Parents, and Mainstreamed Students *(3rd ed., pp. 12–17), by T. E. Heron and K. C. Harris, Austin, TX: PRO-ED.*

mental health model emphasizes the teacher's *feelings* about the problem situation rather than the observable *behaviors* of the child or the class. The mental health model seeks changes in the collaborator's emotional adjustment that will lead to a healthier emotional climate for the students. Proponents of this model believe its advantages to be: (a) the self-actualization concepts (e.g., establishing healthier self-concepts) are applicable in school settings (Friend & Cook, 1996), (b) the approach takes into account school-related factors (e.g., self-concept), and (c) the emphasis is often on preventing further problems. The disadvantages of interventions based on the mental health model are believed to be: (a) mental health techniques are often difficult to define objectively and require special training and supervised practice to implement and (b) empirical data are lacking in support of the effectiveness of the mental health model for school personnel (Friend & Cook, 1996).

BEHAVIORAL MODEL

The behavioral model of consultation uses concepts of applied behavioral analysis. Emphasis is placed on identifying the target behavior of the person in whom the change is needed. In many cases, this is a student with special needs who is having difficulty in the general education classroom. In many school situations, the collaborator (i.e., the person who has unique skills or knowledge that may apply to the situation) is the special educator. The special educator may assist the general education teacher in assessing the problem behavior and generating a set of data to help understand the discrepancy between the desired level of performance and the actual level. Then, the general educator may be involved in planning the intervention and in carrying out the plans. Both the special educator and the general educator are involved in evaluating whether the intervention was successful and the target behavior of the offending child was changed.

For example, a general educator who has a student with behavioral problems in her class may ask the special educator for assistance in planning a behavioral program. The special educator may, after assessing the situation, give suggestions to the general educator concerning the implementation of a behavioral contract with the student in question. After some discussion between the general educator and the special educator, the contract may be implemented in the general educator's classroom and the student's behavior problems in the general education class may be lessened. The special educator and the general educator may meet weekly to evaluate the progress of the plan.

The advantages of a behavioral model of consultation in schools are: (a) that it is based upon well-researched behavioral analysis strategies and (b) it emphasizes the need for data collection that allows for a true picture of what is going on in the classroom as the basis for both planning the intervention and evaluating its impact. The disadvantages of a behavioral model of consultation are: (a) that the format can create a mentor/mentee kind of relationship that is not truly collaborative, (b) the special educator may not be directly involved with the student with difficulties, and (c) the general educator, in many cases, may not feel comfortable asking the special educator for assistance.

ORGANIZATIONAL MODEL

"The organizational model is derived from human relations and organizational theory" (Heron & Harris, 1993, p. 22). The cornerstone of this model is a system self-study focusing on change in formal and informal procedures and processes (Heron & Harris, 1993). Goals are focused on facilitating group processes and interactions among team members in problem solving and decision making. The collaborator's role is to guide the process and focus on modifying policies and group structures.

The goal of interventions in schools using an organizational model of consultation is the improved functioning of the complex social system. Proponents believe that improved school systems have good effects on the special educators and general educators within them. The advantages of this model implemented in schools are (a) there is a coordinated effort to implement collaboration across the entire school system, (b) system personnel build time for collaboration into the schedule of teachers, and (c) more positive feelings toward collaboration are likely to result. The disadvantages of this model are (a) implementing a systemwide collaborative project may take a prohibitive amount of time and expense and (b) opportunities to implement systematically the entire organizational collaborative process in school systems are rare.

CLINICAL MODEL

The clinical model emphasizes the use of diagnosis to determine the problem. Many speech therapists and school psychologists use a clinical model of collaboration or consultation. A special educator may be asked to test or observe a student to identify the problem, then to participate in the prescription of interventions needed to solve the problem. The special educator may not be involved in implementing the interventions. Proponents of the clinical model in schools believe the advantages are (a) it takes a minimal amount of time for the special educators (or other diagnosticians) and (b) it is particularly useful when a complex problem arises and several expert diagnosticians may be needed to clarify the problem. The disadvantages are (a) the diagnostician often has limited involvement in the general educator's classroom and (b) the problem frequently is assumed to be within the student and not related to instructional or curricular issues.

CHOOSING A MODEL

Each of the theoretical models available to the consultant—the mental health, behavioral, organizational, and clinical—is used in today's schools. Choice of model depends on the type of consultation process that is desired, and on the experience and training of the teachers involved. The mental health model is probably the most difficult for two teachers to implement successfully because the consultant must have extensive skills in developing or shaping interpersonal relationships and in acting as a facilitator. These skills are not commonly found in a teacher's repertoire. On the other hand, teachers *are* likely to have been trained in the use of behavioral principles, and may find the behavioral model of consultation a natural choice. It has also been shown to be effective in helping teachers change their own or their students' classroom behavior. The organizational model may be preferred if a "system change" is desired, rather than a change in a single teacher's behavior. A clinical model may be selected if there are specialists who can form part of the consultation team and provide input into the identification and "diagnosis" of student problems.

REFLECTION BOX 3–1

Review the vignette presented at the beginning of the chapter. Which consultation model or combination of models does it appear Ms. Hart is planning to use in working with Mr. Hernandez?

COLLABORATIVE PROCESS

The collaborative process describes the relationship among the participants in a collaboration (Heron & Harris, 1993). The process also describes the stages that educators go through from the onset until the completion of the collaborative relationship or the accomplishment of its goals. Each educator brings to the process different knowledge bases and each should play an active role in the collaboration. Kurpius (1978) outlines the nine stages that assist in defining the pattern of a collaborative process: (1) pre-entry, (2) entry, (3) gathering information, (4) defining the problem, (5) determining solutions, (6) stating objectives, (7) implementing the plan, (8) evaluating the plan, and (9) terminating the process. These stages are defined in Figure 3–2.

The stages in the collaborative process are not necessarily mutually exclusive. Collaborators may complete more than one stage in one meeting or they may take several weeks or months to complete a single stage (e.g., evaluating the plan). Each collaboration process is unique. For any process to run smoothly, the collaborator (often the special educator) must have a certain repertoire of skills.

SPECIFIC SKILLS FOR CONSULTATION

The skills special educators bring to the collaborative consultation are of utmost importance; they need skills that will permit them to work effectively across a variety of educational situations (Berdine & Cegelka, 1995). Special educators and other professionals who collaborate must have not only instructional expertise but also effective interpersonal skills. Conoley & Conoley (1982) believe that a collaborator must be

1.	*Pre-entry*	The collaborators clarify their own orientation toward the consultation process.
2.	*Entry*	The collaborator establishes rapport and determines the conditions of the issue at hand. Roles and responsibilities are addressed.
3.	*Gathering information*	The educators involved gather information that will assist with the problem under discussion.
4.	*Defining the problem*	The educators agree on the definition of the problem; the parameters of the problem are described in observable and measurable terms. If more than one problem exists, the problems are ordered from most critical to least critical.
5.	*Determining solutions*	Several solutions to the problem are generated. Collaborators explore the feasibility of each solution.
6.	*Stating objectives*	Objectives are stated to give clear parameters to the solution.
7.	*Implementing the plan*	The plan agreed on by all collaborators is implemented. Specific responsibilities are outlined.
8.	*Evaluating the plan*	Timely evaluation of the plan takes place to determine if positive change has occurred. A method for monitoring progress is set in place.
9.	*Terminating the process*	The process is terminated by all collaborators when the decision is made that the objectives have been met.

FIGURE 3–2 Nine Stages in the Consultation Process

Note: *From* The Educational Consultant: Helping Professional, Parents, and Mainstreamed Students *(3rd ed.) (pp. 12–17), by T. E. Heron and K. C. Harris, 1993, Austin, TX: PRO-ED*

friendly, open, nonthreatening, and good with groups. Idol-Maestas and Ritter (1985) suggest the following skills are critical for special educators:

- Skills in assessing the behavior of students
- Group interaction skills for participating in staff conferences
- Skills in developing written individual education plans (IEPs)
- Skills in developing plans for decelerating inappropriate social behaviors
- Skills in locating appropriate instructional materials
- Skills in generating activities for specified objectives

To implement a collaborative process effectively, we believe teachers must also have effective skills in the following areas: (a) interpersonal communication, (b) listening, (c) questioning, and (d) observing. These four skill areas encompass several of the skills suggested by Idol-Maestas & Ritter (1985) and are described in greater detail here. Additional important skills involving generating activities, writing objectives, and assessing behaviors will be covered in later chapters.

REFLECTION BOX 3–2

In her brief interaction with Mr. Hernandez, Ms. Hart did several things that illustrate effective consultation skills. Although some of the things she did might seem minor or incidental at first glance, they will go a long way toward setting the stage for a successful collaboration between the two teachers. What do you see as some of the key features of Ms. Hart's response to Mr. Hernandez's situation?

INTERPERSONAL COMMUNICATION SKILLS

It takes more than effort to develop and maintain harmonious and productive working relationships (Bauwens & Hourcade, 1995). With more students with special needs served in general education classrooms, special and general educators are now communicating in the following ways: exchanging student progress information, sharing diagnostic testing information, sharing responsibility for grading, participating in collaborative long- and short-term educational planning, and meeting together with parents and other professionals (Volts, Elliott, & Cobb, 1994). Effective interpersonal communication skills are essential to the smooth-running of these communications. Johnson (1996) identified four interrelated components of interpersonal skills:

1. knowing and trusting each other
2. communicating with each other accurately and unambiguously
3. accepting and supporting each other
4. resolving conflicts and relationship problems constructively

As trust develops, teachers will become more secure and more willing to share information. When teachers feel secure they focus more on the problem than on protecting themselves or their beliefs. Communication focuses on accurate and unambiguous facts instead of on personal differences. Teachers who feel secure in collaborative ventures are confident that their disclosures will remain confidential and they are able to contribute and accept suggestions freely. A sense of trust can be built by accepting and expressing support and understanding. Ridicule, rejection, and criticism lead to the destruction of trust. Good interpersonal skills are needed to resolve conflicts constructively. Such skills can begin with developing good listening skills.

LISTENING SKILLS

Listening is an essential element in many aspects of life. In collaborative ventures, listening is especially critical. When you listen, you show concern and a desire to comprehend what a person is saying (Friend & Cook, 1996). Listening also helps to keep the focus of the consultation where it belongs, instead of on nonrelated issues (e.g., the weather, after-school tasks). Listening can assist in the building of rapport. Listening allows you to gain accurate and adequate information. Educators confirm that good, active listening facilitates collaboration (Idol-Maestas, Lloyd, & Lilly, 1981; Idol-Maestas & Ritter, 1985).

Many responses can interfere with effective listening. Friend and Cook (1996) discuss the following:

- *Rehearsing a response*—you often miss what was said.
- *Daydreaming*—you lose understanding of the other's message.
- *Stumbling on "hot words"*—by concentrating on one or two words such as "pay raise" or "biting" you do not hear all of what was said.
- *Filtering messages*—by assuming you know the topic you may tune out the entire discussion and not hear what is actually being said.
- *Being distracted by extraneous details*—by concentrating on an extraneous detail (such as the speaker's haircut) you may miss what is said.

Most teachers would agree that effective, responsive listening is important in building collegial relationships; however, few teachers have been taught to listen effectively. Being aware of the responses that may hinder effective listening is the first step in improving listening skills. Friend and Cook (1996) list the following as additional strategies for improving listening skills:

- Repeat the information conveyed to you at the completion of the discussion.
- Categorize the information as you receive it, revising your sorting system as more information is given.
- Keep written notes for reference as the information is conveyed to you to help you remember details.
- Select and use a signal to hold your response; write a star or question mark next to the section in which you have a question in your notes. This will remind you of a response you want to make when the time is appropriate.

Effective listening also requires the use of verbal responses that show the other teacher you are following her thoughts and feelings. Verbal responses (e.g., "I see", or "oh" or "uh-hum") added to nonverbal listening responses (e.g., nodding, comfortable eye contact, leaning forward slightly) signal that you are listening to what is being said.

QUESTIONING SKILLS

Questions are often used as the primary source of information during collaborative ventures. It is important to master the skill of phrasing appropriate questions. The way a question is phrased greatly affects the response you receive (Friend & Cook, 1996). For example, a question that seeks information would be phrased differently from a question that provides information (e.g., "What reading textbook have you used with Jessica?" or "What do you think would happen if you asked Michael's parents to take him to a doctor for an examination?").

Questions are tools that can be used to clarify and guide the process of communication. Questions should be specific and designed to elicit information related to frequency, duration, intensity of the problem, and the conditions under which problem behaviors occur.

Although questions are very useful, special education teacher/consultants must be careful that their questions do not sound like an interrogation. For example, in some situations when one teacher comes to another teacher requesting help with a "problem child," the first strategy used is to ask a series of questions. The teacher requesting the help may feel put on the spot. Too many questions may destroy the possibility of developing a collaborative relationship. Yet, it is difficult to avoid the use of questions entirely, and you don't want to. Questions should be one of several communication strategies in a consultant's repertoire. Used along with other strategies, questions can actually encourage collaboration.

Questions serve several purposes in a collaborative relationship: (a) to gain additional information from the other teacher, (b) to check that information has been understood, and (c) to understand what the other teacher is feeling about the situation (see Figure 3–3). Thus, questions can be used to request clarification, to paraphrase what another educator has said, and to check the other participants' feelings about the situation to better understand the situation of concern.

In some collaborative relationships questions can be used appropriately to request clarification concerning information that is provided. Consultants may ask questions to confirm what they already know, or to clarify information they did not understand. For example, "Did I understand your situation to be . . . ?", or "Did I describe your situation accurately?" Another use of questions may be to paraphrase another person's

FIGURE 3–3 Purpose of Effective Questions

Requesting Clarification

The most consistent error is to assume you have understood the other teacher. There are many ways to request clarification. For example, "I am not sure I understand what you have just said?" or "What do you mean by the word *hyperactive*?"

Paraphrasing

It is a good habit to paraphrase the other educator's responses to be certain that your understanding is correct. For example, "I think what you are saying is that Megan has difficulty with completing her homework. Is that correct?"

Perception Checking

An important aspect of maintaining a relationship is to understand not only content, but also the feelings of the communicator. A good perception check communicates that you want to understand the other teacher's feelings. For example, "I bet you are feeling frustrated by Justin's lack of progress in reading!"

statements to convey understanding. In paraphrasing, "the consultant restates in her own words what she thinks another person has just said" (Friend & Cook, 1996, p. 91). Paraphrasing focuses on relatively small units of information and involves little or no inference. By accurately restating what another person has said and asking if your restatement is correct, you communicate that you were attending to and trying to understand what the other person was saying. Paraphrasing may also help to clarify the information the educator related to the consultant. For example, "Did I hear you correctly, that Michael has difficulty with reading independently?"

The third use of questions may be to clarify the perception of the speaker. In perception-checking, consultants confirm what the educators think about the situation they have described. For example, "Does it seem his behavior is upsetting your other students and making it difficult for you to carry out your lesson plan?" By recognizing another educator's anger, sadness, or frustration, consultants can begin to develop trusting and working relationships. Empathy is not always easy to convey. It requires excellent attending and listening skills (Welch & Sheridan, 1995).

Too many or too few questions can hinder effective communication. Yet if used effectively, questions can serve as the primary means through which a consultant seeks information during collaborative activities.

OBSERVATION SKILLS

In addition to listening and questioning, another skill important in the consultation process is the ability to observe in the classroom. Careful observations have long been recognized as integral to the information-gathering phase of the consultation process (Idol, Nevin, & Paolucci-Whitcomb, 1994). Consultants can be of great assistance to general education teachers when they conduct classroom observations of student or teacher behaviors (Heron & Harris, 1993). The general educator may have little opportunity during the school day to isolate and observe a particular student during a class activity. The consultant can provide the observational data from which an intervention can be planned. Data collected on specific behaviors can help set goals, plan programs, and evaluate the effectiveness of interventions (Dettmer, Thurston, & Dyck, 1993). A consultant can select several types of ongoing measurement strategies to observe a student's behavior. (See chapters 5 and 8 for more details on how to observe.)

But observing in another teacher's class is not an easy task. It is often uncomfortable for both parties when a consultant enters a general educator's classroom to observe—especially for the teacher, who can become tense and anxious. Several strategies can facilitate the process of observation and ease the teacher's anxiety. Dettmer, Thurston, and Dyck (1993) suggest the following for consultants:

- Offer a positive comment when entering the room.
- Sit unobtrusively in an area designated by the teacher.
- Avoid getting involved with classroom activities.
- Record behaviors in code.
- Exit with a smile and a supporting glance to the teacher.

- Provide the teacher with positive specific comments about the classroom observation soon after your visit.

A single observation is often not helpful; it is best if repeated observations take place. With multiple days of data, consultants can provide the teacher with many examples and a more reliable understanding of the behavior or problem in question. It is difficult for the observer not to notice teacher behaviors. If instructional issues are in need of modification, the consultant should, in a nonthreatening manner, discuss possible instructional changes.

Effective observation skills are critical to a collaborative relationship.

REFLECTION BOX 3–3

In preparing to observe Jeremy's performance in Mr. Hernandez's classroom Ms. Hart should identify in advance the types of things she will want to focus her attention on. This is an important step since classrooms are typically busy places where lots of things can be going on at one time. What should she plan to look at when she visits the class?

IMPLEMENTING CONSULTATION IN SCHOOLS

Implementing consultation in school settings is not easy. Several roadblocks often need to be circumnavigated. Johnson, Pugach, and Hammittee (1988) discuss pragmatic and conceptual barriers to consultation. Their pragmatic barriers include "(a) the confusing nature of the definition of consultation and the role of the consultant and (b) the lack of time to engage in consultation" (p. 42). Their conceptual barriers include "(a) the credibility of the special educator in relation to the general classroom, (b) the match between the thinking of special education consultants and classroom teachers, (c) the problem of the hierarchy of education professionals, and (d) the knowledge bases of general and special educators" (p. 43). Barriers, whether pragmatic or conceptual, halt the development of effective collaborative relationships. "Recognizing these barriers and becoming aware of how easily they become part of your interactional style is the first step toward eliminating them from your style of communication" (Pugach & Johnson, 1995, p. 89). In the following sections we discuss potential barriers identified as having the greatest influences on impeding implementation of collaborative consultation in schools today. We also give suggestions for eliminating these barriers.

MANAGING RESISTANCE AND CONFLICT

As human interaction increases, so will conflict. Friend and Cook (1996) define conflict as "any situation in which one person (or group) perceives that another person (or group) is interfering with his or her goal attainment" (p. 118). It is natural to be uncomfortable when someone disagrees with you or to be resistant when change is on the way. It is important that educators understand conflict, its causes, and ways to manage it constructively and positively (Welch & Sheridan, 1995).

Many sources of conflict exist in collaboration. In some cases, special educators' understanding of the demands and pressures of the general classroom is in question. Ideas emerging from the consultation process may not seem workable to general classroom teachers; the ideas may be seen as "belonging to" the special educators. Classroom teachers also may believe they are perceived as having less expertise in running a classroom, not more. Newly trained special educators may also feel resistance from the more "experienced" general educators in their buildings. As a new teacher it may not be easy to make suggestions to a veteran. For collaboration to work, the special education teacher/consultant must try to identify the specific sources of conflict and methods of coping with them.

Pugach and Johnson (1995) suggest the following for managing conflict and resistance:

- Avoid giving advice.
- Avoid giving false reassurances.
- Avoid too many questions.
- Do not let your attention wander.
- Avoid interruptions.
- Do not use clichés or quick fixes.

By following this advice, the special education teacher will be able to lessen resistance to the collaborative relationship.

REFLECTION BOX 3–4:

Judging from Mr. Hernandez's comments in the vignette, he does not appear resistant to the idea of entering into a collaborative relationship with Ms. Hart. There is, however, some evidence that he might resist the solutions she may propose. What evidence do you see that supports this view? Knowing that may be the case, what steps would you take along the way to try to address the problem?

MANAGING TIME AND ENERGY

"Collaborative activities require time—often more time than would be needed if the activity were being completed by one person" (Friend & Cook, 1996, p. 13). Thus it should be no surprise that many teachers identify *time* as one of the major barriers to collaboration (Bauwens, Hourcade, & Friend, 1989; Idol-Maestas & Ritter, 1985; Idol, et al., 1994). Finding time to interact may be hard for busy teachers; finding time to reflect may be nearly impossible. Also, teachers are reluctant to seek help from a busy "consultant." The special education teacher/consultant who appears overwhelmed is unlikely to receive many requests for consultation.

West and Idol (1990) reported several solutions for managing time for consultation (See Figure 3–4). Among them, obtaining administrative support for a scheduled planning time is the most essential. Once consultation programs are in place, the requirement for lengthy planning sessions is reduced, but at the beginning there is never enough time to talk and to plan. Consultants can use several strategies to facilitate establishing collaborative relationships; some are listed here:

- Be aware of the limited time and energy all teachers have available; choose priorities carefully (i.e., which concern is of greatest need of attention).
- Eliminate fear of the unknown; describe clearly the role of special education teacher/consultant and collaborator early in the school year and allow teachers to ask questions about the role.
- Be aware that the views of special education teacher/consultants may predispose them to seeing problems differently than general education teachers; make sure all views are heard and discussed before a decision is reached.
- Advertise collaborative activities that have worked; let other teachers know of the successes and work on determining why the failures occurred.

- Regularly bring large groups of students together for special types of school experiences (e.g., guest speakers, films, plays) with few staff supervising.
- Have the principal or other staff/supervisor teach a period a day on a regularly scheduled basis.
- When students are working on the same independent assignment or study activity, arrange for them to be clustered together in large groups (e.g., multipurpose room or library).
- Hire a permanent "floating" substitute (this may be done at no cost to the school district by business community school adopter).
- Utilize aides or volunteers to guide or supervise groups of students at class changing time, lunch, or recess.
- Utilize volunteers (e.g., parents, grandparents, community business leaders, retired teachers).
- Have the principal assign a specific time each week for staff collaboration only.
- Alter the school day to provide staff collaboration time without students.
- Utilize student teachers.
- Have the principal set aside one day per grading period as "Collaboration Day."
- Have the faculty vote to extend the instructional day 2 days per week for 20 minutes to provide a collaboration period for staff.

FIGURE 3–4 Strategies for Increasing Consultation Time for Teachers

Note: *From "Collaborative consultation in the education of mildly handicapped and at-risk students," by J. F. West and L. Idol, 1990,* Remedial and Special Education, *11(1), pp. 22–31. Copyright 1987 by PRO-ED, Inc. Adapted by permission.*

- Time is critical and for collaborative efforts to be successful time needs to be available; talk to the principal about scheduling time for collaborative activities.

None of the strategies listed here will work successfully in every situation, nor are they all needed in every situation. It is important, however, to be aware of these strategies because they help collaborative activities operate more smoothly.

MANAGING CONSULTATION RESOURCES AND RECORDS

Other resources that usually need to be managed are the resources of related service personnel and the keeping of records. Given that many students with special needs use the services of speech and language clinicians, counselors, vocational teachers, and so on, the consultant can orchestrate these separate services into an integrated program.

Every special educator will agree that paper work can be overwhelming. Too much paper work and too little time to complete it is their most common complaint. Yet careful and complete paper work is essential, and time should be allocated for accurate completion of required paper work. The key is for educators to manage their paper work so it does not manage them (Dettmer, Thurston, & Dyck, 1993). Dettmer, Thurston, and Dyck (1993) suggest the use of a consultation log (see Figure 3-5) to help educators keep efficient records of collaborative relationships. Confidentiality of the parties involved, of course, should be ensured.

More and more teachers are using technology to help keep up with their paperwork demands.

Client (coded): ______________________ Consultee (initials): __________

Initiator of consultation: ______________________

General topic of concern: ______________________

____

Purpose of consultation: ______________________

____

____

Brief summary of consultation: ______________________

____

____

____

Steps agreed on—by whom, by when: ______________________

____

____

____

____

Follow-up: ______________________

____

Most successful part of consultation: ______________________

____

Consultation areas needing improvement: ______________________

____

____

FIGURE 3–5 Suggested Format for a Consultation Log

Note: *From* Consultation, Collaboration, and Teamwork *(p. 207), by P. Dettmer, L. P. Thurston, and N. Dyck, 1993, Boston: Allyn & Bacon. Copyright 1993 by Allyn & Bacon. Adapted by permission.*

All teachers should possess consultation and should be provided with the time to seek out individuals they believe have the expertise that will help them solve their problems.

HOW TO GO ABOUT CONSULTATION

As you begin to reflect on the various models of consultation, the skills needed to implement consultation, and the possible barriers to effective collaborative relationships, you may ask yourself, "Now that I know all this information, how do I get started?" or "How do I begin a collaborative relationship with one of my colleagues?" We provide in this next section specific guidelines for teachers beginning their collaborative/consultative relationships. We describe how to build one-on-one collaborative relationships and more formal group relationships.

ONE-TO-ONE COLLABORATIVE ARRANGEMENTS

Collaborations may begin because a general education teacher asks a special education teacher for suggestions on how to solve a problem with a particular student. Or the special education teacher may be asked by the principal to serve as a resource for other teachers. In either scenario, two teachers begin to work together to solve a dilemma (e.g., a child who is having difficulty learning something, or staying on-task). As the two teachers begin to work through the nine stages of collaboration listed in Figure 3–2, several things will make the collaborative arrangement more successful. If the principal has designated the special education teacher as a resource, the principal or special educator might want to send a note at the beginning of the year to all teachers in the building. The note should explain what this teacher's new job entails and inform other teachers in the building of a procedure to use for contacting the special education teacher/consultant. The note may also clarify the orientation toward the consultation process that will be used (i.e., Pre-Entry Stage). Figure 3–6 provides an example of a pre-entry stage note. After contact from one or more teachers, the special educator/consultant should set up a schedule for individual conferences.

BEFORE THE CONFERENCE. As the facilitator of the meeting, the special education teacher/consultant should send a brief note to the general education teacher suggesting a time and place for the meeting. In addition, the note should include a brief description of the purpose of the meeting and a list of any materials the general edu-

FIGURE 3–6 Example of an Introductory Note from a Special Education Consulting Teacher

August 24, 1997

Dear Colleagues,

I have been asked to be a resource teacher during the first two periods of each day. I would like to work collaboratively with each of you to assist some of the learners in your classes who are having difficulty. For example, I can observe and collect data on a student's performance in class, or serve as a co-teacher assisting with accommodations for several students. Please drop a note in my mailbox if I can be of any assistance or if you would like to just brainstorm some ideas.

FIGURE 3–7 Example of a Pre-Meeting Note

> Dear _______________,
>
> I am looking forward to our meeting. I have signed up for **the conference room in the library at 3:00 on Friday the 15th**. Please bring with you any recent instructional work completed by Timothy. If you have any of his recent test scores, bring them also. I hope we can brainstorm for about 20 minutes about some methods that may help Timothy be more successful in your class. If you have any questions or this time is not convenient for you, please drop a note in my box.

cation teacher should bring to the meeting (e.g., the target child's recent test scores). The note does not need to be formal; its purpose is to clarify expectations about the outcome of the meeting. Figure 3–7 is an example of a pre-meeting note.

The special education teacher may also want to plan an agenda for the meeting and bring any materials collected about the student in question. The agenda will serve as a guide during the meeting. The agenda should be flexible, accommodating any last-minute changes. Most meetings between two teachers will seem informal, still the meeting should be structured enough to allow each teacher to share information, brainstorm together, and begin a collaborative relationship.

THE CONFERENCE. As the meeting begins, the special education teacher/consultant will want to begin building rapport by clarifying the purpose of the meeting (i.e., Entry Stage). To do this, the special education teacher would acknowledge appreciation for the participation of the other teacher, demonstrate interest in the other teacher's problems both verbally and nonverbally, and use jargon-free language and the interpersonal skills discussed earlier in this chapter. The special education teacher/consultant and general education teacher may also want to discuss each of their own philosophical orientation toward the consultation process at this first meeting.

An individualized consultation program planner (ICPP) is helpful in defining the issues that arise at this first meeting. An ICPP allows a visual mapping of the student's behaviors that may need changing, the reinforcement chosen for appropriate behavior, and the implementation plan that both teachers decide on. The ICPP also will serve as a guide for evaluating the success of the intervention. Finally, the ICPP is a useful visual summary of the ideas generated during the meeting. Figure 3-8 provides an example of an ICPP.

AFTER THE CONFERENCE. After the meeting, if the student was not present, the special education teacher/consultant may want to spend time reviewing the meeting with the student. The consultant may also want to share the outcome of the meeting

Having the student present when discussing the goals of her ICP facilitates the entire process.

with other professionals who are working with the student. Throughout the process, it is a good idea to record thoughts in a journal that can be referred to later, as necessary. The special education teacher/consultant may also want to follow up on the parts of the ICP that require actions. It may be that the consultant's responsibility is to gather information on the student from past records (i.e., Gathering Information Stage).

FURTHER DEFINITION OF THE PROBLEM. It may be necessary to meet again after all the relevant information is gathered. At this meeting the teachers involved should come to a clear definition of the problem and outline the parameters of the problem in observable and measurable terms. If more than one problem was listed, the two teachers may want to rank them from most critical to least critical (i.e., Defining the Problem Stage). During the second meeting further elaboration of possible solutions might take place. Relevant reinforcers and possible contracts may be listed (i.e., Determining Solutions Stage). Stating the objectives of the plan clearly assists everyone in the implementation of the plan (i.e., Stating the Objectives and Implementing the Plan Stages). It may be the responsibility of the special education teacher/consultant to check with the general education teacher in one week to determine if progress has been made. Finally, timely evaluation of the plan must take place. Always try to remember to share successes and take the time to evaluate and reflect on meetings that do not finish successfully (i.e., Evaluation of the Plan and Termination of the Process Stages).

INDIVIDUALIZED CONSULTATION PROGRAM PLANNER

Date: ____________________

Student name: ____________________

Grade/Teachers: ____________________

Consulting teacher: ____________________

Problem Behaviors	Management Tips Reinforcers/Motivation	Teacher Communication
1.	1.	______ daily
2.	2.	______ weekly
3.	3.	______ other
4.	4.	______ cards
5.	5.	______ contracts
		______ other

Target Behavior	Strategies	Person Responsible	Criterion

Special Notes:

FIGURE 3–8 Example of an Individualized Consultation Program Planner

PROVIDING CONSULTATION TO A GROUP

Frequently, consultants serve as the stimulus for change in a total school program; they help develop the context within which change can be initiated. Consultants and special educators inherit the responsibilities for providing inservice or workshop programs to the faculty in their buildings. Keep in mind that collaboration can be cultivated through carefully designed and well-conducted inservice or workshop activities. Unfortunately, workshops that resemble "those-same-old" staff development programs are not regarded highly by teachers. Yet, staff development should be a fundamental part of any plan for improving education for all students, and it can be a way to extend consultation skills to a larger group.

Special education teacher/consultants who are responsible for developing a workshop for teachers in the building should approach the potential participants as the adult learners and professionals that they are. Most participants not only want part ownership of the inservice process, but also resist all aspects of inservice workshops that appear to be attacks on their professional competence.

PLANNING A WORKSHOP. The first step to preparing a workshop or staff development program is planning. The advantage of providing a program in their own building is that special education teacher/consultants know their school's context and climate, as well as the needs of fellow teachers. Still, suggestions for topics for the workshop should be solicited from colleagues before the announcement that a workshop will take place. Teachers develop ownership of, and interest in, a topic when they have participated in its selection. To solicit teacher input into the topic or subtopic selection, the special education teacher/consultant may want to use a needs assessment. Needs assessments can be conducted by:

- observing in other educators' classrooms.
- speaking with educators, students, and parents.
- visiting successful programs.
- creating task force committees to determine possible topics.
- creating buzz groups to determine possible topics.
- conducting a needs-assessment survey.

A needs assessment instrument can be created and distributed to faculty. The special education teacher/consultant can choose among several formats: checklists, questionnaires or surveys, open-ended questions, or interviews. Always include space for the person completing the needs assessment to add ideas or comments. In addition, the quicker and easier an assessment is to complete, the more likely it will be returned. Of course, there must be clear instructions on when and where the needs assessment is to be returned. Figure 3–9 contains an example of a needs assessment.

After collecting the completed needs assessments, the special education teacher/consultant should write an announcement to all the participants explaining the results of the needs assessment, and highlight the time and place of the workshop. If possible, light refreshments should be provided and mentioned in the

FIGURE 3–9 Example of a Needs Assessment

Dear Teachers:

I have been asked to present a workshop on a topic of your choice during one of the Monday faculty meetings. Please help me choose the topic by completing the needs assessment below.

Please rate the following topics in order of importance to you:

1 = highest (would love to have a workshop on this topic)
2 = okay (maybe)
3 = lowest (already know this information and would not enjoy another workshop on this topic)

1 2 3 behavior management techniques
1 2 3 instructional modifications
1 2 3 attention deficit disorder
1 2 3 modifications for tests
1 2 3 teaching study skills
1 2 3 other: ______________________

Please complete this needs assessment and return to my mailbox by October 15th. I appreciate your help!!!

announcement. The announcement should be posted in a convenient location (e.g., near the coffee pot) and each teacher should be provided with a copy. See Figure 3–10 for an example of a response to a needs-assessment survey.

In planning the workshop, consultants should consider how they will:

- arrange the setting so that participants are comfortable.
- provide the participants with options (e.g., seating, grouping, activities, and so on).
- keep each activity or subtopic to a maximum of 15 minutes in length.
- keep participants informed of the schedule by preparing an outline with time limits for each section.
- list of the materials needed (e.g., name tags, refreshments, handouts).
- plan follow-up and follow-through activities (e.g., related reference lists, addresses or phone numbers, web sites).

PRESENTING A WORKSHOP. When presenting the staff development workshop, it is useful to personalize the topic to meet the needs of the participants, provide a clear outline indicating time needed for each subtopic, and provide time for questions

FIGURE 3–10 Example of a Response to a Needs Assessment

October 16

Dear Teachers:

Thank you so much for your response to the needs assessment. Based on the responses, the topic of **teaching study skills** was selected. The workshop is scheduled for **Monday, November 1st, in the library**. Refreshments and door prizes will be provided!

Thank you for your help and I look forward to seeing you all there!

and interaction with the participants. It is important to know the audience needs, conduct the inservice in an interesting manner, package the materials attractively, and provide follow-up or support, when needed. If there are many participants, it is a good idea to use name tags or name cards. Most participants respond more readily if they are called on by name. When selecting the time for the workshop, keep in mind that time of day affects the presentation. A workshop that takes place before or after

Well-planned workshops provide useful avenues for support.

school might work, but the time will be short and teachers will begin to watch their clock as the hour draws near for school to start or for them to get away after a long day of work. It may be best to ask for time during a regular faculty meeting. It may also be useful to incorporate into the presentation incentives such as take-home materials, refreshments, random drawings for a free class period, provision of a choice parking spot for a month, or even extra teacher aide time.

It is critical that the workshop begin on time. The opening should "hook" the participants' interest. The closing should stimulate inquiry and commitment, but most importantly, the workshop should end on time. The materials used should be presented through more than one sensory channel. Adult learners appreciate handouts, visuals, videotapes, and interactive videodisc activities.

Handouts and visuals should be simple, clear, and in large type. The most effective ones present one main idea per page and use color graphics rather than black and white. Unless the handout is needed as a component of the presentation, it should be given to the participants at the close of the workshop. If handouts are to be distributed during the presentation, plan the distribution so the participants do not become distracted. Always have extras available.

Immediately following the last activity of the workshop, the presenter should provide the participants with an opportunity to evaluate the program. The evaluation should include both objective responses and open-ended responses. A Likert scale of five to seven rating points is preferable to a yes/no format for forced-choice responses. The information gathered in this evaluation will be useful in designing more meaningful activities for the next workshop and will help improve the presentation. Figure 3–11 contains an example of an evaluation form used by a teacher-presenter of a workshop.

Providing a workshop for colleagues or other educators extends the skills of the special education teacher/consultant to a larger audience. It can be rewarding when a thoroughly prepared workshop comes off well. Fellow educators usually will be very invested in a workshop given by a friend whom they respect and who has asked them what their interests are.

SUMMARY

Consultation is becoming an increasingly common approach to solving school and classroom problems. The approach endorsed by the authors of this text views the consultation as a collegial, interdependent, and co-equal process. Several models of consultation described in the educational literature were discussed. As various collaborating groups of teachers work together, they can create mutual empowerment. Using the skills described in this chapter, educators can work together to implement consultation effectively. Effective management of resistance, time, resources, and paper work also will facilitate the use of consultation. Strategies for effective management of such factors were suggested.

Meeting the Instructional Needs of Students
Workshop Presented to the Faculty of Cascade School
November 1

On a scale of 1 to 5 (1 = lowest and 5 = highest) please rate the following statements pertaining to the workshop. Please add any comments you may have.

	Strongly disagree 1	Somewhat disagree 2	Undecided 3	Somewhat agree 4	Strongly agree 5
1. Content of the workshop reflected careful planning and organization.	1	2	3	4	5
2. Presentation was well-organized.	1	2	3	4	5
3. Questions and comments were sufficiently addressed.	1	2	3	4	5
4. Visual aids and handouts were useful.	1	2	3	4	5
5. Participants' needs were met.	1	2	3	4	5
6. Overall, the workshop was helpful.	1	2	3	4	5

Comments:

FIGURE 3–11 Example of an Evaluation of a Workshop

FOLLOW-UP ACTIVITIES

1. Prepare to discuss the model(s) of collaboration used at your school. In particular, be prepared to describe any problems associated with implementation and the reactions of those involved in collaborative efforts. What do participants see as the strengths and limitations of this approach?
2. Watch a television interview show and develop a list of questions posed by the interviewer. Identify the purpose for each question according to the categories presented in this chapter.
3. Tape-record a meeting at your school in which several teachers are discussing the performance of a student from a culturally different background. Develop a list of the questions asked. Speculate as to the purpose for each question and

identify the response it elicited. Examine each question to determine if it was culturally sensitive and if it elicited the type of response desired. If not, how might the question be modified?

4. Briefly describe any teams on which you served as a member. Try to identify specific features that made each team effective or ineffective. Discuss the culturally diverse makeup of the teams.
5. Conduct a collaboration project with a fellow teacher concerning a student for whom you both share some common concerns. Keep an anecdotal record of your meetings to discuss the student. At the conclusion of the project review the anecdotal record and reflect on how well you implemented steps of the consultation process. Which steps were followed successfully and what steps caused some difficulty?
6. Review the nine stages of a collaborative process described in Figure 3–2 and give an example from your own school experiences. Note whether the stages are self-contained or whether they flow together dynamically.

4

CHAPTER

APPROACHES TO EFFECTIVE COLLABORATIVE TEACHING OR CO-TEACHING

KEY WORDS

large-group instruction
small-group instruction
supplemental teaching
independent learning
academic learning time
transition time

OBJECTIVES

After reading this chapter the student will be able to:

1. design a schedule for support services for students across several service delivery options.
2. discuss several physical aspects of the classroom that enhance or impede collaborative teaching.
3. understand instructional grouping plans and when to use them for large-group instruction, small-group instruction, and one-to-one instruction.
4. provide supports for individualization of instruction in general education classrooms.
5. establish roles and responsibilities for collaborative teaching partners.

The Writer's Craft

Dana Williams is one of three special education teachers assigned to Grove Park Middle School. To say that her job keeps her busy would truly be an understatement. On a typical day, she arrives at school at 7:30 A.M. She uses the time from 7:30 to 8:15 to prepare for her day, catch up on paper work, consult with other teachers, and supervise morning study hall activities (when it is her turn in the rotation). At 8:15 she joins the other teachers on hall duty as they supervise the flow of students from homeroom to the first class period. From 8:15 to 9:00 she meets with members of the School Based Assessment Committee to discuss students who have been referred for special education service. From 9:00 to 10:20, Ms. Williams teaches two study skills classes. Because the school is overcrowded, she does not have a classroom of her own and must hold these classes in two different classrooms that happen to be free during this time period. Unfortunately, this means part of her class time is routinely lost to packing and transporting her materials. At 10:20, she co-teaches a language arts class with Ms. Reed.

Her planning time (11:10 to 12:00) is used to complete a variety of activities. On Mondays, Ms. Williams generally devotes her planning time to taking care of the paper work required for her job. On Tuesdays, she tests children who have been referred for special education services. Wednesdays and Thursdays are spent doing joint planning and problem-solving with Ms. Reed and Ms. Cox, with whom she co-teaches. Fridays are used to plan her lessons for the following week. From 12:00-12:45 P.M., she co-teaches a math class with Ms. Cox. Lunch falls at 12:45. At 1:15, Ms. Williams teaches a pull-out math class and at 2:00 a pull-out reading class. The students who attend these two classes are performing significantly below the level of their classmates and require extensive remedial assistance. It was decided their needs could not be met adequately within the regular classroom and that pull-out services were the most appropriate choice. Ms. Williams uses the last 30 minutes of the day to consult with a range of teachers as needed. At times, this involves making a trip to Grove Park High School to discuss transition plans for her students with teachers who will be working with them next year. After school, Ms. Williams often attends professional meetings, works with the drill team, or meets with parents who are not available during the day. Many of her evenings are spent correcting papers or preparing teaching materials. Yes, her day is extremely active. However, her schedule is typical of most special education teachers.

The purpose of this chapter is to offer guidelines for implementing collaborative or co-teaching arrangements in elementary and secondary schools, including the constraints to collaboration that must be overcome, instructional considerations that must be dealt with, and the responsibilities that each of the teachers in the partnership must be willing to take on. Effective teachers make many management decisions every day about the teaching–learning processes that go on in their classrooms. When two people share instructional responsibilities for the classroom, these decisions become even more complex. Teachers need more than a repertoire of sound instructional practices to make co-teaching work. This chapter addresses the additional skills needed for effective collaborative teaching or co-teaching.

Collaborative teaching, or co-teaching, is said to occur when "two teachers, one general education teacher and one special service provider, share physical space in order to actively instruct a blended group of students, including students with disabilities" (Cook & Friend, 1995, p. 2). In co-teaching, "general educators who specialize in understanding, structuring, and pacing curriculum for groups of students are paired with special educators who specialize in identifying unique learning needs of individual students and enhancing curriculum and instruction to match these needs" (Cook & Friend, 1996, p. 2). Co-teaching is undertaken because students with IEPs have instructional needs that will more likely be met if their supports are moved into the general education classroom through this instructional arrangement.

Many issues need to be resolved if co-teaching is to succeed. Some involve practical matters like schedules and classroom space. Others concern more complex issues involving the communications between the two teachers so they can work effectively together. In this chapter we discuss these issues that must be resolved so collaborative teaching can be successfully implemented.

CONSTRAINTS TO COLLABORATION

SCHEDULING CONSIDERATIONS

Schools operate on schedules that help teachers and students be in the right place, at the right time, working on the right curriculum materials. Most special education teachers will admit that one of the most difficult aspects of their jobs is creating a schedule that optimizes the time they spend enhancing the learning opportunities for students with disabilities and minimizes the amount of time the students are pulled away from important educational experiences in the general classroom. Scheduling becomes even trickier when the special education teacher is responsible for serving students with disabilities across several service delivery models (e.g., in a pull-out, resource-room setting; as a consultant to general education teachers; or as a co-teacher in one or more general classrooms). Scheduling is not easy; it is also never perfect! Our best advice is for special education teachers to begin the school year by creating a schedule that meets most of their immediate needs and try it for one semester.

As the task of scheduling begins, it is important to remember that flexibility is a key to success. Fixed schedules offer predictability and consistency; but special education teachers will be more useful to their students and their general education colleagues if the schedule is dynamic and subject to adaptation as new needs arise. At the end of each semester you should review your schedule and the numbers of students and teachers that need to work with you. Temporary changes in the schedule should be accommodated as needs arise, but more permanent schedule changes should take place at the end of the semester to prevent confusion among students and teachers. The following suggestions may help with scheduling:

- From the onset, design the special education schedule collaboratively with general education colleagues.
- Remember that there are only so many hours in the school day.

- Planning time is critical to successful collaborative teaching. Try to schedule planning time during the school day; do not leave all planning time to before or after school. Lack of planning may produce disjointed teaching.
- It is not possible to co-teach with every teacher who has students with disabilities in their classes.

To begin the schedule, the special education teacher should first block in the times for collaborative teaching. Next, block in the times set aside for students who receive direct services in a pull-out setting. Finally, times are scheduled for providing consulting services. See Figure 4–1 for visual displays of options to consider when scheduling services.

It is critical to schedule time for communicating with general education teachers. This time will prove invaluable in assisting collaborative efforts. It is also important to schedule time for observations in general education classrooms in which you share students—particularly those classrooms for which the special education teacher provides consultation services. These observations will alert the special education teacher to the class demands that students with disabilities are facing, and help in planning collaborative programs. (See Chapter 5 for additional information on how to observe in a classroom).

The logistical problems involved in scheduling can be demanding. An example at the middle-school level illustrates this point. Mr. Spencer, a middle-school special educator, spends part of his day teaming with the seventh-grade core content teachers. Each semester, he teams with one core teacher (e.g., social studies) during the two sections of seventh-grade core classes. He also has two pull-out sections of students with disabilities for study skills and extra support. He must also find time to meet with the eighth-grade teachers with whom he consults. In addition, he has a shared planning period with his colleagues on the seventh-grade team. The shared planning period is difficult to fit into his schedule but it is critical for successful teaming; it is during such planning periods that problem-solving can take place. Mr. Spencer meets with the eighth-grade teachers during fifth period. His first two periods are spent collaboratively teaching with the seventh-grade core teachers. During third and fourth period he provides direct instruction to students with disabilities who need strategy instruction. During sixth and seventh period Mr. Spencer alternates between spending time testing students and planning with seventh-grade teachers. Although he often eats lunch on the run he manages to meet with all teachers and students with whom he works.

REFLECTION BOX 4–1

It is clear that Dana Williams' schedule includes a wide range of activities, some of which she can control (e.g., how she will spend her planning time) and many of which depend on others (e.g., when she will co-teach with Ms. Reed and Ms. Cox). Developing this kind of schedule is no easy task even for the most experienced teacher. What factors do you think need to be considered in developing Ms. William's schedule? What strategies might be followed to help facilitate the process?

CODE: ☐ Pull-Out ☐ Collaborative Teaching ☐ Consulting

Period	M	T	W	TH	F
1			C		
2	CT	CT	CT	CT	CT
3			C		
4			C		
5			C		
6			C		
7			C		

C = Consulting
- Consult and co-plan all day, one day a week

CT = Collaborative Teaching
- Collaboratively teach with an additional teacher for five days a week

Subject	M	T	W	TH	F
					C
Lang. Arts	CT	CT	CT	CT	C
Science					C
					C
Math	CT	CT	CT	CT	C
Soc. St.					C
					C

C = Consulting
- Consult and co-plan all day, one day a week

CT = Collaborative Teaching
- Collaboratively teach with two teachers for four days a week

Period	M	T	W	TH	F
1	CT	CT	CT	CT	CT
2			C		
3			C		
4			C		
5			C		
6			C		
7			C		

C = Consulting
- Consult and co-plan all day, one day a week

CT = Collaborative Teaching
- Collaboratively teach with five teachers for one period a week to teach social skills, strategy instruction, and/or curriculum-based assessments. (This model can extend to 10 or 15 teachers a week.)

Period	M	T	W	TH	F
1					C
2	CT	CT	CT	CT	C
3					C
4	CT	CT	CT	CT	C
5					C
6					C
7					C

C = Consulting
- Consult and co-plan all day, one day a week

CT = Collaborative Teaching
- Collaboratively teach with four teachers for two days a week (Monday and Wednesday with two teachers; Tuesday and Thursday with two others).

Subject	M	T	W	TH	F
			C		
Science	CT	CT	C	CT	CT
			C		
Math	CT	CT	C	CT	CT
English			C		
	CT	CT	C	CT	CT
			C		

C = Consulting
- Consult and co-plan all day, one day a week

CT = Collaborative Teaching
- Collaboratively teach with six teachers for two days a week

Subject	M	T	W	TH	F
Lang. Arts	CT	C	CT	C	CT
		C		C	
Math	CT	C	CT	C	CT
		C		C	
Science	CT	C	CT	C	CT
		C		C	
Soc. St.	CT	C	CT	C	CT

C = Consulting
- Consult and co-plan all day, two days a week

CT = Collaborative Teaching
- Collaboratively teach with four teachers for three days a week

FIGURE 4–1 Scheduling Options for the Special Education Teacher

Note: Reprinted with permission from DeBoer, A., & Fister, S. (1996). Working together: Tools for collaborative teaching. Longmont, CO: Sopris West.

TIME CONSTRAINTS

For most teachers, the days pass too quickly and they do not know where the time went. Teachers who co-teach especially complain about a shortage of time; there never seems to be enough time to plan together, meet with their students, and keep up with the paperwork.

Organization and flexibility are keys to success in time management. In addition, keeping track of where time is spent is important. One way educators can understand how their time is being used is to keep a time log. Bauwens and Hourcade's (1995) suggestions on keeping a time log are provided in Figure 4–2. A blank form for developing a time log in 15-minute intervals is provided in Figure 4–3. Entries in the log should include the time, the teacher, the student, and the activity involved.

Keeping track of time can help special education teachers become more aware of their daily schedules and help them manage their time more efficiently. After several days of keeping a time log, teachers are often surprised to see how they spend their

In constructing a time log to meet the unique needs of any educator, the first step is the identification of all activities one engages in throughout the professional day. These obviously will vary from individual to individual. The following possibilities, though far from exhaustive, can serve as a starting point for one's own list of typical daily activities in the school.

- individual professional planning
- directly teaching or working with students
- miscellaneous school duties (e.g., lunchroom duty, playground duty, bus duty)
- athletic coaching or club/activity advisement
- meetings with other school professionals
- meetings with parents
- student advisement and counseling
- miscellaneous paper work (e.g., filling out report cards, attendance forms)
- monitoring students as they work independently (e.g., in cooperative learning activities, at independent seatwork assignments)
- evaluation of students (e.g., grading tests, calculating report-card grades)
- changing the classroom's physical environment (e.g., changing bulletin boards, rearranging student desks or tables and chairs)

The list should be added to as appropriate to reflect the specific activities one typically engages in at the school. Each activity should be recorded in one of the activity columns.

FIGURE 4–2 Suggestions for Keeping a Time Log

Note: *From* Cooperative Teaching: Rebuilding the Schoolhouse for All Students *(p. 229), by F. Bauwens and J. J. Hourcade, 1995, Austin, TX: PRO-ED. Copyright 1995 by PRO-ED, Inc. Adapted by permission.*

	Activity										Notes
Time Period											
8:00–8:15											
8:15–8:30											
8:30–8:45											
8:45–9:00											
9:00–9:15											
9:15–9:30											
9:30–9:45											
9:45–10:00											
10:00–10:15											
10:15–10:30											
10:30–10:45											
10:45–11:00											
11:00–11:15											
11:15–11:30											
11:30–11:45											
11:45–12:00											
12:00–12:15											
12:15–12:30											
12:30–12:45											
12:45–1:00											
1:00–1:15											
1:15–1:30											
1:30–1:45											
1:45–2:00											
2:00–2:15											
2:15–2:30											
2:30–2:45											
2:45–3:00											
3:00–3:15											
3:15–3:30											
3:30–3:45											
3:45–4:00											
4:00–4:15											
4:15–4:30											
4:30–4:45											
4:45–5:00											
Total											

FIGURE 4–3 Sample Time Log

Note: From Cooperative teaching: Rebuilding the schoolhouse for all students, by J. Bauwens & J. J. Hourcade, 1995, Austin, TX: PRO-ED. Copyright 1995 by PRO-ED. Reprinted with permission.

days. The log may reveal that the general education teacher does a great deal of consulting while passing other teachers in the hall. Time logs can be used to support the need for more assistance or for more time per day to collaborate with additional core teachers. Time logs also can be used to determine which students need additional time or support.

Additional suggestions that enhance efforts to be more efficient include arranging the work environment, completing administrative duties, and managing personal time. Smith, Polloway, Patton, and Dowdy (1995) suggest the following:

- Keep the teacher's desk organized and clear of stacks of papers.
- Organize files so that documents and information can be retrieved easily.
- Use color-coded systems if possible.
- Handle most paperwork only once.
- Prepare form letters for all necessary events.
- Prepare master copies of various forms that are used regularly.
- Keep notes of all school-related conversations with parents, teachers, support staff.
- Use a daily to-do list.
- Break down major tasks into smaller pieces and work on them.
- Avoid getting over-committed.
- Use idle time well (e.g., waiting in lines) (pp. 373–375).

ORGANIZING THE PHYSICAL CLASSROOM SPACE

When two teachers are working closely together in one classroom—either co-teaching or with one providing pull-aside instruction—the organization of the physical space is critical. The organization of the physical space of a classroom can enhance or impede student learning and behavior. Careful organization and arrangement of the classroom can decrease noise and disruption, and increase students' time on task. Walls can be used to display decorations and student work, to reinforce appropriate behavior, and to post rules or strategies. Walls can also be used to divide the class into two sections, one for each teacher. The front right wall can usually be seen from all parts of the classroom and can be used to post the daily homework. Walls can also be used to post specific steps of a cognitive learning strategy or to post important instructions or graphic representations of directions that students must follow. Bulletin boards are also useful places to display instructional information. Students' attention should be directed to the information placed in wall postings or on bulletin boards; teachers cannot assume that students will review posted materials without specific instructions to do so.

The physical organization of the general education classroom sends messages about the collaborative teaming that is being implemented. Two teacher's desks in the front of the room denote equity in the teacher's roles in the classroom. A teacher who is always in the corner or in the back may not be seen by students as in control. Arrangement of the students' desks should allow for flexibility in instructional groupings. Groupings of four desks work best for small-group activities. Individual desks in rows provide unobstructed views of the teacher and may be necessary for children with attention deficit hyperactivity disorders. Alternative desk arrangements should be tried depending on the activity.

Bulletin boards can be used to remind students of specific strategies.

Traffic patterns should minimize congestion and disruption of others. For example, the route to the bathroom or the hall should be clear at all times. Movable walls or shelves will make it easier to divide a class into two sections; each section can then be used for a different instructional grouping. Students need to be taught which areas of the classroom are off limits; and the teacher should avoid creating spaces that do not have any clear purpose, as they can lead to problems. Figure 4–4 provides two examples of general education classroom floor plans conducive to cooperative teaching.

REFLECTION BOX 4–2

It is likely that in co-teaching classes with Ms. Reed and Ms. Cox, Dana Williams will recommend they try several of the co-teaching instructional strategies discussed in Chapter 3. To implement these strategies effectively, however, the teachers will need to use several different grouping patterns. What implications will this have for redesigning the classroom space?

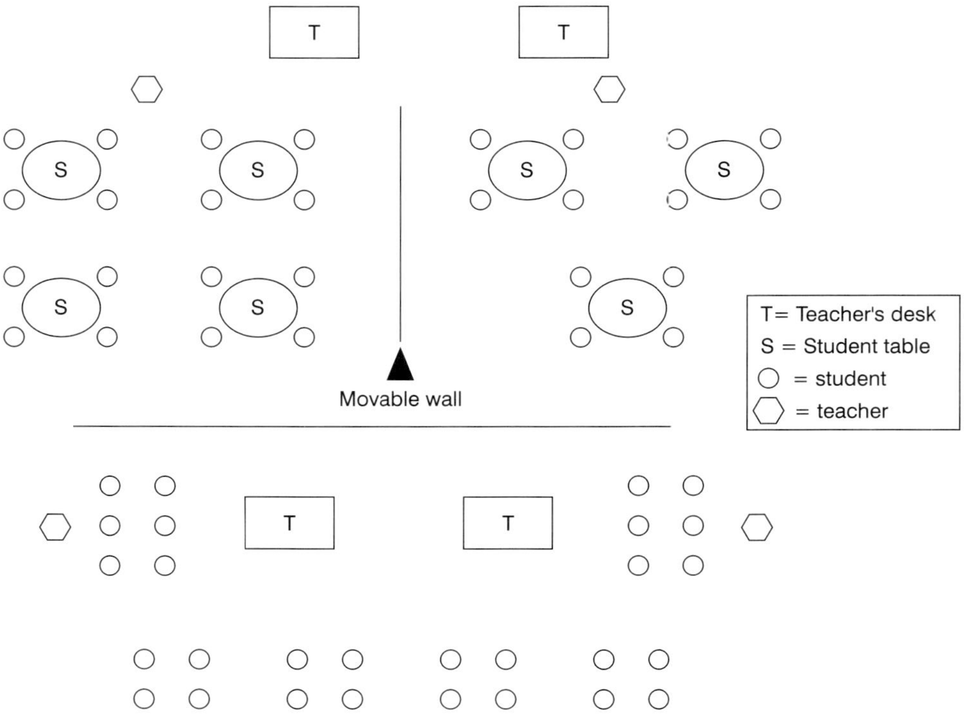

FIGURE 4–4 Two Floor Plans for Cooperative Teaching

CONCERNS THAT REQUIRE ADMINISTRATIVE ATTENTION

In elementary schools, where it is commonplace for all second-grade teachers to be teaching reading at the same time, and all fourth-grade teachers to be teaching math or science at the same time, it is often difficult to arrange a suitable co-teaching schedule for the special education teacher, particularly if the students with special needs are distributed among all the teachers in the school. One solution is to place all students with special needs at each grade level into one teacher's class. This arrangement would appear to make the scheduling of collaborative teaching easier, but it makes managing that classroom much more difficult when only one teacher is available. The first action the administrator of the building needs to take is to determine the number and nature of the students with disabilities in the building. To do that the administrator must (1) list the students who are identified and (2) list the goals specified on their individual educational programs (IEPs). The second decision involves determining whether co-teaching at each grade level is possible and appropriate, given the needs of the students with disabilities. Third, the administrator must identify students whose IEPs specify pull-out special education services. Fourth, the administrator needs to reserve time in the daily schedule of the special education teacher for planning. A major administrative error is to assume the special educator does not need a planning period. Planning time, including time for consultation with paraprofessionals, parents, and other teachers, is critical to successful inclusion at the elementary level.

At the middle and secondary levels, scheduling consulting and co-teaching is often an administrator's nightmare. The task of placing all students in their required classes and selecting the teachers to form the collaborative teams is not easy. The choices often can be narrowed by first thinking about the teachers who may be most open to collaboration. Ideally, they would also be among the strongest teachers in each team. The temptation would then be to overload these classes with high-risk students (Knackendoffel, 1996). To maintain an appropriate balance of more and less challenging students in each class, and to prevent any one class from being perceived as a "dumping ground," it is best to limit the number of students with special needs in any one class to 30% of the total class composition. In addition, the classes that will have two teachers should not be larger than average.

To make co-teaching and collaboration work, the school administration must help create a culture of cooperation, not competition, in the school, and must encourage teachers working together rather than independently. The principal must also remember to create opportunities within the school day for problem solving and planning, so that these are recognized as critical and valued activities in collaborative teaching.

INSTRUCTIONAL CONSIDERATIONS

Sharing responsibility for the same group of students means sharing responsibility for their instruction (Pugach & Johnson, 1995). Responsibilities can be divided up in several ways, but regardless of how they are divided, each teacher must take major responsibility for delivering instruction, at least part of the time. For co-teaching to work successfully, the status of a special educator needs to be changed from someone who works with only the students who have "identified" problems, to someone who teaches all children, or any children; this shift in status will help the students and their parents to see the special education teacher as a "real" teacher and not just a "helping" teacher.

REFLECTION BOX 4–3

Dana Williams has allowed time in her schedule to meet with Ms. Reed and Ms. Cox regularly so they can jointly plan lessons for the classes they co-teach. A key instructional consideration they must address in developing these plans is to decide who will be responsible for teaching what. What guidelines do you think they might follow in making this decision?

Coordinating instructional responsibilities is a critical aspect of successful teaming (Pugach & Johnson, 1995). When planning for instruction in diverse classrooms, both teachers in the pair should learn to vary methods of presentation, methods of practice, and methods of testing.

GROUPING FOR INSTRUCTION

Grouping patterns refer to how students are organized for instructional purposes. For the students with disabilities in general education classrooms, the primary concern should center on their individual needs and IEP goals. Smith et al. (1995) suggest that teachers do the following:

- Give serious consideration to the makeup of instructional groups.
- Make sure that group composition is not constant. Vary membership so that students do not become stereotyped by the grouping arrangements.
- Use different grouping arrangements, sometimes based on skills sometimes based on interests or some other variable.
- Use cooperative learning arrangements on a regular basis, as this approach, if structured properly, facilitates successful learning *and* socialization.
- Determine the size of groups based on ability levels; the lower the ability, the smaller the size of the group (p. 370).

Mercer and Mercer (1998) suggest six instructional arrangements that take advantage of collaborative teaching: (1) large-group instruction, (2) small-group instruction, (3) one-to-one instruction, (4) independent learning, (5) collaborative learning, and (6) peer teaching. Cook and Friend (1995) divide them up in a slightly different way (refer to Figure 2–7).

Large-group instruction frequently consists of one teacher providing the instruction or the information. In collaborative teaching, during large-group instruction the two teachers can take turns presenting information or one teacher can "drift" throughout the classroom assisting students and keeping others on task while the other teacher leads the lesson. Cook and Friend (1995) call this the *one teach–one drift* model. Another way the teachers can share large-group instruction is through what Cook and Friend label *team teaching*. Here, the two teachers fully share the teaching responsibilities of the classroom; they take turns presenting the content material or leading the discussion. In team teaching, one teacher might speak while the other models or demonstrates note taking on the overhead projector; or the second teacher might role-play and model appropriate ways of asking questions while the first teacher delivers the lesson.

In **small-group instruction**, one teacher may work with part of the class, the co-teacher may work with a second group of students, and the remaining students may participate in independent learning, cooperative learning, or peer tutoring. Cook and Friend (1995) call this arrangement *station teaching*. Students and teachers are arranged in stations, so that eventually all students work with each teacher, and, if appropriate, work independently or with each other, as well. Station teaching reduces the student–teacher ratio during instruction but retains for each teacher separate, substantive teaching responsibilities. An alternative small-group instructional model suggested by Cook and Friend is *parallel teaching*. This time, each teacher works with half the group for a designated period but not with the other half; again, each teacher delivers a lesson to a heterogeneous group consisting of half the class.

In yet another approach to small-group instruction, **supplemental teaching**, a small group of students is pulled aside from the large group to accomplish a specific instructional purpose such as pre-teaching or reteaching, enrichment, or assessment; again, each teacher has a defined responsibility. To accomplish *one-to-one instruction*, one teacher may provide individual instruction while the co-teacher provides instruction to the rest of the class; or they may both provide one-to-one instruction while the other students work independently. **Independent learning** is used to provide students with an opportunity to practice, independently, a skill for which they have already received instruction. During this time, co-teachers may both "drift" and provide assistance when needed; or they may use independent learning time to work with a student one-to-one. *Cooperative learning* (also described in Chapter 2) provides opportunities for students to work together to accomplish a goal. Teachers act as facilitators and monitor time on task. *Peer tutoring* provides opportunities for students to work in pairs, coaching each other. Students need training to do either cooperative learning or peer tutoring successfully. Teachers should not only provide the training but also

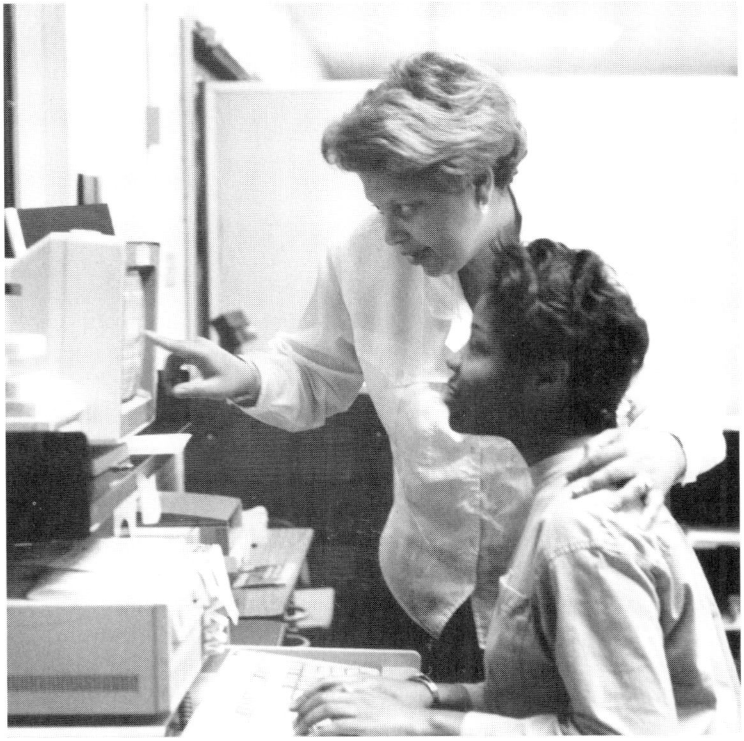

One teacher can provide one-to-one instruction while the other teacher provides small-group instruction.

supervise the activities. Deciding which instructional arrangement to use will depend on the needs of the students and the curriculum area. Refer to Chapter 2 for more discussion of in-class collaborative arrangements.

MANAGING INSTRUCTIONAL TIME

The amount of time students are successfully engaged in academic activities in school is referred to as **academic learning time**. Research has shown that the greater the academic learning time the more students learn. **Transition time** is defined as the time it takes to change from one activity to another. Transition time can occur when students remain at their seats and change from one subject to another or move from their seats to an activity in another part of the classroom or another part of the school. Well-managed, efficient transitions will increase the time available for instruction and academic learning. Teachers should provide time reminders that are both visible and audible so that students will know how much time is remaining (Smith et al., 1995). Modeling appropriate ways to transition between activities (Rosenberg, O'Shea, & O'Shea, 1991) helps students stay focused and on task. In addition, providing activities to be accomplished during transition times increases students' academically engaged time. For example, if students change rooms when they change classes, the receiving teacher might project a focus question, using the overhead, for students to consider as they move into the class. The teacher would also instruct students on procedure: Enter the classroom and immediately begin working on the daily focus question. The question could be an advanced organizer for the material to be covered that day, or it could be a review question on material covered the previous day. The purpose of the focus question is to eliminate the off-task transition time that usually occurs as students move from one activity or classroom to another.

SUPPORTS FOR INDIVIDUALIZATION

For many classroom teachers, the thought of modifying instruction to accommodate individual student needs seems overwhelming. In their commitment to move the entire class through the entire curriculum, there is little time in general educators' mindset or daily schedule for designing individual instructional programs beyond, perhaps, individual behavior management plans. However, a special education teacher working in collaboration with a general education teacher can assist in the design, development, and implementation of support programs that facilitate instruction to meet the needs of individual students in the class. Initially, both teachers should work together to identify the curriculum adaptations that might be effective with the student, or might have been effective in the past. Next, co-teachers should develop, jointly, a plan to implement the curriculum adaptations in the general education class. Then, the special educator should assist in monitoring the implementation of the adaptations; and finally, both teachers should evaluate the effectiveness of the plan. Using the guide that follows, teachers can meet and determine what adaptations are

Name: ____________________	Date: ____________________
Subject: ____________________	Grade: ____________________

Teachers: ____

Area of difficulty: ____

____

Instructional objective: ____

____

Adaptations to use: ____

____

____

Evaluation measure: ____

____

By whom: ____________________	Duration: ____________________

Next meeting date to review: ____

FIGURE 4–5 Summary of Adaptation Needs

needed, how long the adaptations will be implemented, and the basis for evaluation (see Figure 4–5).

PLANNING FOR COLLABORATIVE TEACHING

Just because collaborative teaching or co-teaching *can* be beneficial doesn't mean it always *will* be; it takes considerable work on the part of both teachers to make co-teaching successful. The collaborative structure requires that each teacher on the team be willing to change teaching styles and preferences, work closely with and rely on another adult, and share responsibility to perform tasks previously done alone (Friend & Cook, 1995). Teachers who are planning to implement collaborative teaching should consider a number of issues to judge their readiness for developing a collaborative relationship. The questions included in Figure 4–6 have proved to be a useful guide to many teachers.

As general and special educators work together they often find that new or modified skills are needed to make the inclusive and collaborative programming successful for their students and for themselves. The greatest area of frustration between educators appears to be their expectations about respective roles and responsibilities (Polloway & Patton, 1997). Role ambiguity occurs when either member of the team is uncertain about his or her purpose for being involved (Pugach & Johnson, 1995).

Topic	Questions
Philosophy and beliefs	What are our overriding philosophies about the roles of teachers and teaching and about students and learning? How do our instructional beliefs affect our instructional practice?
Parity Signals	How will we convey to students and others (e.g., teachers, parents) that we are equals in the classroom? How can we ensure a sense of parity during instruction?
Classroom routines	What are the instructional routines for the classroom? What are the organizational routines for the classroom?
Discipline	What is acceptable and unacceptable student behavior? Who is to intervene at what point in students' behavior? What are the rewards and consequences used in the classroom?
Feedback	What is the best way to give each other feedback? How will we ensure that both positive and negative issues are raised?
Noise	What noise level are we comfortable with in the classroom?
Pet peeves	What aspect of teaching and classroom life does each of us feel strongly about? How can we identify our pet peeves so as to avoid them?

FIGURE 4–6 Questions for Creating a Collaborative Work Relationship in Co-Teaching
Note: *From "Co-Teaching Guidelines for Creating Effective Practices," by L. Cook and M. Friend, 1995,* Focus on Exceptional Children, 28*(3), p. 53. Adapted by permission.*

Bauwens and Hourcade (1995) suggest that both teachers need constant reminders that, in co-teaching, "all teachers are responsible for all students" (p. 48).

REFLECTION BOX 4–4

One factor that will greatly influence how effective Dana William's co-teaching activities are, is how well she and her fellow teachers define their roles and responsibilities. What guidelines do you think they should try to follow as they approach this task?

SUMMARY

Many teachers involved in collaborative teaching describe their role as "evolving" (Nowacek, 1992). They learn to work together by observing and watching each other, rather than by planning their roles explicitly, at least in the beginning. They offer suggestions tactfully until a level of trust and respect is reached. Because most teachers have a history of working alone, this level of trust and respect does not occur overnight.

Collaborative teaching, with its provision of two teachers in the classroom, eases the classroom-management burden of the general education teacher, allowing for greater emphasis on student learning (Bauwens & Hourcade, 1995). In addition, teachers have found that through co-teaching, they learn valuable professional skills (Bauwens, Hourcade, & Friend, 1989).

FOLLOW-UP ACTIVITIES

1. Visit a general education classroom where co-teaching strategies are being used. How has the physical space been arranged to support co-teaching activities?
2. Talk with several teachers who participate in co-teaching activities. Find out how they established roles and responsibilities with their co-teaching partners. Ask them to identify aspects of this task that were the most difficult and strategies they used to address any problems.
3. Interview a special educator whose daily schedule must accommodate a range of activities such as co-teaching, pull-out instruction, planning, observing, completing required paper work, and meeting with others. Find out how this teacher developed a schedule to address so many needs.
4. Discuss the issue of scheduling time for collaborative teaching with an elementary- and secondary-level special education teacher to determine how each teacher approaches the task of developing a schedule. Identify factors that present the greatest problems for each teacher. Are these factors essentially the same for both teachers?
5. Complete an observation in several general education classrooms. Try to identify strategies being used to facilitate transitions among tasks and promote high rates of academic learning time.

PART 3

PULLING IT ALL TOGETHER

CHAPTER 5 EVALUATING INSTRUCTIONAL CONTEXTS

KEY WORDS

diagnostic data
examination of products
time-based recording system
error analysis
event-based recording system
item analysis
checklist
orienting strategies
rating scale
instructional mode
case study methods
scope and sequence

OBJECTIVES

After reading this chapter you should be able to:

1. provide examples of formal and informal approaches that can be used to describe classroom environments.
2. discuss variables that might be considered in analyzing instruction in general education classrooms.
3. discuss variables that might be considered in analyzing evaluation tasks and activities.
4. describe a model that can be used to guide evaluation of instructional contexts at the elementary and secondary level.

The Writer's Craft

Carlos, a sixth-grade student at Jones Middle School, seems to be having extraordinary difficulty in Ms. Pope's social studies class. Carlos has been identified as having a learning disability in written language, but the disability is not severe enough to account for the amount of trouble he is having. Both Carlos and Ms. Pope are frustrated. She has asked Mr. Stout, the special education teacher, to help her figure out what to do about this situation so she and Carlos can get some relief.

Mr. Stout decides to use a four-step plan. First, he will try to get a better sense of the problem by interviewing both Ms. Pope and Carlos. Next, he will spend some time reviewing samples of Carlos' work and observing his performance during class time. Then he will analyze this information to see if he can pinpoint the source of Carlos' difficulties, knowing that more than one factor likely is involved. Finally, he will meet with Ms. Pope and Carlos and share his findings so that together they can develop an action plan to help Carlos be more successful in social studies.

As Mr. Stout implemented the first two steps in his plan, he obtained several important pieces of information. As a result of his interview, he learned that Ms. Pope believes Carlos is lazy and could do better if he would only show a little effort. She says he daydreams during class and that he never takes notes. When he isn't daydreaming he is usually drawing, whispering to those around him, tapping his pencil, or being disruptive in other ways. According to Ms. Pope, Carlos never turns in any homework and rarely finishes his class work. He never has his materials for class and does poorly on tests. This surprises her, because his participation in class discussions suggests he understands the material. He also seems to do well when she gives the class "team learning" assignments. He is always a contributing member of his team. But he is currently failing social studies.

In his interview with Carlos, Mr. Stout learned that Carlos believes Ms. Pope hates him; she always seems to be yelling at him. He thinks that the harder he tries in her class the more he fails. Nothing he does is good enough. He also feels confused because he doesn't understand many of the homework assignments. The assignments that he does do often get lost between home and school. He thinks someone is going into his locker and taking them. He really wants to do well but just can't seem to get ahead.

When Mr. Stout examined Carlos' work products, he found that Carlos' locker, book bag, and notebooks were a jumble of papers with absolutely no organization or pattern to them. Things were crammed in wherever they fit. He found that the written work that Carlos had attempted was sloppy and incomplete. His answers were as short as possible and much of the work received a grade of "F". Carlos did, however, complete every project-type assignment that was given. His projects were creative, colorful, and extremely well done. But because they had to be accompanied by a written report, his project grades were generally marginal. It was unclear from the project directions how much weight each project carried in determining the course grade.

Mr. Stout will use the information he obtained from the interviews and product examination to help guide his classroom observations.

The previous two chapters focused on critical competencies for those who want to implement effective in-class programs for students with disabilities. In those chapters, we described a variety of approaches to consultation and collaborative teaching. We emphasized that the foundation for teaching students with special needs in general education settings consists of effective communication among professionals and working together as instructional partners. However, while this is the foundation of in-class programming, it is not sufficient. The second building block is pinpointing students' problems and determining their needs. Teachers must to be able to identify what and how to teach each student. They must also be able to analyze their own classroom practices to determine where modifications may be needed to better meet the needs of particular students. In short, teachers must understand approaches to assessment and evaluation if they are to develop effective in-class programs for students with disabilities. This chapter and chapters 6 and 8 address these concerns.

WHY EVALUATE CLASSROOM CONTEXTS?

To understand the importance of evaluating classroom environments, one must understand the nature of instruction. First, instruction is interactive. It involves the interplay between a learner and the context in which instruction takes place. As illustrated in Figure 5–1, instructional contexts involve variables related to teachers, environments, and instructional or evaluation tasks. As you will learn later in this chapter, each of these variables is composed of a number of subcomponents that vary considerably from one context to the next, just as students vary considerably from one another.

The three instructional context components and the student interact with one another during instruction. The ways in which they interact change, depending on the type of instructional event taking place at that moment. Thus a second important feature of instruction is that it is dynamic.

When students with disabilities are taught in general education settings, the regular education classroom is the context for their instruction. Because such classrooms can vary significantly in many ways, each having the potential to greatly affect student achievement, an essential step toward effectively teaching these students is an assessment or evaluation of the instructional context. What is needed is a clear "picture" of what happens in each class setting that students encounter. This picture is the basis for developing educational plans, in that it serves as the framework against which a student's profile of strengths and weaknesses can be compared. The more

FIGURE 5–1 Components of Instructional Contexts

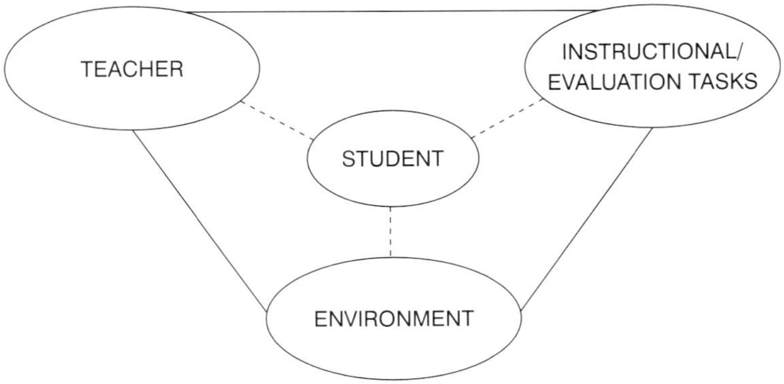

that is known about the instructional context, the easier it is to identify "mismatches" between the demands of the classroom and the capabilities of the student. Instructional adaptations can then be tailored to minimize mismatches between student and context. Without this framework, plans for instructional modifications and accommodations will be loosely targeted and not likely to achieve the best possible results.

This chapter introduces approaches to determining instructional contexts. It will include a discussion of various formal and informal methods that can be used to gather data. It will also include a discussion of specific targets of focus in analyzing an instructional context. These same two themes will be addressed in chapters 6 and 8 with respect to determining the academic and behavioral needs of students.

GATHERING DATA TO EVALUATE INSTRUCTIONAL CONTEXTS

Teachers have a number of tools that can be used to gather information about students. These tools are also useful for exploring the parameters of an instructional context. The difference is not in the tools that are used but in *how* they are used—that is, in *why* the information is being gathered. In the first case it is to provide insights into a student's specific educational needs. In the second case it is to provide a clearer picture of what is happening during instruction and to pinpoint where the instructional process breaks down for a particular student.

In this section we discuss important evaluation tools that can be used to gather diagnostic data. The term **diagnostic data** is used here to mean any information gathered for the purpose of identifying areas of critical concern. Diagnostic data might be related to student concerns or they might be related to instructional contexts. In either case, the same set of evaluation tools can be used.

Evaluation tools involve three broad categories of activity (see Table 5–1). The first of these involves gathering information simply by *asking*, either through a pencil-and-paper survey or through some form of interview. The second involves gathering information by *direct observation*, using procedures that can vary in their structure or focus. Finally, information can be gathered through systematic **examination of products** (e.g., things routinely collected in classrooms like homework, seat assignments, or weekly tests), or contrived products (e.g., a criterion-referenced test administered to explore subtraction skills), specifically collected to evaluate an area of concern. Each of these strategies for gathering classroom context data is described in the following sections.

ASKING

If information is to be collected using an *asking* strategy you should keep several important points in mind. First, asking often takes the form of an interaction between two or more people, but it can also involve a single individual using self-questioning.

TABLE 5–1 Strategies and Tools for Gathering Evaluation Data

Strategy	Tool
Ask	survey interview
Observe	event-based recording time-based recording rating scale or checklist case study
Examine	routine products contrived products

For instance, a special education teacher is working collaboratively with a general educator to identify adjustments in the instructional context that might better meet the needs of a student with disabilities in the class. The two teachers decide to gather diagnostic data by having the classroom teacher respond to a survey specifically designed by the special education teacher to explore this concern. Afterward, the two teachers might discuss the general educator's responses for clarification and elaboration. Alternatively, the two teachers could have used an interview in place of the survey; in this case, the special education teacher develops a set of open-ended questions that tap into the same kinds of concerns addressed in the survey and would interview the general education teacher. In each of these cases use of the asking strategy involved two professionals working together.

Either of these teachers also might have chosen to examine the instructional context independently. Each could have explored the same concerns reflected on the survey or in the interview by using a self-questioning strategy. To do this, each teacher would examine the items on the survey or the set of open-ended interview questions. The special education teacher would respond to the items based on knowledge of the general education classroom gained through direct and indirect contact over time. The special educator would ask, "What do I know about the teacher and classroom with respect to this item?" The general education teacher would answer based on direct knowledge of what occurs, daily, in the classroom. The teacher would ask, "How do things in my class operate? How do I organize and manage things with respect to this item?" Self-questioning can be an equally effective method of gathering diagnostic data to describe instructional contexts (Emmer, Evertson, Clements, & Worsham, 1997). But, if self-questioning is used, responses should be confirmed by seeking input from others who are familiar with the target classroom and have directly observed the instructional context in action (Emmer et al., 1997).

A variety of commercial surveys and interviews are available to help implement the asking strategy. Teacher-made alternatives also can provide insights into the dynamics of students and instructional contexts, if they are carefully constructed. Anderson and Burns (1989) say two critical features should be addressed in designing surveys and interviews. The questions asked should be related to specific and well-defined purposes, and a number of questions should be asked relative to each area of concern to get a clear picture of what is occurring. Later in this chapter, a summary of important elements of instructional contexts will be presented. This summary can serve as the guide for developing teacher-made surveys and interviews for gathering diagnostic data on classrooms. A number of commercially available options will also be presented later in the chapter.

OBSERVING

The second strategy for gathering diagnostic data is *observation*. This strategy involves collecting data through direct means. While both asking and observing approaches have merit in helping teachers analyze instructional problems, many believe that direct observation is necessary for planning effective interventions because it is the only approach that permits critical features of problem behaviors to be studied within the setting in which they are occurring (Gelfand & Hartman, 1984; Sugai & Tindal, 1993; Wolery, Bailey, & Sugai, 1987).

Observation data can be collected in many ways. Some methods are highly structured in terms of the rules and procedures that must be followed in gathering the data. Some are highly focused in terms of the specific behaviors that will be observed and recorded. Other approaches are either less structured, or less focused, or both.

Two types of fairly structured and focused observation methods are **event-based** and **time-based recording systems**. In event-based recording systems an observer records the *number of instances* of specific target behaviors or characteristics. Time-based systems provide an estimate of the *level or rate* at which a specific behavior occurs based on observations made over time. For example, a teacher interested in the number of times a student was out-of-seat during the fifth-period math lesson might carry a 3-by-5-inch card during a week of math classes, making a check mark each time the target child got up. This is an example of an event-based recording system.

But if the observation target were the student's off-task behavior during independent seat assignments, the teacher might select a time-based recording system instead. The teacher might choose three half-hour portions of the day when students work independently, and develop a record-keeping form dividing these 30-minute periods into 5-minute segments. The student might be observed for 5 seconds at the start of each 5-minute segment with the teacher noting on the form whether the student was on or off task. At the end of the day the teacher would have a count of the number of 5-second intervals the student was off task, and could estimate the percent of intervals or amount of time during three half-hour periods the student was off-task. The teacher would repeat this procedure over several days and average the results to get an estimate of the student's typical rate of off-task behavior.

If the teacher were interested in how long the student stays off task, or how long it takes the student to get back to work after being redirected by the teacher, other time-based systems of observation could be used:

A *duration recording system* can reveal how long specific behaviors last; the teacher records the start time and the stop time of off-task behavior during the three half-hour periods each day.

A *latency recording system* tells the amount of time that passes between an antecedent and the desired behavior; the teacher records the amount of time it takes for the student to get back on task after being reprimanded.

Regardless which observation system is used, the observer must specify the exact nature of behaviors to be studied, when observations will occur, and the rules to be followed in conducting the observation (Sugai & Tindal, 1993). Chapter 8 presents additional information to guide the selection and design of structured observation systems and shows examples of forms that might be used to record outcomes from event-based and time-based (rate, duration, or latency) measurement systems.

Checklists and rating scales are less-structured observation methods that typically involve fewer procedural rules and tend to provide more of a summary impression of what is happening, rather than a quantitative score. **Checklists** show the presence or absence of target behaviors, without regard to their degree or frequency; **rating scales** involve judgments on the extent to which, along a pre-defined continuum, a particular behavior or characteristic was observed (Herron & Harris, 1993). Both checklists and rating scales are especially useful in the initial stages of data gathering; they are not, however, recommended as definitive sources of observation data (Wallace, Larsen, & Elksnin, 1992). Furthermore, although described here as direct observation methods, checklists and rating scales can also be used as indirect measures, as would be the case, for example, if they were incorporated into an interview. A number of published rating scales and checklists are available, many of which are reviewed in the *Twelfth Mental Measurements Yearbook* (Connoley & Impara, 1995).

A third observation approach involves the use of **case study methods** (Heron & Harris, 1993), sometimes referred to as qualitative observations (Stake, 1978). The goal here is to provide an in-depth narrative description of what is occurring in the classroom. Its focus includes characterizing the behavior of individuals, the setting in which behaviors occur, and the dynamic interaction between these two. According to Heron and Harris (1993), the case study method is useful when one wants to understand the context in which behaviors are being measured, define problems to be studied, or gather information to help target subsequent evaluation activities. Thus, like checklists and rating scales, the case study method may be best suited for initial identification of problems.

While the case study method is somewhat less structured and focused than other observation methods, it is not totally unstructured. A number of procedures have been recommended for establishing boundaries or parameters for the observation (Stake, 1978) and for systematically collecting and analyzing the data (Wilson, 1977).

REFLECTION BOX 5–1

Consider the information Ms. Pope provided concerning Carlos's general behavior in her social studies class. Clearly, this will be one area Mr. Stout will want to explore further when he observes in Ms. Pope's classroom. How might this observation be structured? Are there particular things Mr. Stout should try to focus on during his visit to the class?

EXAMINING

A final strategy that can be used to gather diagnostic data is **examination of products**. Examination may involve two types of products: routine classroom products and contrived classroom products. Routine products are things that students work on daily in classrooms. They might involve instructional materials such as workbooks, worksheets, seat assignments, teacher-made tests, and homework assignments. Routine products also might include teacher materials such as a planning book, grade and attendance records, written rules for behavior, grading standards, printouts summarizing performance on computer-based activities, and anecdotal notes on students. Contrived products are gathered for a specific reason, not reflected in the day-to-day operation of the class as a whole. For example, the teacher might wish to explore a particular student's problems in multiplication and division. Routine products such as daily workbook pages and homework may not seem adequate, so the teacher decides to administer a criterion-referenced test in multiplication and division. The test is a contrived product; it is an attempt to get a more focused look at student performance beyond what can be gleaned from daily assignments. Similarly, a teacher who wants to study a student's composing abilities in depth might have the student prepare a special portfolio of writing samples that goes beyond typical classroom writing tasks. In another case, a special education teacher might wish to get a better insight into the nature of a teacher's daily instructional plans. That teacher might be asked to provide written or taped reflections on the purpose behind various lesson activities or the rationale for certain assignments. Such a commentary is not typically included in instructional plans and would, therefore, not be apparent from review of the teacher's plan book; it is a contrived product.

REFLECTION BOX 5–2

Mr. Stout's preliminary examination of Carlos's work products pointed to a number of potential problem areas. He plans to explore these concerns further by examining a broader sampling of Carlos' work. What products do you think Mr. Stout should plan to examine? Should he look at anything in particular as he examines these work samples?

A wealth of diagnostic information can be obtained from examination of classroom products (Wood, 1998; Choate, Enright, Miller, Poteet, & Rakes, 1995; Olson & Platt, 1996), but several considerations should be kept in mind when using this strategy. First, whether looking at routine or contrived products, the examination of the product needs to be systematic. Examination should begin by specifying a set of questions that will guide the analysis. Figure 5–2 presents a sampling of questions generated by a special education teacher who wanted to better understand *the nature of the instructional focus* for a target student and the approaches to evaluations being used. These questions provided the framework for examining the various classroom products listed

1. What is the specific focus of instruction; what objectives are being addressed?
2. What exactly is the student being asked to do on assignments?
3. What reading, writing, and related skills are necessary to complete assignments?
4. What is the typical length of assignments; how much time is given to complete them?
5. What grouping patterns are used for in-class assignments?
6. How is instructional content presented in terms of mode, pacing, grouping patterns, and so on?
7. What is the format of evaluation activities? How are they structured?
8. What reading, writing, and related skills are necessary to complete evaluations?
9. To what extent do evaluation activities match class assignments and practice activities?
10. What procedures are used to grade evaluation activities? What weight is placed on evaluations in determining course grades?

Sources to be examined:

seat assignments
teacher's plan book
homework assignments
teacher-made unit tests and quizzes

FIGURE 5–2 Questions to Guide a Product Examination: Instructional Focus

at the bottom of the figure. In contrast, if the purpose of the product examination had been to focus on *learning more about the student*, questions like the ones shown in Figure 5–3 might have been used to guide the product analysis.

Several other considerations enhance the quality of information obtained from product examination. One involves the use of **error analysis** to pinpoint specific skill strengths and weaknesses (Choate et al., 1995; Olson & Platt, 1996; Cegelka & Berdine, 1995). The series of steps involved in conducting an error analysis is shown in Figure 5–4. Following these steps will not only help a teacher understand the probable source of a student's difficulties, but will also help the teacher design probes to confirm the accuracy of initial "diagnosis." Figure 5–5 presents a helpful summary form which can be used when conducting an error analysis.

A second important strategy for product examinations is referred to as **item analysis**. In this technique, items on work samples or teacher-made tests are examined critically to determine what skills they address (see Figure 5–6). Having a clear sense of the skills reflected in a particular product provides the framework for judging student mastery of specific skills. (Error analysis and item analysis techniques can also serve as useful guides in interpreting outcomes from assessments involving standardized tests.)

It should be apparent that each of the methods for gathering diagnostic information discussed in this section can provide important information to guide development of highly targeted educational programs for students with disabilities in general education classrooms. To decide which tool to use in a particular situation, it may be helpful for

1. Do specific types of assignments exist with which the student is most successful?
2. What types of assignments present the greatest problems for the student?
3. Is the student able to complete assignments during the allotted time?
4. Is the student more successful when certain instructional grouping patterns are used?
5. Is the student more successful when certain response modes are used?
6. Does the student appear to understand directions for completing assignments?
7. Does the student appear to have the necessary reading, writing, and related skills necessary to complete assignments?
8. Is the student more successful in dealing with certain types of questions (e.g., factual vs. interpretative, recognition vs. recall, conceptual vs. procedural)?
9. Does the student's pattern of errors suggest specific skill weaknesses?
10. Does the student's performance pattern indicate skills that have been mastered?

Sources to be examined:

seat assignments completed independently
seat assignments completed in small group or with partner
completed homework
completed tests and quizzes
examples of creative projects

FIGURE 5–3 Questions to Guide a Product Examination: Student Focus

special education teachers to consider several factors. First, determine where you are in the process of gathering information; that is, are you just beginning to study a problem, or do you already have a preliminary idea of the areas of concern? According to Heron and Harris (1993), two levels of activity are involved in exploring educational problems: survey and specific. *Survey*-type activities are appropriate in the early stages of diagnosing problems. But once the parameters of a problem begin to emerge, more *specific* information should be obtained through highly targeted assessments.

FIGURE 5–4 Steps in Conducting an Error Analysis

1. Isolate the errors on the sample.
2. Group errors according to common patterns.
3. Form a preliminary hypothesis as to the source(s) of errors.
4. Look for examples of nonerrors to help confirm hypothesis.
5. Administer probes as necessary to further confirm suspicions.
6. Plan and implement an intervention to address problem.
7. Revise hypothesis as necessary based on intervention outcomes.

Student John Ford   Date 3-15-99

Class Language Arts   Teacher Smith

Product (attached) Composition on Field Trip

Error Pattern Summary

Error Type: Mispells phonetically irregular words

Examples: peces/pieces sinse/science ignsun/ignition cemcals/chemicals suspshen/suspicion

Non-examples: Friends, acid, people

Comments: Over-reliance on phonics; problem especially apparent with multisyllable words.

Error Type: sentence fragments

Examples: The many pieces of equipment. The assistant gave us.

Non-examples: Remaining sentences are properly formed.

Comments: Total # sentences = 12

Error Type: word usage

Examples: to/too; there/their

Non-examples: misused in all cases

Comments:

FIGURE 5–5 Sample Error Analysis

The next thing teachers must determine is how much time they have. Some methods described in this section take more time to gather information than others. Again, consider where you are in the process of gathering information. If little is known about a problem, it may be wise to use methods that will not involve too much time. Methods that are more time consuming might best be used to follow up on preliminary impressions, so that these activities can be more targeted to address specific concerns.

Finally, teachers should consider using more than one approach to gather diagnostic data. Whether just beginning to explore a problem at the survey level or following-up on preliminary impressions through specific probes, the most accurate picture is likely to emerge if a combination of data gathering tools is used. For instance, if a spe-

Student Arla Bright	Task Oral Reading of Word Cards
Item	**Target Skill(s)**
near	CVVC pattern vowel digraph 'ea'
plow	CCVV pattern consonant blend 'pl' vowel dipthong 'ow'
hive	CVCe pattern long vowel 'i'
softly	root word w/ suffix two syllable
umbrella	three syllable/predictable
patient	two syllable/irregular
parachute	three syllable/irregular

FIGURE 5–6 Sample Item Analysis Based on Graded Word List

cial education teacher has identified several possible problem areas through the asking strategy (interviewing the classroom teacher), these suspicions might be confirmed by doing a brief observation or an examination of routine classroom products related to the areas of concern. Assuming that data from the second source are consistent with outcomes from the teacher interview, the special education teacher could plan follow-up activities to explore the problem in greater detail.

Specific examples of how these approaches to gathering diagnostic data can be used to explore instructional contexts will be presented throughout the remainder of this chapter. Examples of how these same approaches can be used to determine the academic and behavioral needs of students will be presented in chapters 6 and 8.

ANALYZING INSTRUCTION

As pointed out earlier in this chapter, instructional contexts involve a wide variety of variables related to teachers, classroom environments, and instructional/evaluation tasks, all of which interact and change throughout the day. A number of ways exist to describe the components of instruction (see Table 5–2). The discussion of approaches that follows was framed using the components described in Table 5–2 as a broad context. We begin by considering factors related to how subject matter is presented, which includes discussion of variables such as teacher style and instructional delivery.

TABLE 5–2 Interacting Components of Classroom Instruction

Anderson & Burns	Gump	Weil/Murphy	Barr/Dreeben	Stodolsky
Subject matter	Concern		Curriculum content	Subject matter
Task demands	Pupil activity	Instructional activities	Intellectual and social demands	Cognitive level
Instructional format	Teacher leadership pattern	Source of instruction		Instructional format
Grouping arrangements	Group quality	Group size	Class organization	Expected student interaction
Time and pacing	Action sequencing	Duration	Content Coverage Pacing	Pacing
Classroom behaviors/ interactions	Teacher and student behaviors	Teacher and student behaviors	Patterns of interaction	Student behavior and student involvement

Note: *From* Research in Classrooms *(p. 10), by L. W. Anderson and R. B. Burns, 1989, Oxford: Pergamon Press. Copyright 1989 by Pergamon Press. Adapted by permission.*

This is followed by a discussion of factors to consider in analyzing the curriculum. The final section concentrates on analyzing instruction in terms of the approaches to evaluation employed.

PRESENTATION OF SUBJECT MATTER

Studies on teacher effectiveness have demonstrated conclusively that teachers who employ certain teaching skills are more effective than teachers who do not. An excellent summary of outcomes from this body of work is presented in Wittrock's (1986) review of research on teaching. According to Mastropieri and Scruggs (1994), research on teacher effectiveness has several implications for teaching students with disabilities. Specifically, it suggests that instruction will be most effective when (1) students are actively engaged and on task during instruction, (2) information is presented clearly and concisely, (3) students are asked questions that relate to instructional objectives, (4) student involvement is maintained through participation in relevant instructional activities, and (5) student performance is monitored.

The extent to which these features are addressed in a teacher's presentation of subject matter will depend on several factors. For this discussion we have grouped these factors into two categories: those that are related to the teacher's general instructional style and those that are reflected in the teacher's approach to instructional delivery. Obviously it would follow that because these concerns can greatly influence how effective instruction will be, they should provide the context for analyzing the presentation of subject matter.

TEACHER'S STYLE. Teachers are likely to exhibit certain characteristics and behaviors that cut across their teaching regardless of the subject matter or the nature of the activity involved. For example, some teachers may appear more enthusiastic than others, or some may have a higher tolerance for movement and activity than others. Some may have an easy-going manner or an obvious sense of humor. Each of these characteristics is likely to be reflected in the way the teacher presents subject matter.

Orienting strategies. One element of a teacher's style that will have a considerable effect on student learning involves the teacher's use of **orienting strategies**, that is, the extent to which the teacher prepares students for lessons that will follow. Orienting strategies might involve asking a set of key questions regarding the instructional content, discussing students' experiences related to the topic, or introducing key terms to be discussed. In each case the goal is to create anticipation so that students' interest is heightened and their attention is focused with the help of the advance organizers.

Clarity of instruction. A second aspect of teacher style that influences instructional effectiveness is the clarity of instruction. Certainly, the teacher's use of language will be a key concern, especially in terms of how explicit the teacher tends to be during instruction and the complexity of the language structures used. According to Berliner (1987), teachers should avoid using vague terms and rely instead on words whose meanings are clear. Instruction should also be characterized by slow, elaborated explanations that include verbal links—prepositions, conjunctions, and other verbal markers used to explicitly point out causes, results, means, and purposes; highlight relationships; and show transitions. In short, a teacher's use of language during instruction should provide a systematic framework that helps students see how information is organized and how ideas are related together.

Clarity of instruction will also be influenced by the extent to which a teacher tends to couple the use of effective verbal explanations with the use of concrete supports. This might involve demonstration and modeling techniques so that students can see exactly how to perform a particular skill or process, or it may involve concrete examples to show how a rule can be applied or how new information can be linked to prior knowledge. Another type of concrete support are graphic organizers which, like verbal markers, helps students see how information is organized and how ideas are linked.

According to Sugai and Tindal (1993), several types of graphic organizers should be considered, including maps, structural illustrations, hierarchical illustrations, and chronological charts. The literature also includes descriptions of several mapping formats that can be used to help students analyze various text structures (see Grassen & Carnine, 1992). While primarily intended for use with printed material, these formats can be adapted easily for use during verbal instruction. A sampling of graphic organizers that could complement a teacher's verbal explanations is provided in Figure 5–7. Other examples of concrete supports that can help clarify instruction will be discussed in Chapter 7.

An overhead projector can be used to provide examples of graphic organizers, graphs, and other concrete supports.

Concrete supports of the type described in this section can be useful when teaching students with disabilities in general education classrooms because many of these youngsters have significant problems understanding and processing spoken language as well as difficulties with concept formation and memory. By pairing good verbal explanations with concrete supports, teachers can give these students a sound framework and help guide their understanding and recall.

Questioning strategies. Another important factor to explore when analyzing instructional style is the teacher's approach to questioning. Asking questions allows a teacher to see how well students understand the information and what further explanations are needed. Questions also give students opportunities for immediate practice. If students are unable to respond to questions with a high degree of accuracy, the teacher should infer that the instruction must be modified.

To understand the value of questioning, one might liken an instructional situation to a game of catch. The teacher may repeatedly toss the ball to students, but until they can catch it and toss it back they are not really playing the game. When teachers "toss" instructional content to students they do not know if learning is occurring until students can demonstrate that they "caught it" by responding successfully to questions.

Several factors should be considered when exploring a teacher's questioning style. (1) How often does the teacher ask questions? In general there should be a fairly high rate of

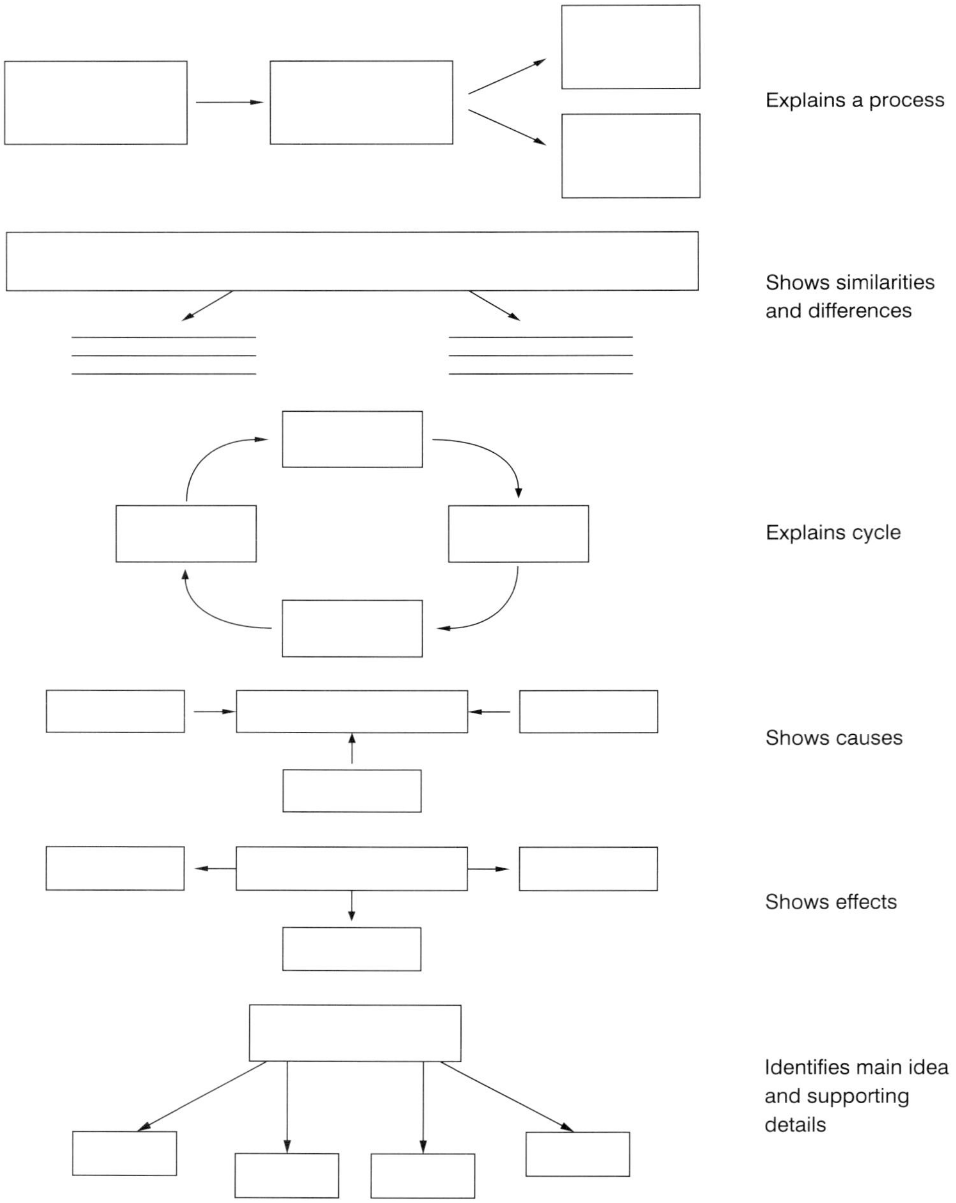

FIGURE 5–7 Sample Graphic Organizers

questioning during instruction to provide the teacher with continuous evaluative feedback on which to base adjustments to the instructional plan. (2) How varied are the types of questions being asked? How well do they match the instructional content? According to Mastropieri and Scruggs (1994), when instruction focuses on basic skills, questions should call for direct, literal responses (e.g., What is the rule for using commas in a series?). But when instruction involves evaluation or application objectives, or is designed to promote inferential reasoning, questions that call for higher cognitive skills are more appropriate (e.g., How can the writing strategy TOWER help you do better on tests? In what way do you think the industrial revolution might have contributed to the Civil War?).

Another factor to consider is whether the teacher involves everyone in the questioning, either by directing questions to students at random or by asking students to comment on the correctness of another student's response. Or does the teacher tend to question students according to a predictable routine, calling primarily on students who raise their hands or moving up and down rows? When patterns such as these are used, students who know they are unlikely to be called on become less attentive.

An analysis of questioning style should also include how a teacher provides feedback to students on their responses. Feedback should be overt, prompt, direct, and positive (Sugai & Tindal, 1993). Teachers can vary the types of feedback they give based on the nature of a student's response. Table 5–3 summarizes strategies suggested by Mastropieri and Scruggs (1994), which a teacher can use to lead students who are unable to respond correctly to a question.

Attention to cultural and linguistic differences. A fourth important factor to consider in examining instructional style is the extent to which teachers are responsive to cultural

TABLE 5–3 Types of Feedback to Student Responses

Response	Feedback
Correct	Overt acknowledgement ("That is correct"). Not overly elaborate; appropriate to response. Should be more limited during rapid-pace drill activities.
Partially correct	Acknowledge correct aspect of response. Provide answer or call on another student if necessary. Repeat question later in the lesson.
Incorrect	State simply that the response is incorrect. Do not prod or probe students who obviously do not know the answer. State correct response or call on another student. Do not criticize the student unless incorrect response is due to inattention, lack of effort, or refusal to follow directions; be judicious with criticism.
Lack of overt response	Question further to determine source of nonresponse. Elicit an overt response, even if "don't know" is most appropriate. When response is overt—whether correct or incorrect—respond as described above.

Note: *From* Effective Instruction for Special Education *(p. 16), by M. A. Mastropieri and T. E. Scruggs, 1994, Austin, TX: PRO-ED. Copyright 1994 by PRO-ED. Adapted by permission.*

and linguistic differences among students. Teachers who are sensitive to such diversity recognize the effect such differences can have on student learning and adjust their teaching style to take these differences into account. They realize that every culture has a set of values and beliefs that influence the behavior of its members, and that an effective teaching style accommodates multiple cultural perspectives. For example, unlike students from cultures in which spoken and written words are the dominant form of communication, Native American students may feel more comfortable expressing themselves through actions. This cultural difference would have important implications for such things as the teacher's use of questioning strategies, selection of instructional tasks, or performance expectations. Lewis and Doorlag (1999) present an excellent summary of differences between the dominant U.S. culture and a variety of other cultures; their analysis provides a useful context for examining a teacher's responsiveness to cultural and linguistic differences. Gersten and Jimenez (1998) also provide a good overview of strategies that can be used to promote learning among culturally and linguistically diverse students.

Student motivation. A final consideration in analyzing a teacher's style is how the teacher motivates students. In this age of fast-pace television shows and interactive video games, students are likely to find the typical routines of a classroom fairly uninteresting and uninspired. Thus it is important for teachers to use a variety of strategies to motivate students and keep them involved.

Cultural differences should be considered in developing instructional and evaluative tasks.

Verbal praise, privileges, token economies, and tangibles all have been shown to be effective in motivating students (Cegelka & Berdine, 1995). Other strategies that appear to be effective include the use of graphing and self-monitoring techniques, cooperative learning methods, games and simulations, and computer-assisted instruction (Bos & Vaughn, 1998; Lewis & Doorlag, 1999; Mercer & Mercer, 1998). While it may not be necessary for a teacher to use all of these approaches to motivate students, instruction should incorporate some combination of these techniques.

REFLECTION BOX 5–3

Based on the information Mr. Stout obtained when he interviewed Carlos, what type of teaching style might be a good match for Carlos?

Each of the methods for gathering diagnostic data discussed earlier in this chapter (i.e., asking, observing, and examining) can be used to gain a clear picture of a teacher's style. In some cases commercially available materials can be used, or teachers can develop their own materials.

One example of a teacher-made data collection tool is presented in Figure 5–8. It shows how many of the elements of teacher style described in this chapter can be turned into a simple rating scale. Items shown on the scale could be discussed with a target teacher to determine the extent to which that teacher emphasizes certain procedures during instruction. Or the rating scale could be used to summarize impressions formed as a result of several observations of the teacher in action. Both approaches would provide insight into the teacher's style; those data could then be used to guide intervention efforts for a particular student.

Another example is presented in Figure 5–9. It shows how one special education teacher developed an **event-based observation** system to explore the questioning patterns used by a classroom teacher. The special education teacher wanted to study several important aspects of questioning. The form she created provides space for keeping track of the questions being asked and who is being queried. Each time a question is asked during an observation, the teacher places a tally mark in the appropriate categories to indicate question type and target. At the end of two or more observation periods, results are examined to determine the teacher's questioning style. Several patterns are apparent in the example shown in Figure 5–9. The target teacher tends to ask more literal questions than any other type. Also, while questions appear to be evenly distributed among male and female students, the teacher does seem to favor questioning students who raise their hands. The special education teacher may wish to explore these patterns further by conducting additional observations. The special education teacher might also decide to use a similar version of this observation system to study the response patterns of particular students. This would simply involve keeping track of the types of questions a target student tends to answer (i.e., literal, inferential, evaluative) and whether the answer was volunteered.

Teacher: ______________ Date: ______________					
Subject: ______________ Data Collection Method: ______________					
	Estimated Frequency of Use				
Orienting Strategies	**Seldom**				**Always**
• Introduces key questions related to topic	1	2	3	4	5
• Explores students' experiences	1	2	3	4	5
• Introduces key terms and new vocabulary	1	2	3	4	5
• Provides advance organizers	1	2	3	4	5
Clarity of Instruction					
• Uses explicit language	1	2	3	4	5
• Provides slow, elaborated explanations	1	2	3	4	5
• Provides concrete supports (examples, demonstrations, models)	1	2	3	4	5
• Uses graphic organizers	1	2	3	4	5
• Explicitly shows relationship among ideas/concepts	1	2	3	4	5
Questioning Strategies					
• Uses a high rate of questioning	1	2	3	4	5
• Varies the types of questions asked	1	2	3	4	5
• Provides prompt feedback	1	2	3	4	5
• Varies feedback based on nature of response	1	2	3	4	5

FIGURE 5–8 Analysis of Teaching Style

INSTRUCTIONAL DELIVERY

In addition to involving variables related to a teacher's style, presentation of subject matter also involves a number of key concerns related to how instruction is delivered. One aspect of instructional delivery involves the mode or delivery system being used.

INSTRUCTIONAL MODE. One of the most common instructional modes is the lecture format, but several other possibilities can also be used. Anderson and Burns (1989) have identified 10 instructional delivery systems: (1) lecture, (2) recitation, (3) demonstration, (4) discussion, (5) question/answer, (6) oral drill/practice, (7) textbook/worksheet, (8) audio-visual, (9) game/contest, and (10) project/computer. Because these approaches are linked to various instructional purposes, teachers likely will use different combinations of delivery systems at different times. Students also likely will vary with respect to how well they respond to different approaches. So when a student is having difficulties, it is important to study the nature of the delivery systems being used in his/her classroom.

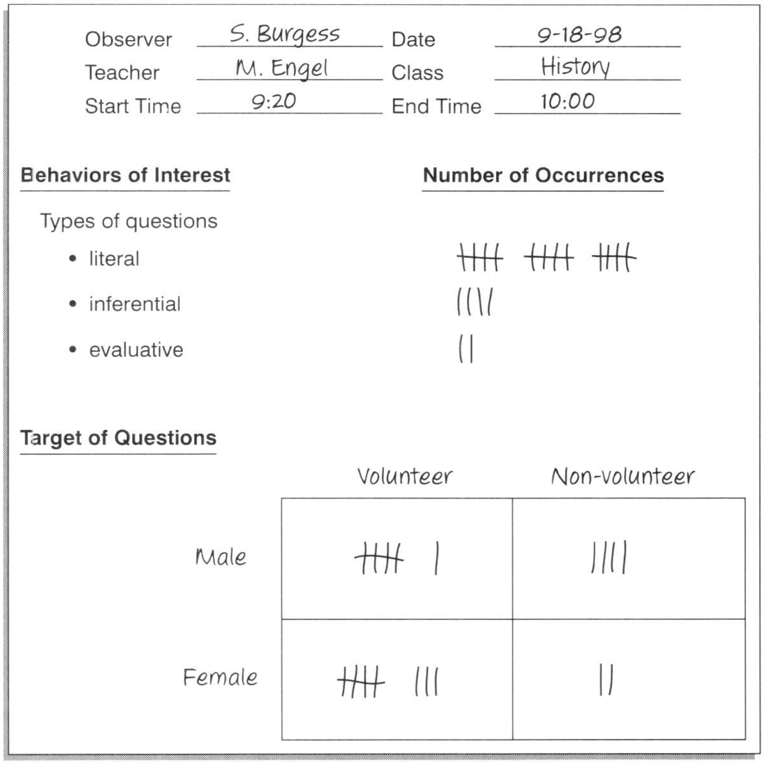

FIGURE 5–9 Event-Based Observation System

One way to do this is to complete several direct observations of the class, guided by the checklist of questions shown in Figure 5–10. By comparing results from observations conducted on more than one occasion, a picture will emerge of the range of delivery systems typically employed in the class.

INSTRUCTIONAL PROCEDURES. A second important dimension of instructional delivery concerns how instruction is carried out. This refers to the overall structure a teacher follows in delivering lessons: beginning with a review, presenting new information, providing for guided and independent practice, and evaluating student understanding. It also refers to specific characteristics of instruction such as the teacher's pacing or rate of movement through material. Clearly, if all students are expected to move through material at roughly the same rate, the pace at which instruction progresses from one objective to the next is likely to affect students with disabilities.

Instructional procedures also involve a teacher's systematic use of prompts, cues, and modeling. In analyzing this aspect of the instructional context, it is important to consider the extent to which these features are routinely reflected in instruction, how quickly these supports are faded, and whether they are used in different ways with different students.

Format	Questions to Ask	Comments
Lecture	How long are the lectures?	
	What are the levels of engagement?	
	Are the knowledge forms within the lecture well balanced?	
Recitation	Is the material well suited (oriented toward facts) for recitation?	
	Do students recite individually or in groups?	
	How is the correctness of recitation monitored?	
Demonstration	Is the model well displayed?	
	Are the requisite steps explained during the demonstration?	
Discussion	Is the information appropriate (personal, evaluative) for discussion?	
	Do students stay on the topic?	
	Is the content monitored? Are interactions structured to ensure involvement by everyone?	
	How is the topic maintained?	
	Is a "conclusion" reached?	
Question/Answer	Are the questions convergent or divergent?	
	What knowledge forms are represented in the questions?	
	How are students called on to answer questions?	
	Does the teacher exhibit an appropriate "wait time"? after asking a question?	
	How are correct responses from students handled?	
	How are incorrect responses handled?	

FIGURE 5–10 Checklist of questions Addressing Instructional Delivery

Format	Questions to Ask	Comments
Oral	Is the material appropriate for oral versus silent practice?	
Practice/Drill	How long are the responses?	
	How are they distributed among students?	
Film/AV/TV	What is the reason for watching a film?	
	How does it fit into the lesson?	
	Does the information match the interactively taught information?	
	The curriculum?	
Textbook/Worksheet	How does the textbook or worksheet extend the lesson?	
	What is the range of student responses represented?	
	What behaviors are exhibited? How long are students engaged?	
Games/Contest	How does the game fit into the lesson?	
	What types of student responses are necessary?	
	What decision-making skills are required?	
	What rules or algorithms are being learned?	
	What are the consequences for engaging?	
	How are students paced through the lesson?	
	What feedback is presented?	
Project/Computer	How does the textbook or worksheet extend the lesson?	
	What is the range of student responses represented?	
	What behaviors are exhibited?	
	How long are the students engaged?	
	What contingencies are present for feedback?	
	For mistakes? For correct responses?	

FIGURE 5–10 *continued*

Note: *From* Effective School Consultation: An Interactive Approach *(pp. 310–311), by G. M. Sugai and G. A. Tindal, 1993, Pacific Grove, CA: Brooks/Cole. Copyright 1993 by Brooks/Cole. Adapted by permission of Wadsworth Publishing Co.*

GROUPING PATTERNS. Another important aspect of instructional procedures to investigate involves grouping patterns. As we pointed out in Chapter 4, students are usually taught using one of the following grouping arrangements: (1) as a whole class (large group), (2) in smaller groups, (3) one to one, or (4) using independent learning activities. Each of these approaches is well suited to different types of instructional activities and delivery systems. For instance, Lemlech (1988) has suggested that large-group instruction is an efficient way to introduce new skills or content because it reduces the need for repetition. Large-group instruction is also a good choice when instructional delivery features lecture, recitation, demonstration, or audio-visual techniques; when the content is similar for all students; or when the purpose is to invite input from the whole class, as in a discussion. On the other hand, in a large-group arrangement students typically get fewer opportunities to respond and less corrective feedback (Bos & Vaughn, 1998).

Small-group arrangements allow for a higher rate of student involvement. They are often used when students need more intensive, teacher-directed instruction, either to help them keep pace with the larger group or to address unique skill deficits. Small-group arrangements are also beneficial when the goal of instruction is to make instruction more student-directed, or to enhance student involvement and participation in their own learning. One method that uses small groups is cooperative learning, which was introduced in Chapter 2 and will be discussed again in Chapter 7.

According to Lemlech (1988), effective classrooms feature a combination of both large- and small-group instructional arrangements. For some students with disabilities however, one-to-one instruction will also be needed from time to time. One-to-one instruction is useful for students who may require even more teacher direction than can be achieved in a small group, or who need to learn a particular skill that the rest of the class has already mastered. A one-to-one approach could be delivered by the teacher or, to offset the demand on a teacher's time, through use of peer tutoring. Peer tutoring was also introduced in Chapter 2 and will be discussed again in Chapter 7.

Finally, instructional procedures might also feature use of independent learning activities, that is, activities that students complete with minimal assistance. According to Bos and Vaughn (1998), independent learning activities should be used primarily to provide practice on skills for which a student has already developed some proficiency. We believe independent learning activities can also be used to help students acquire new skills, if the assignments are carefully controlled. For example, many software and multimedia programs are available that are specifically designed for self-instruction. Commercially available texts and workbooks, as well as teacher-made learning centers, can also be used to guide independent acquisition of new skills, if the activities progress in manageable increments and provide adequate cues, models, and corrective feedback.

REFLECTION BOX 5–4:

Based on the information Mr. Stout obtained when he interviewed Carlos, what type of instructional delivery might suit Carlos well?

In gathering diagnostic information to characterize the grouping patterns used in a target classroom, several things should be kept in mind. Obviously, it is important to note the range of grouping patterns employed and their frequency. But it is also important to get a sense of how well the grouping patterns match instructional purposes. As we have said, certain grouping arrangements are better suited to particular purposes and/or conditions than others. And finally, it is useful to consider whether the physical arrangement of the room supports the use of different grouping patterns. Is the room arranged so that students have space to work in small groups as well as independently, away from distractions? Can several types of grouping patterns occur simultaneously? Are materials and equipment accessible to students and can they be used independently? It is not uncommon to find classrooms in which the range of grouping options is limited by the arrangement of the physical space or because students have not been taught how to access and use instructional materials independently.

Information characterizing classroom grouping practices can be gathered easily through teacher interview, direct observation, examination of instructional plans, or from a combination of these approaches. One simple tool that can be used to analyze classroom grouping patterns, as well as to gather information on the other instructional procedures discussed in this section, is presented in Figure 5–11. It is designed as a rating scale that can be completed in several ways. In the example shown, a special education teacher used the rating scale to summarize the results of four classroom observations. Based on these observations, the special education teacher indicated the extent to which each of the instructional procedures listed seemed to be emphasized in the class. As an alternative, items listed on the form could be turned into questions for a teacher interview, or they could provide a context for examining lesson plans.

CHARACTERISTICS OF THE CURRICULUM

No attempt to analyze classroom instruction would be complete without careful consideration of the curriculum. Our discussion to this point has focused on *how* instruction takes place. Now we address another important concern, analyzing *what* instruction takes place. We will focus on what students are being asked to learn and what tasks they are being given to help them learn that material or content. This section describes a number of issues that should be considered in examining the curriculum.

SCOPE AND SEQUENCE. The **scope and sequence** of a curriculum refers to the amount of information covered and the order in which information is introduced. A good starting point is to consider how much variation exists in the curriculum. For instance, are all students expected to cover the same amount of material? If the teacher has planned a history unit involving several chapters in the textbook, as well as a number of supplemental activities and an interactive video clip, will everyone in the class have to move through all of this material? Or will the teacher reduce the amount some students have to cover, perhaps by having them read only selected parts of the assigned chapters or complete fewer of the supplemental activities.

In a similar vein, it is also important to consider the variation in the number of objectives or skills students are expected to master. Continuing with our example from

Teacher: M. Robinson

Subject: World Cultures

Dates of Observations: 10/2/98, 10/5/98, 10/12/98, 10/15/98

Dates of Interview: N/A

Instructional Procedure	Estimated Frequency of Use						Comments
	Seldom					Always	
Lesson Formats							
Begins with review	0	1	2	3	4	(5)	Lessons typically follow this same pattern
Provides for guided practice	0	1	2	3	(4)	5	
Provides for independent practice	0	1	2	(3)	4	5	
Evaluates student work standing	0	1	2	(3)	4	5	
Lesson Designs							
Provides specific prompts	0	1	2	(3)	4	5	
Incorporates cues	0	1	2	3	(4)	5	
Includes modeling	0	1	2	3	4	(5)	
Provides specific examples	0	1	2	(3)	4	5	
Varies instructional support based on student need	0	(1)	2	3	4	5	
Grouping Patterns							
Large group	0	1	2	3	4	(5)	Majority of lessons emphasize large group work followed by independent seat activities
Small group / Teacher directed	0	1	(2)	3	4	5	
Small group / Student directed	0	1	(2)	3	4	5	
One-to-one / Teacher directed	0	1	(2)	3	4	5	
One-to-one / Student directed	0	(1)	2	3	4	5	
Independent learning activities	0	1	2	3	4	(5)	

FIGURE 5–11 Instructional Procedures Rating Scale

the history class, one would want to know if the teacher expected all students to master all of the objectives established for the unit, or if some students would be responsible for a smaller number of key objectives.

It would also be useful to consider the variation in the sequencing of the curriculum; that is, do all students study the same things at the same time and in the same order? This is an especially relevant concern in classes emphasizing development of fundamental operations in reading, writing, and mathematics, the so-called basic skills. But sequencing also should be considered in content subject classes where students may differ in their levels of background knowledge.

Each of these concerns can have important implications for the success of students with disabilities in general education settings. Unfortunately, it is often the case that there is far *too little* variation in the scope and sequence of the curriculum to adequately meet the needs of youngsters with mild disabilities.

ACADEMIC TASKS. Another critical factor to consider when analyzing the curriculum involves the academic tasks students are given to help them master curriculum objectives. We recommend examining these from a number of perspectives. First, look at the cognitive demands academic tasks place on the learner. Table 5–4 summarizes the types of academic tasks students typically complete in school. These tasks vary considerably in the kinds of cognitive processes they involve. For instance, memory tasks require simple verbatim recall of information, but procedural tasks require the ability to apply rules. Comprehension tasks are even more demanding in that they require an understanding of conceptual structure. To complete an opinion task one must be able to establish a point of view and a rationale to support it. If all the assigned tasks are at the same level, some students with different cognitive practicing skills may have difficulty demonstrating competence.

A second important dimension of academic tasks is the nature of the instructional materials used. Determine if tasks have been designed so that they are responsive to different cultural and linguistic perspectives. Examine the range of class assignments. See if directions are stated clearly, and get a sense of the reading level of assigned tasks and worksheets. Examine the extent to which materials include cues and examples, or if they provide for any corrective feedback. Another aspect to consider is the type of response students must provide (e.g., oral, written, demonstration) and how extensive the response must be (e.g., single word, sentence, essay). Also consider the extent to which the form and content of assignments overlap with the type of evaluation to be given. Often there is not a good match between the academic tasks students are asked to complete during the acquisition stage of learning and what they are asked to do to demonstrate mastery.

A third critical factor to consider when analyzing academic tasks is how accessible and involved the teacher is in the activity. According to Wood (1998), teachers assign two broad types of academic tasks, *control* and *no control* assignments. *Control* assign-

TABLE 5–4 Types of Academic Tasks

Type	Requirements
Memory tasks	Students must recognize or reproduce information.
Procedural task	Students must apply a rule, formula, or algorithm to come up with an answer.
Comprehension tasks	Students must recognize transformed or paraphrased information, apply known procedures to new problems, or draw inferences based on previously encountered information.
Opinion tasks	Students must state a preference and support it with an appropriate rationale.

Note: *From "Academic Work," by W. Doyle, 1983,* Review of Educational Research, 53*(2), pp. 162–163. Copyright 1983 by the American Educational Research Association. Adapted by permission.*

ments include a range of activities over which the teacher maintains some level of involvement or control. These include class discussions, seat assignments, group projects, and so on. When students work on controlled assignments, the teacher has the power to make adjustments, like answering questions, clarifying directions, or changing the length of the assignment. Controlled assignments offer teachers the opportunity to observe students as they work and immediately address problems. In contrast, *no control* assignments are tasks that students complete without direct supervision from the teacher. The most common example of this is homework. Because homework is so problematic for many students with disabilities, it needs to be carefully examined when a student with disabilities is having trouble. Table 5–5 identifies four common types of homework assignments and provides examples of each type. This table can be a useful guide in analyzing classroom homework patterns, and in making suggestions for adaptations.

ANALYZING EVALUATION

Another important component of instructional contexts involves how student performance is evaluated. According to Doyle (1983), evaluation activities provide a basic accountability structure for making several types of judgments. For instance, teachers routinely use evaluation activities for assigning report card grades, verifying that required competencies have been met, or making promotion decisions. Evaluation activities are also commonly used to determine whether instruction is having the desired effect and can be used to modify instructional plans. In each case, judgments made as a result of evaluation activities will have important implications for students, particularly those with special educational needs.

In this section we will discuss a number of factors to consider in analyzing the evaluation practices used in classrooms.

DETERMINING WHAT IS BEING EVALUATED

An important first step in analyzing evaluation activities is to determine *what* is being evaluated. This can be done by considering the types of knowledge reflected in evaluation tasks and the type of intellectual operations they require of students.

According to Kameenui and Simmons (1990), when teachers teach, they are always teaching about "something." That something is the knowledge contained in the academic domains of language, reading, mathematics, writing, and the content subject areas. It is the basis of the curriculum and comes in many forms. For instance, knowledge can involve concepts, facts, operations, rules, or procedures.

Over the years, a number of models have been presented that attempt to classify various knowledge forms. These *taxonomies of knowledge* show how knowledge can be grouped into categories just as one might classify objects. The following discussion reflects one taxonomy of knowledge we believe is especially well suited to analyzing

TABLE 5–5 Homework Patterns and Adaptations

Type of Homework	Definition	Examples	Suggested Adaptations
Preparation	Homework assigned to assist students' preparation for the next day's lesson/class	Reading a chapter Reviewing a film	Provide recorded materials for materials to be read. Before the lesson, review in class to assist students who could not prepare ahead of time. Allow students to prepare with a buddy. Provide a summary of material to be read. Provide a checklist for steps on procedures to be reviewed.
Practice	Homework assigned to reinforce the skills taught during the day's lesson	Working on math problems Answering questions about class lecture	Be sure that the student understands the assignment. Review assignment directions. Review the assignment. Provide a model. Provide guided practice before independent practice. Check for student's functional level and match assignment to level. Provide alternative amounts of assignments to students who cannot complete the same quantity as others.
Extension	Homework assigned to extend or transfer skills taught	Book reports Practicing computer skills	Provide models for required reports. Provide a checklist of procedures. Allow buddies to work together on a shared assignment. Be sure that students have been taught for acquisition and retention before requiring transfer.
Creativity	Homework that requires synthesis of skills and concepts previously taught	Projects Term papers Research assignments	Allow partners to work on projects. Provide a clearly explained checklist with examples for all projects. Do class projects that model each independent project. Remember that students who have difficulty with structure need guidance with assigned projects, papers, research projects. Consider alternative assignments for students who may not be at this level.

Note: *From* Adapting Instruction to Accommodate Students in Inclusive Settings *(p. 411), by J. W. Wood, 1998, Upper Saddle River, NJ: Merrill/Prentice Hall. Copyright 1998 by Merrill/Prentice Hall. Adapted by permission.*

evaluation activities in classrooms, because it is both comprehensive and uncomplicated. It was developed by Kameenui and Simmons (1990) based on the earlier work of Gagne (1985) and is illustrated in Figure 5–12.

The taxonomy shown in Figure 5–12 describes four broad categories of knowledge forms. These have been arranged hierarchically, with the simplest forms of knowledge at the lowest level and more complex knowledge forms shown at the upper level. Thus, verbal associations represent one of the least complex forms of knowledge, whereas cognitive strategies involve much more complex knowledge forms. To use this taxonomy as a context for analyzing evaluation activities, it is important to have a clear understanding of what is meant by each category label.

Verbal associations involve connecting a specific response with a specific stimulus. According to Kameenui and Simmons (1990) verbal associations consist of three types: simple facts, verbal chains, and discriminations. Simple facts involve associations among names, objects, events, and places that use *singular exemplars*. That is, there is only one correct answer. Such is the case when a student is asked to name a specific color or indicate the date on which a particular event took place. Verbal chains involve *sequences* of simple facts, such as naming the days of the week in correct order or reciting the alphabet. Discriminations involve the ability to *differentiate* between two or more stimuli, such as when a student is shown three word cards and asked to point to the one that says "stop."

The next level of the taxonomy involves *concepts*, which are defined as objects, events, actions, or situations that are part of a class based on common attributes or

FIGURE 5–12 Taxonomy of Knowledge Forms

Note: *From* Designing Instructional Strategies: The Prevention of Academic Learning Problems *(p. 66), by E. J. Kameenui and D. C. Simmons, 1990, Upper Saddle River, NJ: Merrill/Prentice Hall. Copyright 1990 by Prentice Hall. Reprinted by permission.*

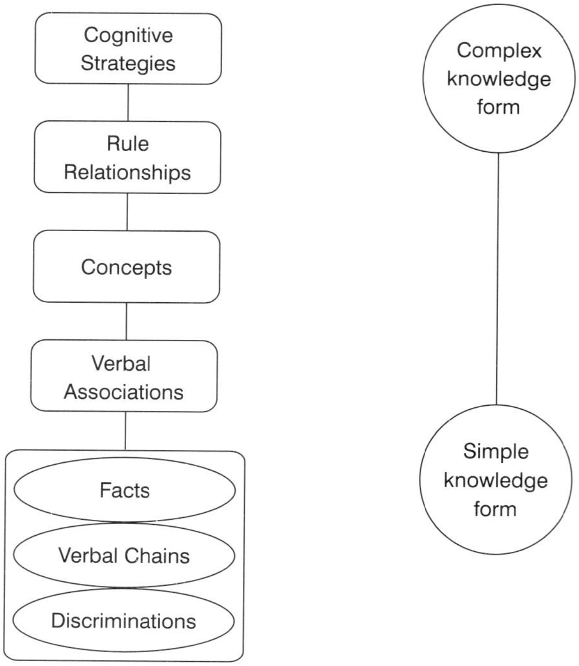

characteristics. Concepts are organized around rules or formulas that specify the relevant features differentiating members of the class from nonmembers. Examples of tasks that involve conceptual knowledge include having students select proper nouns from a word list, circle the odd numbers on a worksheet, name four communist countries, or list five types of reptiles. In each case the student must understand the rule around which the concept is organized: What attributes must be present for something to fit the category of proper noun, odd number, communist, or reptile?

Rule relationships constitute the next level of complexity on the taxonomy. These may be thought of as principles that describe "if–then" or "cause–effect" connections between and among facts or concepts. For example a rule relationship is emphasized when students are taught that fire requires oxygen to continue burning. A teacher might assess students' understanding of this relationship by showing a picture of a candle placed under a glass covering and asking, "Why wouldn't this be a good way to keep the candle from going out?"

The final and most complex knowledge form represented on the taxonomy involves *cognitive strategies*, which are defined as multistep associations and procedures used to bring about a response to specific problems. Cognitive strategies might be likened to "procedural knowledge," whereby one must be able to manipulate multiple pieces of information (i.e., facts, concepts, or rules) and implement a sequence of steps to solve a problem. An example of a task that requires the use of cognitive strategies or procedural knowledge is to ask a student to write a paragraph about a particular topic. To do this, the student must be able to decide what to say about the topic, organize those ideas into a coherent plan, apply the rules and conventions of writing to express the plan correctly in print, evaluate the written product for clarity, monitor it for technical writing errors, and revise the composition as necessary. Clearly, the numerous skills and pieces of information that must be drawn on to complete this task are quite complex.

Once one has a clear understanding of what is meant by each element shown in Figure 5–12, the taxonomy can be used as a backdrop against which to gather diagnostic data on the types of knowledge emphasized in a particular teacher's evaluation activities. While this can be done by employing any of the data-gathering strategies discussed earlier in the chapter (i.e., asking, observing, and examining), it is especially time-efficient to initially concentrate on collecting this information by directly examining the evaluation tasks and activities the teacher is using. You will want to determine not only the types of knowledge forms the teacher tends to include in evaluation tasks, but also which of these, if any, seem to be especially problematic for a target student. To get a clear sense of this, a substantial number of evaluation activities should be analyzed, with the results of each analysis summarized so that patterns can be identified. An example of a simple form that might be used to record results from an examination of evaluation tasks with respect to determining "what is being evaluated" is shown in Figure 5–13.

EXAMINING THE NATURE OF EVALUATION TASKS

The second important component in analyzing classroom evaluation practices is to examine the *nature* of the evaluation tasks students are given. Clearly, evaluation tasks can vary significantly in terms of their design. They can also vary with respect to their purposes.

Student: Jean Scamp　　Subject: History
Date: 10-15-98　　Teacher: J. Clark

Type of Evaluation Task

Quiz	____	Presentation	____
Unit test	____	Demonstration	____
Mid-term	X	Oral drill	____
Final exam	____	Written drill	____
Homework	____	Other	____
Seatwork	____		____

Knowledge Forms Addressed

Type	Amount of Emphasis					
	Limited					Extensive
Verbal Associations						
Facts	0	1	2	3	4	(5)
Verbal chains	0	(1)	2	3	4	5
Discriminations	(0)	1	2	3	4	5
Concepts	0	1	2	(3)	4	5
Rule relationships	0	1	2	(3)	4	5
Cognitive strategies	(0)	1	2	3	4	5

Cognitive Demands

	Limited					Extensive
Recognize or reproduce information	0	1	2	3	(4)	5
Apply rule, formula, or algorithm	(0)	1	2	3	4	5
Recognize paraphrased information	0	1	2	3	(4)	5
Apply known procedure to new problems	(0)	1	2	3	4	5
Draw inferences	0	1	2	(3)	4	5
Support a point of view	0	1	(2)	3	4	5
Other ____						

FIGURE 5–13 Evaluation Analysis Form: Content Analysis

Evaluations commonly have two purposes. *Formative* evaluation provides ongoing feedback to teachers on student progress, while *summative* evaluation is used to determine educational outcomes. For example, a teacher who has introduced a list of 15 new science vocabulary words might ask a target student to read, spell, or define the words each day after working on them. By keeping track of the student's daily performance, the teacher would know if the instruction was effective or if adjustments in the instructional plan were warranted. In this case the teacher would be using evaluation data for formative purposes.

In contrast, having the student complete a test at the end of the 10-day science unit to measure mastery of those new words is an example of using evaluation for *summative* purposes. The exam shows the teacher the "bottom line" of what was accomplished as a result of the instruction. Other examples of summative evaluations include teacher-made mid-term and final exams, as well as standardized achievement measures.

It should be clear from these examples that each type of evaluation is closely linked to how often it occurs. Because formative evaluation is most useful if student progress is monitored on a fairly continuous basis, it must occur with a high rate of frequency. Because summative evaluation focuses on attainment of goals, it typically occurs less often.

Classrooms serving students with special educational needs should feature both types of evaluation activities if they are to adequately meet the needs of these students. Traditionally, general education teachers have primarily emphasized summative evaluation. Their practices need to be broadened. Procedures should be in place to permit teachers to monitor student progress regularly so that instruction can be modified as necessary. Otherwise, teachers have no way of knowing who didn't "get it" until the mastery test is given. In Chapter 6 we discuss strategies for implementing continuous progress monitoring in general education settings.

A second important factor to consider in examining the nature of evaluation tasks is the form they take. For example, one would want to know how much overlap there is between the types of evaluation tasks a teacher gives students and the types of practice activities they completed during instruction. In theory, there should be a good match between the two, but in practice, this is not always the case. It is not uncommon for students to complete a variety of academic activities during the practice stage of an instructional cycle that are not reflected in evaluation, either in terms of the specific content or design of the evaluation tasks. For instance, students who are learning a list of new spelling words may be asked to do such things as write sentences using the words, look up the words in a dictionary, or participate in spelling bees. Yet to evaluate their mastery of the words they may be asked to produce correctly spelled words in writing from dictation. The students had been given virtually no opportunity to practice doing the very thing that will be used to determine their mastery of the words.

An analysis of evaluation practices should also include consideration of task structure or general design, just as one might examine the structure of academic tasks given to students during the practice stage of instruction. It is important to examine input and output demands that an evaluation task places on students. Does the task require the student to read? Are listening skills involved? Does it emphasize information that must be processed visually? Is a written response required? Does the student respond orally or is some type of physical response involved, such as pointing, marking, or demonstrating? A wide range of alternatives can be used in evaluation tasks, and these options will vary considerably with respect to how well suited they are for particular students.

Several other factors mentioned previously in connection with analyzing academic tasks should also be addressed in examining the structure of evaluation tasks. It is important to explore such things as the clarity of directions, sensitivity to cultural and linguistic differences, time constraints, and readability of materials. Also some emphasis should be placed on studying the amount of information involved, both in terms of

Formative evaluation provides ongoing feedback about student progress.

how much information is covered and with regard to how extensive student responses must be. Finally, it is useful to consider the overall quality of the materials. It is not uncommon to find evaluation tasks that are visually cluttered, do not provide adequate space for responses, or are poor quality copies. Figure 5–14 presents a sample form that can be used in examining the quality of evaluation tasks.

> **REFLECTION BOX 5–5**
>
> Consider what Mr. Stout has learned about Carlos from his preliminary interviews and product examinations. What might this suggest to him in terms of designing evaluation tasks for Carlos?

EXAMINING CLASSROOM GRADING SYSTEMS

A final area that should be considered in examining classroom evaluation practices is the grading system. As we pointed out earlier, evaluation activities provide the account-

Student: Karen Osborne Subject: Geography
Date: 12-3-98 Teacher: P. Smart

Type of Evaluation Task

Quiz	____	Presentation	____
Unit test	____	Demonstration	____
Mid-term	____	Oral drill	____
Final exam	____	Written drill	____
Homework	X	Other	____
Seatwork	X		____

Purpose

Formative X Summative ____

Overlap with Practice Activities Poor ____ Fair X Good ____

Judgment based on:
- Review of assignments ____
- Review of plan book X
- Teacher interview X
- Student interview X
- Other ____

General Structure or Design	Comments
Input demands	– Read worksheet and textbook – examine map
Output demands	– written responses (sentences & paragraphs)
Clarity of directions	– good example provided
Time constraints	– 10 minutes of class time; remainder to be completed as homework for next day
Readability level	– sixth or seventh grade
Amount	– 20 items
Quality of materials	– good, clear reproductions, ample space for response provided

FIGURE 5–14 Evaluation Analysis Form: Structure Analysis

ability structure for making several types of judgments. One key form of judgment is the assignment of a report card grade. Although this decision typically places greatest emphasis on student test performance, a number of other factors can come into play.

It is important to determine the full range of elements that contribute to a classroom grading system, as well as the relative weight placed on each of these elements. While test performance may be the principal consideration, grades may also reflect homework assignments, classroom discussions, special projects and demonstrations, and class notebooks. Other factors that have been suggested as a basis for assigning grades include the extent to which students have mastered specific IEP goals, their apparent effort, evaluations provided by others such as a special education teacher, or products and self-reflections included in students' portfolios (Choate et al., 1995).

Classrooms that feature grading systems based on multiple sources of information, with the relative weight of each carefully balanced, are well suited for students with special educational needs. These classrooms provide numerous opportunities for students to demonstrate what they have learned. This is critical because many of these youngsters encounter significant problems in taking tests, often not because they have failed to master the material but because of the way the test has been designed. In such cases student achievement may be greatly underestimated. Broad-based grading systems offer a more equitable method of judging achievement for these students.

According to Wood (1998), however, an important preliminary question to answer when considering the issue of grading is whether alternative grading procedures are necessary for a particular individual. Often students with mild disabilities can be graded using the same methods applied to others in the class, assuming steps have been taken to make appropriate adaptations in the learning environment, format of the content, teaching techniques, and testing procedures. In cases where such steps are not sufficient, an alternative grading system may be needed. Care should be taken to specify any necessary grading accommodations on the student's IEP, including the exact criteria and weighting procedures that will be applied in determining the student's grade, as well as an indication of who will be responsible for assigning the grade. Chapter 7 presents several useful strategies that can be followed in developing alternative grading systems.

REFLECTION BOX 5–6

Consider what Mr. Stout has learned about Carlos from his preliminary interviews and product examinations. What might this suggest to him in terms of how to design an appropriate grading system for Carlos?

Information to document classroom grading systems can be gathered rather quickly by using an "asking" strategy. This might be accomplished using a questionnaire like the one shown in Figure 5–15 which also incorporates use of a rating scale. The special education teacher and classroom teacher could complete the questionnaire together, or the classroom teacher could be asked to respond using the self-questioning technique.

COMPREHENSIVE DATA-GATHERING TOOLS

In discussing approaches to evaluating instructional contexts we have presented a number of tools that can be used to gather information. Several comprehensive tools

Teacher: M. Robinson Subject: World Cultures

Respondent(s): M. Robinson Date: 2-12-99

J. Stern (student)

Various factors might be considered in determining report card grades. Indicate the amount of emphasis placed on each of these items.

Factor	Amount of Emphasis (Limited)					(Extensive)	Comments
	0	1	2	3	4	5	
Quizzes	0	1	2	3	(4)	5	lowest score not considered in averaging grade
Unit tests	0	1	2	3	4	(5)	
Mid-term exams	0	1	2	3	4	(5)	
Final exams	0	1	2	3	4	(5)	
Seat Assignments	0	(1)	2	3	4	5	
Homework	0	(1)	2	3	4	5	
Class discussions	0	1	(2)	3	4	5	
Presentations	0	1	(2)	3	4	5	
Demonstrations	(0)	1	2	3	4	5	
Special projects	0	1	2	(3)	4	5	
Student portfolios	(0)	1	2	3	4	5	
Mastery of IEP goals	(0)	1	2	3	4	5	
Effort	0	(1)	2	3	4	5	
Behavior	0	(1)	2	3	4	5	

Other ____________________

FIGURE 5–15 Grading System Rating Scale

also are available commercially that focus on many of the same concerns we have discussed. One popular tool is *The Instructional Environment Scale* (TIES) (Ysseldyke & Christenson, 1993) which uses all three methods of gathering diagnostic data that we have discussed. Protocols are provided for conducting teacher and student interviews, completing structured classroom observations, and examining student work products. Outcomes from these activities are recorded on a form that identifies areas in which instructional adjustments may need to be made. Another commercially available tool is the *Intervention/Transition Checklist* developed by Wood (1998). This checklist outlines, in considerable detail, key elements of classroom contexts as well as important features of related school environments such as the library, media center, and cafeteria.

Respondents complete the checklist by indicating whether behaviors listed have been mastered, are currently being developed, or cannot be performed. Information from a variety of sources can be obtained to complete the checklist, including student, teacher, and parent interviews; direct observation; or review of school records. The design of the checklist facilitates identification of clearly defined instructional goals and also allows for easy progress monitoring.

SUMMARY

In this chapter we have emphasized that student learning does not occur in a vacuum, but is affected by a number of critical classroom variables. To be effective in teaching students, especially those with learning difficulties, these situational factors must be examined carefully. In many cases these variables may explain student learning problems. We have also described three broad strategies that can be used in gathering information to evaluate instructional contexts: asking, observing, and examining.

A chart that summarizes the classroom variables discussed in this chapter is presented in Figure 5–16. It provides an overview of critical classroom concerns and can serve as a framework for gathering information.

A number of additional sources offer detailed information on evaluating instructional contexts. Among these we recommend texts by Wood (1998), Choate et al., (1995) and Sugai and Tindal (1993).

FOLLOW-UP ACTIVITIES

1. Obtain three examples of homework assignments. Use the questions presented in Figure 5–2 to analyze the assignments in terms of their instructional focus.
2. Obtain two examples of homework assignments for any subject area. Conduct an item analysis to determine the specific skills addressed in each assignment. Your analysis should also include a listing of skills required of the student to complete the assignment.
3. Use the event-based observation system shown in Figure 5–9 to complete an observation in a content subject class. The focus of the observation should be on examining the teacher's questioning patterns. Be prepared to discuss your findings.
4. Select three sample homework assignments for any content subject area. Tell how you would redesign each assignment to reduce the writing requirements and increase the diversity among item types.

INSTRUCTIONAL CONTEXT

INSTRUCTIONAL DESIGN

Presentation of Subject Matter

- Teacher's Style
  - orienting strategies
  - clarity of instruction
  - questioning strategies
  - cultural/linquistic sensitivity
  - student motivation
- Instructional Delivery
  - mode
  - lesson structure
  - pacing
  - prompts, cues, modeling
  - grouping patterns

Characteristics of the Curriculum

- Scope and Sequence
  - amount
  - variation
- Academic Tasks
  - nature
  - structure

EVALUATION PRACTICES

Knowledge Types

- verbal associations
- concepts
- rule relationships
- cognitive strategies

Structure and Design

- overlap with practice
- input/output demands
- clarity of directions
- time constraints
- amount
- readability
- overall quality

Grading Systems

- range
- relative weights

FIGURE 5–16 Dimensions of Instructional Contexts

5. Obtain two examples of teacher-made tests for any content subject area. Use the form in Figure 5–13 to analyze each test in terms of its content.
6. Interview two teachers concerning the grading system used in their classroom. The rating scale in Figure 5–15 should be used as a guide. Be prepared to describe each system and provide your impressions as to where improvements could be made.

CHAPTER 6 EVALUATING ACADEMIC PERFORMANCE

KEY WORDS

referral process
instructional planning
criterion-referenced tests
curriculum-based assessments
commercially available
APPLY *model*
performance assessment
strategic learning behaviors

OBJECTIVES

After reading this chapter you should be able to:

1. differentiate among purposes for evaluating academic performance.
2. provide examples of formal and informal strategies that can be used to document students' academic skill needs.
3. discuss components that might be included in an evaluation of basic "tool" skills.
4. discuss components that might be included in an evaluation of related academic skills.
5. apply error-analysis procedures in assessing basic skills.
6. describe a variety of techniques for monitoring academic progress.

Three weeks ago Ms. Camp was informed that a transfer student, Tim Cannon, had been assigned to her class. Her principal indicated that the teachers at Tim's previous school described him as being generally well-behaved, although in need of some academic assistance. According to his former teachers, Tim was about to be evaluated for a possible learning disability when his family moved out of the area. Ms. Camp learned that plans were under way to proceed with the evaluation once Tim was settled at his new school. In the meantime, she would do her best to assess Tim's abilities within the context of her fifth-grade class. She knew the information she gathered would be useful to those who would be completing Tim's formal evaluation. She also knew this information would be essential to her as she planned Tim's instructional program.

In the three weeks that Tim has been a student in her class, Ms. Camp has formed a number of impressions about his strengths and weaknesses. She has kept an anecdotal record of her observations so that she will be prepared to meet with Tim's evaluation team. Her notes suggest Tim is struggling in a number of areas, although happily his behavior does not appear to be one of them, as was also the case at his previous school.

Ms. Camp's anecdotal record indicates her belief that Tim may have problems in the area of oral expression. As evidence to support this belief she has described a number of instances in which Tim's behavior clearly indicated that he understood what was said, but was unable to provide an appropriate oral response. Instead his responses were quite short and disjointed.

Ms. Camp also noted a number of inconsistencies in Tim's reading performance. She described situations in which he had extreme difficulty completing reading assignments from social studies and science textbooks. Yet she described other instances in which he seemed to have no problem working from library books that dealt with sports legends or mysteries.

She noted similar inconsistencies in Tim's writing performance. Her records described numerous examples of writing assignments that showed he had significant problems with spelling and with producing compositions of adequate length, but no apparent problems applying punctuation and capitalization rules, nor in writing legibly.

Ms. Camp's record also documented numerous occasions in which Tim's work was incomplete. At first she suspected this was because the work was too difficult for Tim, but she noted there were many times when Tim seemed to be making good progress—he just ran out of time.

Using this information as a guide, Ms. Camp plans to carry out a number of additional activities that will help her evaluate Tim's academic performance.

In Chapter 5 we discussed approaches to assessment that can be used to analyze classroom instructional practices and that contribute to developing effective programs for students with disabilities in general education settings. In this chapter we apply these same approaches to examining students' academic needs.

WHY EVALUATE ACADEMIC PERFORMANCE?

Student achievement is affected by a number of factors, particularly the instructional ones discussed in the previous chapter. Indeed, Ysseldyke and Christenson (1987) have suggested that educators should always systematically examine the role of instructional factors before categorizing or labeling students as having learning problems. But because instructional factors interact reciprocally with student characteristics, an assessment of student needs cannot stop with the assessment of the instructional environment. It is equally important to conduct a thorough assessment of a student's academic abilities to determine what the learner brings to an instructional situation.

These two evaluations, of the instructional environment and of the student's abilities, provide the essential framework for developing effective intervention plans. No matter how much one knows about the instructional context, it is impossible to develop interventions that are appropriately targeted without a clear sense of who the learner is. It is only when one examines the interplay between what the learner brings to the classroom and the parameters of instruction in that classroom that effective strategies can be planned.

GATHERING DATA TO EVALUATE ACADEMIC PERFORMANCE

In Chapter 5 we introduced a number of important evaluation strategies that can be used to gather diagnostic data on instructional contexts. We grouped these evaluation tools into three broad categories (asking, observing, and examining) and discussed essential considerations when using each approach. We also indicated that these same evaluation tools can be used to gather information about student abilities. To understand this point, it is useful to think of the three categories of evaluation tools as three types of lenses for a microscope, each designed to provide a different "picture" of a specimen slide. Our two "specimen slides" are the instructional contexts and student performance; the three evaluation tools give us different information about each.

This chapter focuses on gathering data about students' academic performance. The methods described rely on asking, observing, and examining as strategies for collecting the data. In Chapter 7, we will show how these same data collection strategies can be used to characterize students' social and behavioral status.

TYPES OF ACADEMIC EVALUATIONS IN SPECIAL EDUCATION

We begin our discussion by clarifying the role of academic evaluations for students with special needs. As shown in Figure 6–1, academic evaluations might be done for one or two purposes. Some are conducted as part of the special education **referral process**, either in conjunction with prereferral screening efforts or as part of the formal process to verify the presence of a disability and determine eligibility to receive special services. Other academic evaluations are conducted to serve as the basis for *planning instructional programs*, such as the annual Individualized Education Plan (IEP), weekly or monthly instructional goals, or daily teaching plans. Evaluations conducted

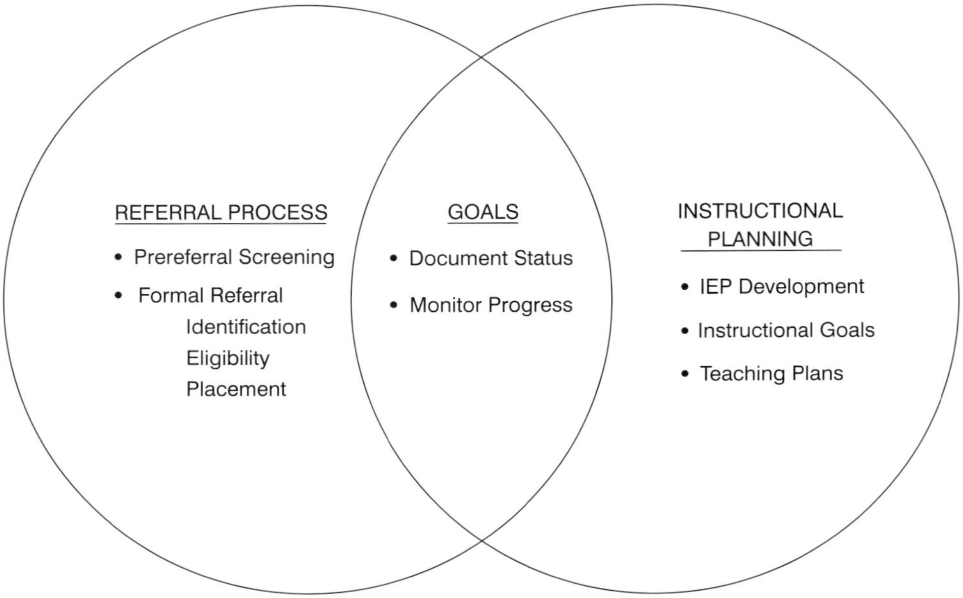

FIGURE 6–1 Role of Evaluation in Special Education

as part of the referral and placement process in special education often rely heavily on traditional standardized tests; results of such tests generally do not offer enough functional information to guide instructional planning. In contrast, assessments for instructional planning rely heavily on alternative and more informal approaches to assessment that show clearly what students have learned and lead directly to instructional decisions.

The focus of this chapter is on evaluating student performance for the purpose of **instructional planning**. Throughout, we will assume that evaluation efforts involve the active and on-going participation of both the special education teacher and the general education teacher, since both professionals are sharing responsibility for teaching students with disabilities. Moreover, because they bring different perspectives to the assessment, each is in a position to make unique contributions.

A number of alternative assessment strategies have been described in the literature; our focus will be on three that are especially useful for general education settings: (1) criterion-referenced tests, (2) curriculum-based assessments, and (3) performance-based assessments. Note that these approaches employ the data collection strategies of asking, observing, and examining introduced in Chapter 5.

CRITERION-REFERENCED TESTS

Criterion-referenced tests are designed to measure the extent of a student's mastery of a skill based on an established criterion. Such tests compare the student's performance with expected levels of mastery, rather than with the performance of other students (as is the case with norm-referenced measures). Results obtained from criterion-referenced tests provide teachers with information on what skills have been mastered, the student's rate of progress, and objectives that still must be addressed. Criterion-referenced tests lead directly to instructional decisions. They can be used to guide the design and delivery of instruction and they provide important information for evaluating the effectiveness of educational programs.

A variety of **commercially available** criterion-referenced tests are available for a range of academic and vocational areas. Some of these are designed to assess a single subject area. For example, the *Spellmaster Assessment and Teaching System* (Greenbaum, 1987) involves a series of dictated spelling tasks that provide information on strategies students use in spelling and the spelling patterns they have (or have not) mastered. Other criterion-referenced tests are multiskill batteries that contain subtests for measuring skills in several academic areas; the popular *Brigance* diagnostic inventories (Brigance, 1977, 1981, 1983), which include subtests in reading, spelling, and mathematics are examples of such multiskill batteries. Other commercially available criterion-referenced tests will be presented later in the chapter as they relate to various subject areas.

If a commercial test will be used, be sure to consider carefully the curriculum scope and sequence for the target subject area in which you plan to test, paying special attention to grade level differences. For example, if you are looking for a test to assess a second-grader's knowledge of punctuation and capitalization rules, it would be important to identify the types of rules introduced in *your* curriculum up to and including second grade. Your list of rules might include punctuating sentence endings, using commas to separate words in a series, and capitalizing proper names or the first word in a sentence. Armed with this list, you would try to locate a test that includes these items. Although the test you find might also include items that address more "advanced" skills such as applying correct punctuation for abbreviations, quotations, and contractions, or rules related to capitalizing names of months, holidays, titles, and salutations, these portions of the test need not be administered. In short, the criterion-referenced test you select and the parts of it you choose to administer should be a good match with curriculum objectives for *your* student in *your* setting.

A second factor to keep in mind when choosing a commercial test is that the guidelines and directions provided by the publisher need not be followed explicitly. The goal of criterion-referenced testing is to gain a clear picture of what a student can do and the conditions under which performance was elicited; the testing procedure can be adapted to accommodate individual differences and to provide the most accurate assessment of the student's true abilities, as long as those adaptations are carefully noted and are used to explain the test results. You may decide, for example, to complete an assessment over several short sessions to accommodate a child who has difficulty sustaining attention. Or you may elect to interrupt testing periodically to ask questions about how answers were derived or to conduct follow-up probes in apparent problem areas. You might even decide to see what happens to a student's performance when prompts, cues, or examples are provided. Adjustments such as these can have a positive effect on the student's performance and provide the teacher with important insights about student capabilities and needs.

A final factor to keep in mind when choosing a commercially available test involves setting the criteria for mastery, that is, the level at which a student must be able to perform to demonstrate that a skill has been mastered. Is an accuracy level of 100% required, or are somewhat lower levels acceptable? Christenson, Ysseldyke, & Thurlow (1989) suggest an accuracy level of 80% is appropriate during the acquisition stage of instruction, but that a level of accuracy between 90% to 100% should be required at the stage of independent practice. Commercial test makers frequently provide criteria for determining mastery, but these do not have to be followed rigidly. The mastery criterion you adopt should be appropriate for your situation and should reflect consideration of overall learner needs and the relative importance of particular skills. Thus you may decide to establish a lower mastery criterion for skills that are lower priority concerns and a higher criterion for really important skills. Often school districts establish minimum student performance standards; these might assist you in establishing mastery criteria.

As an alternative to using commercial tests, teachers can develop their own criterion-referenced measures. According to Sugai and Tindal (1993), this can be accomplished by following these steps: First, parameters for the domain of assessment items should be clearly established. For instance, one might specify that the assessment domain will focus on math computation involving addition of three-digit numbers with regrouping, or that it will involve literal reading comprehension of facts and details in short passages, or that it will focus on concepts related to photosynthesis covered in a particular science chapter. In each case an exact set of boundaries for the assessment domain is established.

Once parameters for the domain have been identified, a strategy for sampling the domain should be developed. In essence, the sampling plan addresses the question, "How many items from the domain should be administered to support the assumption that a student's performance on similar items would be the same?" At least three to five items should be selected for each subskill.

Finally, criteria for mastery or proficiency must be established against which student performance will be deemed either acceptable or unacceptable. Sugai and Tindal (1993) recommend considering mastery within three zones: (1) clear mastery, (2) uncertain mastery, and (3) clear nonmastery. For clear mastery, the student demonstrates a high level of correct performance; the evidence shows that the student is proficient in the skill area. In clear nonmastery, the evidence shows that the student is experiencing considerable difficulty. Uncertain mastery refers to inconsistent student performance; while there is evidence of correct performance, there are also quite a few instances of error. According to Sugai and Tindal, the outside two zones (i.e., clear mastery and clear nonmastery) are usually easy to establish. Greater disagreement is found in the "uncertain mastery"; however, all three zones should be considered in summarizing performance.

CURRICULUM-BASED ASSESSMENT

Curriculum-based assessment (CBA) is an overall approach to evaluation characterized by several critical features: (1) test items are drawn directly from the curriculum, (2) student performance is evaluated frequently across time, (3) assessment outcomes are recorded on graphs, and (4) these visual representations of student progress are used to guide instructional decisions. CBA is an "individual" referenced evaluation system for judging progress; each time a student's performance is measured it is compared not with some mastery criterion but with the student's previous levels of performance on the same task.

A number of CBA models have been described in the special education literature, including *curriculum-based measurement* (CBM) developed by Deno, Fuchs, Mirkin, and their colleagues (Deno, 1985). CBM is a type of curriculum-based assessment that has standardized techniques for the creation, administration, and scoring of measurement samples, as well as for monitoring progress. CBM procedures have been developed in the areas of reading, spelling, written expression, and mathematics. Readers who are interested in a detailed discussion of the CBM model should consult Deno (1985) and Fuchs and Fuchs (1986). A good summary of procedures for using the CBM model in classrooms also has been provided by Mercer and Mercer (1998). Our discussion will focus instead on curriculum-based assessment in a broader context, that is, as a data collection strategy to measure student progress within the curriculum and to guide educational decision making.

Several procedures for implementing a curriculum-based assessment system in classrooms have been described in the literature (Choate, Enright, Miller, Poteet, & Rakes, 1995; Mastropieri & Scruggs, 1994; Sugai & Tindal, 1993). While differences can be found in the number and types of procedural steps outlined by various proponents of CBA, the suggested methods overlap considerably. Most approaches to using CBA begin with attention to the curriculum and end with how to use the results.

One procedural model that we have found especially useful was developed by King-Sears (1994). The model uses the mnemonic APPLY to synthesize the steps involved in developing and using a curriculum-based assessment. Elements of the **APPLY model** are presented in Figure 6–2 and discussed in the remainder of this section.

The first step in the APPLY model involves careful examination of the curriculum. Effective academic assessment requires an understanding of both the scope and sequence of the academic subject and how it relates to an individual student's needs. In short, the evaluator needs to be aware of what skills or sets of skills are being taught, the order or hierarchy in which they are typically introduced, and adaptations to that order that might be planned for a particular setting.

Using the curriculum as a guide, the teacher begins the assessment process by selecting short- or long-term objectives as benchmarks for monitoring student

FIGURE 6–2 Elements of the Apply Model for Developing and Using Curriculum-Based Assessment

Note: *From* Curriculum-Based Assessment in Special Education *(p. 17), by M. E. King-Sears, 1994, San Diego, CA: Singular Publishing Group. Copyright 1994 by Singular Publishing Group. Reprinted by permission.*

1. Analyze the curriculum
2. Prepare items to match curriculum objectives
3. Probe frequently
4. Load data using a graph format
5. Yield to results by making revisions and decisions

progress. Although a curriculum will comprise *many* objectives, not all of them must be assessed in a CBA system. Each teacher needs to determine which of the broad array of curriculum objectives are critical benchmarks for a particular student. This decision will obviously require consideration of instructional priorities for the student, both in terms of the student's remedial needs and successful integration into the general education curriculum, and in terms of planning for post-school transitions.

The second step in the APPLY model calls for the evaluator to prepare assessment items or probes to match the curriculum objectives (i.e., the short- and long-term goals) established for a given student. Probes can be developed in a variety of formats and will be highly dependent on the type of curriculum objective involved. Materials and procedures used to probe student skills might include items like the following:

- lists of words to be read
- checklists of steps to be completed
- sets of problems to be solved
- passages with questions to be answered
- teacher directions that prompt student responses such as story starters for written compositions or oral stories
- checklists of student behaviors that are contextually/socially appropriate (King-Sears, 1994).

Several factors should be considered when developing probes. First, CBA is characterized by frequent measurement; probes should be brief, easy to administer, and easy to score so it will not be onerous to administer them regularly. For example, if the target objective is to improve the student's ability to read words containing the CVCC pattern, the teacher could develop probes consisting of 1-minute timed readings of word lists taken from the basal reader, to be administered 3 times each week, with the number of words read correctly in 1 minute as the score. This would clearly be a quick and easily administered and scored CBA. Secondly, all assessment targets must be directly measurable and items should match the target objective exactly. The precise behavior, the conditions under which it should be performed, and the performance criteria specified in the instructional objective must be reflected in the assessment probe. In other words, if the objective specifies production behavior at a particular fluency or mastery level, test items must be designed to address this. Similarly, if the objective calls for application of a skill or ability to demonstrate the skill using particular curriculum materials, these elements should be addressed in the probes. Some consideration might also be given to randomly selecting from a pool of appropriate probe items to ensure greater reliability of outcomes.

The third step in the APPLY model calls for evaluating student progress regularly using the probes developed in the second step. How often teachers choose to probe and how much time each probe takes can vary considerably. In developing a strategy for probing, however, teachers should keep in mind that an underlying assumption of CBA is that student performance and progress will be measured much more frequently than is customary, but that each assessment activity will require only brief amounts of time. One common approach is for teachers to develop a schedule for administering short probes, each usually lasting between 1 and 3 minutes, which can be completed daily or, at the very least, several times a week (Germann & Tindal, 1985; King–Sears, 1994; Rosenfield, 1987). This strategy can be quite effective because the amount of time spent on probing is limited, but much more information is obtained than in the more traditional end-of-week, end-of-unit, or end-of-chapter testing routine. Frequent probing is useful in monitoring student progress and making adjustments to instruction, as necessary.

Step four of the APPLY model involves displaying the data obtained from the probes. This data display is more than traditional record-keeping in a grade book or log. It involves displaying probe results in a graph format to facilitate interpretation of findings.

Graphs can be easily constructed by marking two axes on graph paper, a vertical line which depicts performance scores and a horizontal line which shows measurement dates. Each of these axes should be labeled to indicate what they represent and the objective in question should be specified at the top of the graph. Figure 6–3 presents an example of a teacher-made graph constructed to display a student's progress towards the curriculum objective of correctly spelling 15 out of 15 words containing the CVCC pattern. On this graph, the vertical axis represents the number of words Todd spelled correctly, from 1 to 15. If the probes contain a large number of responses, such as in a probe for measuring the number of words a student reads correctly in a 3-minute period, the vertical axis could be marked in larger units (e.g., 5, 10, 15, and so on). The horizontal axis of the graph shown in Figure 6-3 represents the dates when probes were administered. Ideally, this axis should mark off the number of days elapsed since the last test and not just equally spaced test sessions. Outcomes

FIGURE 6–3 Teacher-Made Graph Showing Todd's Spelling Performance During a 3-Week Period.

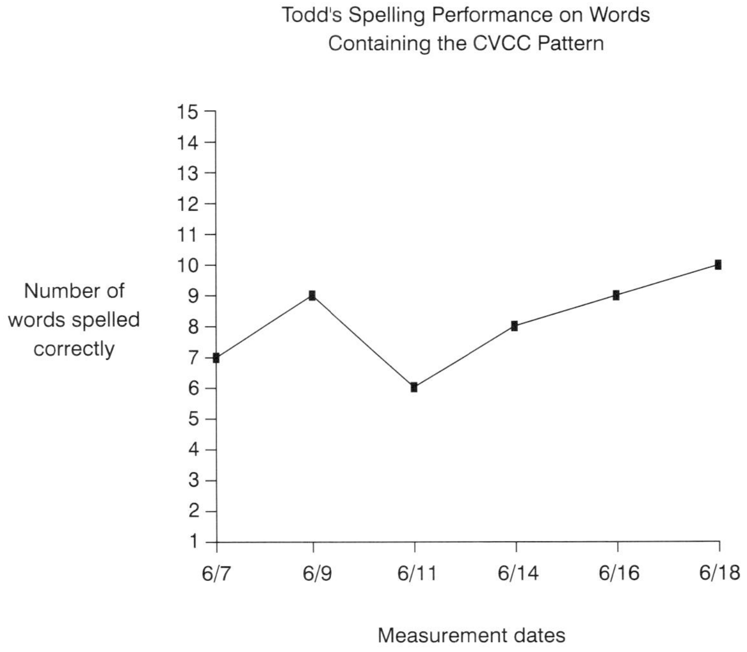

from the probes are recorded on the graph. Data points are connected to illustrate the flow of the student's progress.

The final step in the APPLY model calls for the teacher to "yield to results." This means that the teacher critically evaluates data shown on the graph and decides whether to make an instructional change. The data may show that good progress is being made, suggesting that the current instructional approach is effective. Or the data may show that insufficient progress is being made, suggesting that the teacher should revise the instructional program. Such an outcome might also lead the teacher to reconsider the appropriateness of the curriculum objective selected for the student, or to reexamine the materials used as probes to make certain they accurately reflect the instructional objective.

A number of guidelines and decision rules for interpreting CBA data have been suggested in the literature. (See guidelines suggested by Deno, 1985; Fuchs & Fuchs, 1986; Olson & Platt, 1996; and Sugai & Tindal, 1993).)

PERFORMANCE ASSESSMENT

Another approach to assessment gaining in popularity has been broadly termed **performance assessment**. This calls for direct examination of student performance on tasks that reflect the goals or desired outcomes of the curriculum. Because performance assessment is closely linked to instruction, it often involves analysis of work samples such as in-seat written assignments, oral readings, participation in class discussions, homework assignments, and notebooks, to name a few. The term *performance* refers to the type of response the student must provide (Meyer, 1992); tasks used in performance assessment call for students to produce, demonstrate, apply, solve, plan, illustrate, or explain. When performance assessments are designed so that in evaluating curricular objectives they require application to real-life situations or demands, they are termed *authentic* performance assessments. Figure 6–4 presents examples of authentic performance assessment tasks for several subject areas.

Performance assessment tasks can take many forms, as long as they meet the criteria of being closely linked to the curriculum and requiring some form of "production" response. Performance assessments are especially useful when designed to provide insight into both the content of a student's response and the thought processes used to arrive at that response.

REFLECTION BOX 6–1

Tim's teacher believes he may have some weaknesses in the area of oral expression. What type of performance assessment tasks might she have him complete to obtain additional information about his oral language skills? Why do you think it would be important for his teacher to have several of Tim's classmates complete the same tasks?

An increasingly popular form of performance assessment involves the use of assessment portfolios. These are systematic collections of performance evidence over time and

Reading
- Videotape of reading to peer
- Critiques of books read
- Book reviews

Science
- Original investigation and report of findings
- Journal of observations of moon, stars

Oral Expression
- Phone call to request information
- Debate on current issues
- Persuasive speech

Social Studies
- Map of school or community
- Advertising campaign for political candidate

Written Expression
- Article for school paper
- Written resume and job application
- Letter to editor

The Arts
- Design and decoration of bulletin board
- Submission of art to contest
- Performance in a play

Mathematics
- Solving real-life problems using math knowledge
- Monitoring a savings account
- Personal budget

Generic
- Reflective journal of learning progress
- Planning and teaching a lesson to peer

FIGURE 6–4 Examples of Authentic Assessment Tasks

Note: *From* Performance Assessment and Special Education: Practices and Prospects, *by J. A. Poteet, J. S. Choate, & S. C. Stewart, 1996, in E. L. Meyen, G. A. Vergason, & R. J. Whelan (Eds.),* Strategies For Teaching Exceptional Children In Inclusive Settings *(p. 220), Denver, CO: Love Publishing Co. Copyright 1996 by Love Publishing Co. Reprinted by permission.*

under varying conditions, all related to curricular objectives for a particular content area (Poteet, Choate, & Stewart, 1996). Assessment portfolios often, although not always, include demonstrations of authentic tasks and they typically call for students to provide self-evaluations of their work products. Many believe that assessment portfolios are especially valuable because they show the depth, breadth, and development of a student's abilities over time. This is only true, however, when clear guidelines for constructing and evaluating portfolio entries have been established. A number of excellent sources are available to assist teachers in developing procedures for using assessment portfolios; see, for example, guidelines suggested by Arter and Spandel (1991) and Wolf (1991).

DEVELOPING AN ACADEMIC SKILL PROFILE

The discussion that follows shows how criterion-referenced assessment, curriculum-based assessment, and performance assessment can be used to determine students'

Having students debate a current issue is an authentic assessment task that can provide insight into oral expression task.

academic skill needs and set instructional priorities. In organizing this section, we have made two assumptions. The first is that to be successful in school students need to develop certain basic or "tool" skills. These involve skills in the areas of oral language (including English as a second language), reading, written expression, and mathematics; the focus in each of these areas changes as a student progresses through the grade levels. In the primary grades, emphasis is placed on helping students develop a functional foundation in each of these areas. Later, students are expected to expand their abilities by using this functional foundation to deal with information in a variety of content subjects. Our second assumption is that academic success also requires the development of a number of **strategic learning behaviors**. These involve learning strategies and study skills, some of which are taught explicitly as part of the typical school curriculum, but many of which are not.

Given the important role that basic skills and strategic learning behaviors play in school success, it follows that these would be critical areas to explore in developing an academic skills profile.

ASSESSING ORAL-LANGUAGE PERFORMANCE

That oral language plays an important role in school learning is obvious. It is central to being able to understand what occurs during instruction and is one of the principal methods by which students communicate and share knowledge with others. Students also use language to help them organize new information into long-term memory so it can be retrieved and used at a later time. Moreover, oral language serves as the basis for printed language, so students who have oral-language problems are likely to also experience difficulty in reading and writing.

To conduct an analysis of oral-language abilities it is important to understand the range of skills that constitute the oral-language domain. This understanding provides an essential context or "road map" for gathering diagnostic information.

The term *language* refers to a code or system of arbitrary signals used to communicate ideas. In the case of oral language the system involves a speaker's use of vocal signals to communicate ideas and thoughts to a listener. The speaker's ability to correctly send messages using the code is referred to as *expressive language* or production, while the listener's ability to correctly interpret the code is called *receptive language* or *comprehension*. These two terms identify the principal aspects of the oral-language domain. Each of these can, in turn, be subdivided into a number of component skill areas (see Figure 6–5, and Bloom & Lahey, 1978; Bos & Vaughn, 1998; Lewis & Doorlag, 1999).

Language form refers to the structure and sounds of language, and consists of phonology, morphology, and syntax. *Phonology* is the system of rules that governs the sounds and sound combinations of each oral-language system. Units of sound that can be combined with others to form words are *phonemes*; phonemes are the smallest linguistic units of sound that can signal a difference. When phonemes are interchanged within words, they alter word meaning, such as in the case of shifting from *stop* to *spot*.

There are about 45 phonemes or speech sounds in the English language. Students must be able to identify these sounds and understand the rules for combining and

FIGURE 6–5 Components of Oral Language

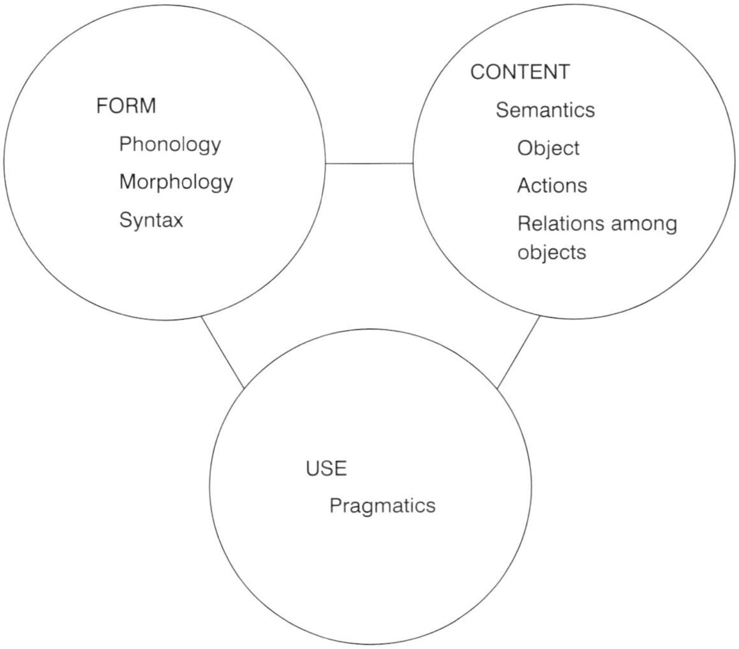

patterning them. They also must understand the relationship between these sounds and written letters. Phonemic awareness is not only an essential part of oral-language development, it also plays an important part in learning to read and spell. For instance, a growing body of research evidence suggests that many serious reading and spelling difficulties experienced by students with learning disabilities are related to problems with phonemic awareness (Lerner, 1997).

A second aspect of language form involves morphology. A *morpheme* is the smallest unit of language that conveys meaning. Two types of morphemes exist in our language: root words and affixes. Root words can stand alone; affixes cannot. When affixes in the form of a prefix or suffix are attached to a root word, the meaning of the word changes. Students need to understand the rules for word formation as a basis for determining word meanings.

The final aspect of language form involves *syntax*, the system of rules for determining the order of words in sentences. According to Owens (1992), the rules of syntax specify word order, sentence organization, and the relationships between words and word classes or types and other sentence constituents. These rules vary across languages; they specify which word combinations are acceptable for a particular language. In short, syntax represents the rules of grammar that govern a language.

Another major component shown in Figure 6–5 involves language content or the meaning conveyed by individual words and word combinations. This aspect of language is generally referred to as *semantics* and it can also be divided into three categories: objects (e.g., bell, cap, teacher), actions (e.g., running, jumping, thinking), and relationship among objects (e.g., Bill and his dog) or events (e.g., the relationship between hearing a joke and laughing). Development of semantic abilities is a slow and complicated process that begins as children acquire their first words and continues into adulthood. Throughout this process, children increase their vocabulary and expand their ability to understand and talk about abstract concepts. They not only learn more words, but also develop the ability to group words by abstract features, understand multiple meanings of words, and understand figurative uses of language, such as idioms, metaphors, and similes (Bos & Vaughn, 1998).

The final component shown in Figure 6–5 is language use or what is commonly referred to as the *pragmatic* aspect of language (Owens, 1992). Pragmatics involves the functional use of language as a means of affecting the behavior of others or carrying out one's intentions (Bruner, 1975). As children develop their pragmatic abilities they become increasingly adept at understanding the rules that govern how language is used in a variety of contexts, including social situations, developing an appreciation for sarcasm and jokes, or being able to appreciate a variety of perspectives (Schultz, 1974).

If oral language appears to be a problem area for a particular student, an oral-language assessment would be in order. Because such an assessment could focus on a wide range of skills, it is a good idea to begin the assessment by determining the parameters of the problem. It is helpful to conduct a survey assessment to identify the *specific* aspects of oral language that seem to be involved. Also, if the assessment will focus on a student for whom English is not the native language, the survey can help the teacher differentiate between language patterns that suggest real deficiencies and those that are primarily related to cultural or linguistic differences. A survey assessment can be done rather quickly by interviewing the classroom teacher to describe observations of the student's oral language performance during routine classroom activities. Note taking during the interview can be greatly enhanced by using a checklist like the one shown in Figure 6–6; the checklist also helps make certain all important components of oral language are discussed in the interview. The checklist was developed using the categories presented in Figure 6–5, and can help a teacher identify areas where a student might be experiencing particular difficulty. Note that care was taken to include items which address the specific, often unique, language demands of content area subjects.

Results of an initial assessment survey can also provide a general indication of the *extent* to which a student has oral-language difficulties. If a problem does appear to be present, a more extensive probe can be conducted using one of the alternative assessment approaches described earlier (criterion-referenced tests, criterion-based assessment, and performance assessment). For instance, when Julian's eighth-grade teacher was interviewed, her responses suggested that Julian had problems with oral expression involving both the content and use of spoken language. To explore this problem further Julian's special education and general education teachers decided to have him complete several "authentic" performance assessment tasks. Julian was asked on three different occasions to describe in as much detail as possible events that were well known to him: (1) the general routine followed in his eighth-grade English class, (2) a visit his class took to the middle-school science fair, and (3) how he celebrated his last birthday. The teachers chose these familiar settings or events to provide a structure that would help Julian organize his thoughts and limit his need to think up something to say.

The special education teacher tape-recorded Julian's descriptions and analyzed them later using the error analysis technique described in Chapter 5. Judgments about his performance are summarized in Figure 6–7. Several problems were noted, confirming his English teacher's suspicion that Julian has difficulties with oral expression and that a focused instructional program or other accommodation would have to be considered.

Because oral-language problems are often quite complicated, Julian's teachers planned to use the information they gathered as the basis for discussing his problem with the school's speech/language pathologist. This individual has the special expertise necessary to continue the assessment and would know when professionals from other disciplines should be involved. Julian's teachers know that the speech/language pathologist is in the best position to develop an instructional plan to address Julian's needs. While the special educator and classroom teacher could come up with a plan on their own, and would if the area of concern were reading or mathematics, it makes good sense to seek out the speech/language pathologist and follow this individual's lead when oral-language difficulties are involved. The speech/language pathologist may need to show Julian's teachers how to use special instructional techniques with which they have limited experience.

ASSESSING READING PERFORMANCE

About 10% to 15% of the general school population experiences some difficulty in reading (Harris & Sipay, 1990). Indeed, more students are referred for special educa-

Student ______________________________ Date ______________

Teacher ______________________________ Class ______________

Areas to be addressed during a teacher interview are listed below. Boxes should be checked to indicate teacher's impressions of the target student's abilities.

A. Form

The student can do the following:	Yes	No	Comments
1. Identify sounds heard in words.	____	____	
2. Segment words into sound units.	____	____	
3. Identify rhyming words.	____	____	
4. Replace sounds in words.	____	____	
5. Identify root words and affixes.	____	____	
6. Identify root words and affixes in content area vocabulary.	____	____	
7. Use appropriate word forms and sentence structure (i.e., demonstrate appropriate oral grammar).	____	____	

B. Content

The student can do the following:	Yes	No	Comments
1. Use appropriate vocabulary to describe common objects and actions.	____	____	
2. Correctly use specialized vocabularies associated with school subjects.	____	____	
3. Describe relationships among objects, events, or ideas.	____	____	
4. Discuss abstract concepts.	____	____	
5. Discuss relationships among ideas or concepts as pertains to content area subjects.	____	____	
6. Understand multiple meanings of words.	____	____	
7. Understand figurative uses of language (e.g. metaphors, similes, and idioms).	____	____	

C. Use

The student can do the following:	Yes	No	Comments
1. Use appropriate language for a classroom (or similarly formal) situation.	____	____	
2. Make needs known.	____	____	
3. Effectively seek assistance or ask a question.	____	____	
4. State a point of view.	____	____	
5. Understand sarcasm and jokes.	____	____	

FIGURE 6–6 Oral Language Skills Checklist

Student: Julian Date: 9-25-98

Assessment Area: Expressive Oral Language

Target Skill: Content

Vocabulary tended to be fairly concrete and included limited use of color words (adjectives/adverbs). Also somewhat limited use of "specialized" vocabulary related to classroom or school situations, particularly in relation to the science fair experience (e.g., referred to class schedule chart as "that thing that tells us what to do," test tubes called "mixing things", calculator and number line called "math helpers," referred to science experiments as "the games"). Teacher prompts had little effect.

Target Skill: Use/Pragmatics

Did not appear to adjust his use of language to meet the demands of assessment task (i.e., school assignment), especially with respect to choice of vocabulary.

Target Skill: ______________________

FIGURE 6–7 Summary of Assessment Outcomes for Julian

tion services because of problems in reading than for difficulties in any other academic area (Bos & Vaughn, 1998). Because reading is a basic tool for accessing all academic subjects, those who have problems reading are at a serious disadvantage; failure in reading often results in school failure and dropping out (Carnine, Silbert, & Kameenui, 1990; Lerner, 1997).

It is not surprising that learning to read is so challenging for so many students. Reading is a very complicated skill. To assess and teach reading effectively, it is important to understand the complexity of the reading domain. In this section we describe elements of the reading process and explore the role of meta-linguistic and meta-cognitive skills in the reading process. This division of reading into elements, each described as a separate entity, is, of course, artificial. Reading is actually an integrative process that requires concurrent use of these many related elements or skills.

We approach our discussion of the reading domain by addressing three broad categories of reading skill: word recognition, reading fluency, and reading comprehension. *Word recognition* is the processes of understanding phoneme–grapheme relationships (i.e., the match between sounds and symbols) and translating printed words to their oral-language equivalent. *Reading fluency* is the ease with which an individual can move

Direct observation during oral reading can provide valuable information on word attack strategies and reading style.

through print so that it parallels the patterns and rhythms of spoken language. *Reading comprehension* involves an understanding of the meaning of printed words in isolation and in context.

REFLECTION BOX 6–2

Based on Ms. Camp's description of Tim's reading performance, which broad categories of reading skill do you think she might need to examine further? Because it is possible that the inconsistencies in Tim's performance are related to motivational issues, how might she address this concern in developing assessment tasks?

Figure 6–8 illustrates how each of these broad categories of reading skill can be further subdivided into component skills. For example, word recognition involves the ability to use a variety of strategies to analyze or attack unknown words. One common word recognition strategy is phonetic analysis, in which the reader analyzes unknown words by applying the alphabetic principle to make connections between units of print and units of sound (Stanovich, 1992). Another approach involves the use of structural cues, identifying root words, prefixes, suffixes, plurals, and compound words to figure out unknown words. The ability to use context cues is yet another word analysis strategy. Contextual analysis involves the use of text meaning, grammatical cues, and pictures to identify unfamiliar words.

Word recognition also involves sight vocabulary. Cooper, Warncke, and Shipman (1990) describe two types of sight vocabulary words: those that become instantly recognizable to the reader as a result of repeated exposure; and those that become recognizable because they were purposely introduced as whole words in reading instruction. Early reading instruction commonly focuses on words that are likely to occur with

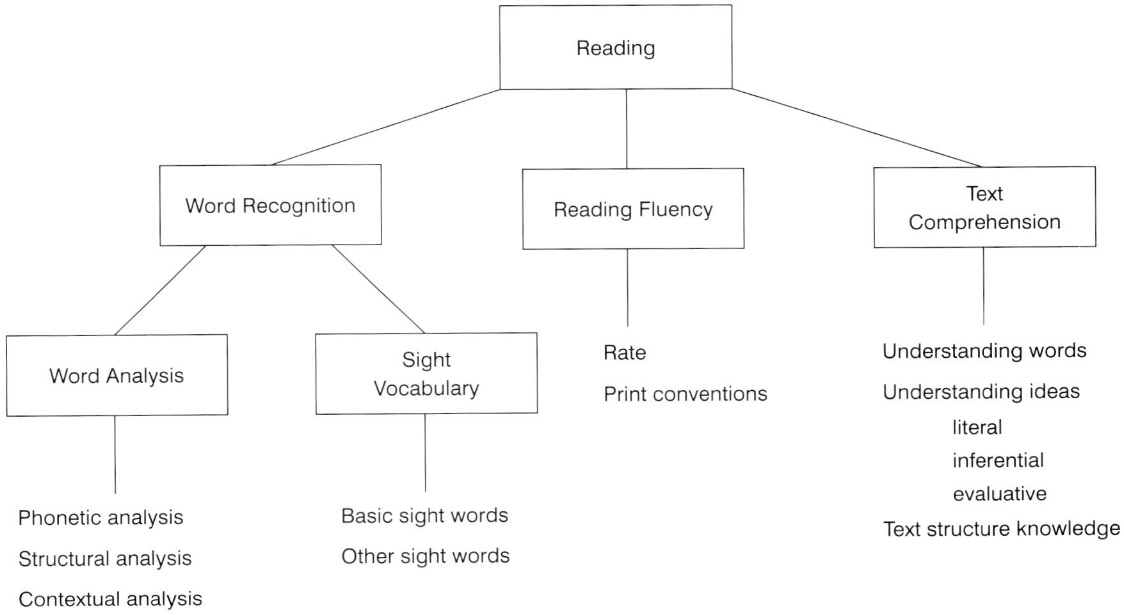

FIGURE 6–8 Organizational Framework of the Reading Domain

great frequency (often referred to as *high frequency* words), the theory being that one way to help beginning readers become more fluent is to teach them to automatically recognize words that appear often in print. Words with irregular spelling patterns that do not follow predictable phonic rules also are commonly taught as sight words. The number and types of words that become part of an individual's sight vocabulary continues to grow as access to print increases and sight vocabulary gradually expands to include more "specialized" vocabularies such as might be associated with various school subjects.

The second broad category of reading skill shown in Figure 6–8 is reading fluency or "the ability to read with speed and effortlessness" (Rivera & Smith, 1997). To read fluently one must be able to recognize most words automatically, without needing to stop and attack unknown words (i.e., fluency requires an adequate sight vocabulary). Fluency also requires an understanding of print conventions so that the reader will pause at appropriate points and use correct intonation. Fluency is influenced by other factors as well, including understanding of the author's purpose, familiarity with the topic, and the purpose for which the text is being read. Failure to develop reading fluency is one of the most common forms of reading difficulty and one that will have direct bearing on an individual's ability to understand what is read (Lyon, 1995).

The final broad category of reading skill shown in Figure 6–8 is text comprehension, the ultimate goal of reading. Adequate word recognition and reading fluency are necessary prerequisites for text comprehension, but readers also must be able to understand the meaning behind individual words and groups of words to grasp the message the writer is trying to convey.

In Figure 6–8, we have further divided comprehension into three component areas. First is student knowledge of the meaning of words. According to Heilman, Blair, and Rupley (1998), students' reading comprehension will be greatly facilitated or impeded by their vocabulary knowledge, that is, the pool of words an individual can correctly define or use appropriately. Vocabulary knowledge is not the same as sight vocabulary, as it is possible to recognize and pronounce certain words correctly without knowing what those words mean. While an individual's language background and experiences can have a substantial impact on vocabulary knowledge, understanding of words can be developed and extended through classroom instruction.

A second component of reading comprehension is the ability to understand ideas. Within this component are (1) *literal* comprehension, the ability to recognize and recall explicitly stated information such as main ideas, facts, details, and sequences of events; (2) *inferential* comprehension, the ability to go beyond what is printed on the page and use stated information to form hypotheses, understand cause-and-effect relationships, predict outcomes, and draw conclusions; and (3) *evaluative* comprehension, the ability to form opinions and judgments about a text based on personal experience, knowledge, and values, or to assess the validity of ideas, judge the difference between fact and opinion, make moral judgments, or analyze the author's intent (Mercer & Mercer, 1998).

A final component of reading comprehension shown in Figure 6–8 involves *text structure knowledge* or the extent to which the reader is aware of devices commonly used to frame and organize text. In expository text, these devices include transition words and phrases that alert the reader to important information and show how ideas are linked. In narrative or story text, they include key elements such as time frame, settings, characters and their reactions, conflicts to be resolved, episodic events, and resolutions. From experience, capable readers expect these devices or elements in the texts they read and they use their text structure knowledge to help them understand relationships in text and recall what was read. When students do not have a good understanding of text structure cues, their ability to comprehend text can be seriously compromised (Englert & Thomas, 1987; Idol, 1987; Laughlon & Morris, 1989; Vallecorsa & deBettencourt, 1997).

In addition to these elements of the reading domain, depicted in Figure 6–8, meta-linguistic ability and meta-cognitive ability must also be addressed in both assessment and instruction of reading. *Meta-linguistics* has to do with an individual's understanding of the structure of language and its use. As pointed out earlier in our discussion of oral language, a learner's understanding that ideas are represented by words and that words can be segmented into sounds and individual phonemes (i.e., phonemic awareness) has particular relevance in learning the sound-symbol relationships involved in reading. Research in the area of meta-linguistics indicates that successful acquisition of reading skill requires the ability to segment words into syllables and phonemes as well as the ability to blend sounds together to form words (Ball & Blachman, 1991; Cornwall, 1992; Stanovich, 1991; Tangel & Blackman, 1992).

Meta-cognition refers to an awareness of one's own thinking processes and the ability to monitor these processes for successful learning and task completion. Lerner

(1997) describes meta-cognition as "thinking about thinking" or being able to organize and oversee one's own mental activity in ways that help manage the thinking process. In the case of reading, meta-cognition might involve deciding which word analysis approach to use in a given situation, which memory strategies will aid recall of words, or which strategic behaviors will help to organize text content for understanding, retention, and subsequent recall. Skilled readers employ a variety of meta-cognitive routines, while students with reading difficulties have been shown to be deficient in the use of meta-cognitive strategies (Mann, 1991; Torgesen, 1985; Wong, 1987; Zabrucky & Ratner, 1992).

Understanding the skills involved in reading and how they interact with one another is critical to a meaningful assessment of reading performance. With this knowledge as a backdrop, teachers can follow the same general approach to assessment as recommended earlier. Assessment can begin with screening or survey activities designed to identify which aspects of reading skill may be problematic for the student. Special care should be taken if the assessment involves students from different cultural or linguistic backgrounds. It is important that such differences be taken into account, not only in selecting or developing assessment materials, but also in analyzing outcomes, so that differences in background are not misinterpreted as deficits in need of remediation. Once problem areas have been identified, assessment should focus on obtaining a more detailed picture of student strengths and weaknesses through the use of one or more of the assessment strategies we have presented.

Several standardized diagnostic tests can be used for the initial screening or skill survey and to draw a preliminary profile of student reading performance in the areas of word recognition, fluency, and comprehension. Among them are the *Diagnostic Reading Scales* (Spache, 1981), the *Durrell Analysis of Reading Difficulty* (Durrell & Catterson, 1980), the *Doren Diagnostic Reading Test of Word Recognition Skills* (Doren, 1973), the *Gates-McKillop-Horowitz Reading Diagnostic Tests* (Gates, McKillop & Horowitz, 1981), and the *Brigance Diagnostic Inventory of Basic Skills* (Brigance, 1977). Several of these tests also include auditory analysis and discrimination subtests that can provide useful information about phonemic awareness abilities.

As the assessment goal shifts toward determining more precisely what needs to be taught, teachers may wish to follow the procedures for constructing criterion-referenced tests or curriculum-based assessments outlined earlier in this chapter. These strategies will help to pinpoint students' instructional needs and will provide benchmarks against which to monitor students' progress. These methods are particularly well suited to reading assessment of word recognition and fluency.

A number of performance assessment activities are also quite effective and easy to implement. For example, teachers can obtain a wealth of information about word recognition abilities, reading fluency, and meta-cognitive skills by simply having students read graded passages out loud. These passages should begin at a level well within the student's reading ability range, then increase in difficulty to challenge the student. The latter is critical as it permits the teacher to document what becomes problematic for the student and what strategies the student employs when "stuck." Care should be taken to select passages from a variety of sources such as basal readers, content area texts, and high-interest materials to determine if a student's performance varies depending on the type of material being read. Selection of materials should also reflect consideration of multicultural and linguistic differences.

If oral readings will be used, it is helpful to tape-record the student's performance so the teacher does not have to concentrate on marking errors while the student reads. That leaves the teacher free to focus on observing the student's overall reading behaviors. It also is a good idea to have available a checklist of things to consider while observing the student read. An example of one such checklist is shown in Figure 6–9. The checklist helps focus the observation and identifies areas that might be explored in a follow-up probe or interview. Then the teacher can review the tape and

Student: Date:

Checklist of Behaviors	**Always**	**Sometimes**	**Seldom**
Reads with expression			
Reads clearly, with good pronunciation			
Reads word by word			
Observes punctuation			
Reads for meaning (tries to make sense of material)			
Skips or refuses unfamiliar words			
Substitutes linguistically appropriate words			
Perseveres with task			
Is easily frustrated			
Knows consonant sounds			
Knows short vowel sounds			
Knows long vowel sounds			
Knows vowel and/or consonant pairs			
Knows most basic sight words			
Guesses at words			
Tries various methods of word attack			
Frequently loses place			

FIGURE 6–9 Checklist of Oral Reading Behaviors

TABLE 6–1 Oral Reading Error Pattern Guide

Category of Error	Patterns Noted
Poor knowledge of sound/symbol associations	• Consistently misses words containing particular sound/symbol combinations • Errors within words involve specific sound/symbol combinations
Poor word attack skills	• Random guessing at words • Problems blending sounds together • Guessing based on first sound • Limited attempts to "sound out" • Repetitions • Requires frequent teacher assistance (doesn't attempt words)
Poor word attack on multisyllable words	• Same patterns as above • Gets "lost" in middle of words • Omits syllables
Poor structural analysis skills	• Misses words with affix • Misses compounds • Misapplies syllabication rules
Visual processing problems	• Misses many nonphonetic words or word parts • Generally poor sight vocabulary • Frequent omissions of words
Limited attention to context	• Inappropriate word substitutions • Random guessing
Rate and fluency problems	• Word-by-word reading • Generally poor sight vocabulary • Frequent stops to attack unknown words
Reading miscues	• Limited attention to punctuation • Word insertions based on miscue • Word substitutions based on miscue

analyze student error patterns using the general error analysis guidelines presented in Chapter 5. An "error pattern" guide shown in Table 6–1 can be used in interpreting results from oral readings and in suggesting areas for follow-up.

The combined use of observation, error analysis, and follow-up interviews can provide the teacher with explicit information about the student's approach to reading and specific skill needs. For instance, students struggling with unknown words might be asked in follow-up interviews to describe the strategies they used to figure out "tough words." Follow-up probing or interviewing are especially useful ways to assess meta-cognitive abilities, because they provide direct information on students' thought processes during reading tasks.

Performance assessments that focus on comprehension skills also can be constructed rather easily. For example, the teacher may have a student read passages and answer questions about what was read. If this approach is used, however, four important factors should be kept in mind. First, give students the choice of reading the passages silently or aloud, because some may find it easier to concentrate on meaning when they use one mode or the other. Second, because the principal assessment goal is to determine how well the student *understands* what is read, make certain that the student can indeed *read* the text without too much difficulty. Passages should be well within the student's general reading ability range. Passages at higher readability levels can be administered later as listening comprehension tasks to assess the student's ability to understand more complicated material. Third, develop questions that tap into the full range of comprehension skills shown in Figure 6–8, including comprehension of words, ideas, and structures. Finally, permit the student to answer either orally or in writing to minimize the effects of any writing problems that may be present. Oral answers also provide an opportunity for the teacher to interview the student to gain additional insights into the responses.

Another popular performance-based approach to comprehension assessment involves "retellings" or "think alouds" (Wade, 1990). The teacher has the student read a selection, silently or aloud, and retell it in as much detail as possible, preferably on tape to facilitate later analysis. By matching the student's retelling against the selection the teacher can learn much about the student's strengths and weaknesses. For example, when the target selection involves a story, the teacher can determine which elements of story form the student included in the retelling and which were omitted. The student's recollection of correct sequence, facts, details, and important events will also be apparent. During or after the retellings, the teacher can gather additional information by interviewing the student about what was read.

Regardless of which assessment strategy is used, it is critical for the teacher to prepare a written summary of all outcomes. This can involve little more than a listing of findings and observations such as the one shown in Figure 6–10. Or it might be a checklist like the one shown in Figure 6–11, which identifies key skills and allows the teacher to summarize findings at several points over time. It also can be a narrative report. In each case the written summary provides a record of the teacher's judgments and evaluations relative to the student's performance on the assessment tasks.

ASSESSING WRITTEN EXPRESSION SKILLS

Written expression is one of the most important and complex language skills. According to Lerner (1997), competent writing requires many related abilities, including a solid foundation in the English language, adequate reading ability, skills in spelling, sufficient visual and motor memory to carry out the complex eye-hand movements necessary for legible handwriting, knowledge of usage rules and conventions, and cognitive strategies for organizing and planning. The complexity of written expression is further underscored by the fact that each of these component skills is fairly complicated in its own right, and all of them must be performed simultaneously when writing.

Given this complexity, it is not surprising that writing difficulties appear to be especially common among students with learning problems. Such students have been shown to make more errors in spelling, handwriting, capitalization, and punctuation

Student Jonathan Kraft

Date 10/13/98

Task Read three graded passages spanning grades 4.0 – 5.0; one selected from social stud es text

	Strengths	Weaknesses
• Word Analysis	attempts most words	multisyllable words are consistently difficult
• Sight Vocabulary	few problems with single syllable words	usually gets first syllable correct, then gets lost in word or predictable patterns
• Reading Fluency	generally adequate	some problems noted with proper nouns
• Comprehension	no real problem with lower grade level passages correctly answered all questions (all types) for lower level passages	rate drops off considerably as reading level increases difficulty with inferential questions for higher level passages

Areas to explore further: Probe knowledge of word-attack strategies for multisyllable words. Interview as he attempts graded word list—what strategies is he using to figure out unknown words?

FIGURE 6–10 Summary of Outcomes from Oral Reading of Graded Passages

than their peers (Deno, Marston, & Mirkin, 1982; Gerber, 1984; Gerber & Hall, 1987; Graham, Boyer-Schick, & Tippets, 1989). They also appear to have difficulty organizing ideas and developing themes in their compositions (Englert, Raphael, Fear, & Anderson, 1988; Harrell & Vallecorsa, 1987; Nodine, Barenbaum & Newcomer, 1985; Vallecorsa & Garriss, 1990). These problems have been shown to persist over time and often continue into adulthood (Gerber & Reif, 1994; Harris & Graham, 1992).

As in other academic skill areas, the first step toward conducting a thorough diagnostic evaluation is to develop a clear understanding of skills that constitute the written expression domain. Components of written expression have been described a number of ways in the literature. We have chosen to describe written expression in terms of the three broad components shown in Figure 6–12; these three components have been further divided to show a sampling of key subskills involved.

The first broad component shown in Figure 6–12 is *ideation*, which is concerned with the ideas underlying a writer's purpose and intent and with the writer's ability to

Reading Diagnosis Sheet

Name ______________________ Teacher ______________________

Grade ______________________ School ______________________

No.	Item	1st Check	2nd Check	3rd Check	Area
1	Word-by-word reading				
2	Incorrect phrasing				Oral Reading
3	Poor pronunciation				
4	Omissions				
5	Receptions				
6	Inversions or reversals				
7	Insertions				
8	Substitutions				
9	Basic sight words not known				
10	Sight vocabulary not up to grade level				
11	Guesses at words				
12	Consonant sounds not known				
13	Vowel sounds not known				
14	Vowel pairs and/or consonant clusters not known (digraphs, diphthongs, blends)				
15	Lacks desirable structural analysis (morphology)				
16	Unable to use context clues				
17	Contractions not known				
18	Comprehension inadequate				Oral Silent
19	Vocabulary inadequate				
20	Unaided recall scanty				Study Skills
21	Response poorly organized				
22	Unable to locate information				
23	Inability to skim				
24	Inability to adjust rate of difficulty of material				
25	Low rate of speed				
26	High rate at expense of accuracy				
27	Voicing-lip movement				Other Abilities
28	Lacks knowledge of the alphabet				
29	Written recall limited by spelling ability				
30	Undeveloped dictionary skills				

FIGURE 6–11 Summary of Performance Outcomes

Note: *From* Locating and Correcting Reading Difficulties *(7th ed., p. 6), by J. L. Shanker and E. E. Ekwall, 1998, Upper Saddle River, NJ: Merrill/Prentice Hall. Copyright 1998 by Prentice Hall. Reprinted by permission.*

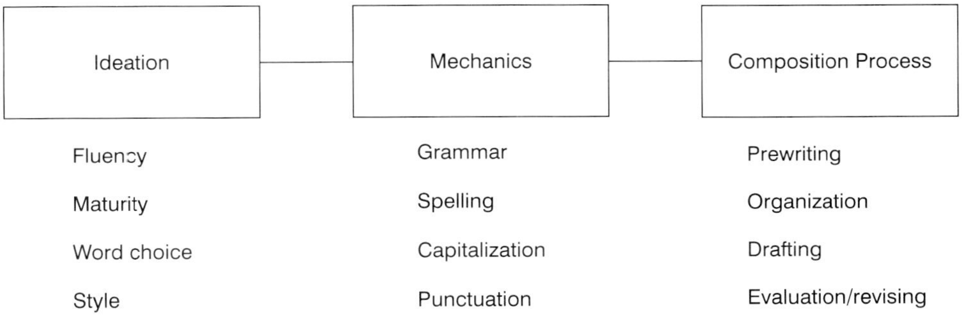

FIGURE 6–12 Components of the Written Expression Domain

express those ideas in words (Choate et al., 1995). Several factors influence how well ideas are communicated. The writer must be fluent, able to choose a sufficient number of words to express ideas clearly, without including so many words that it clouds the writer's intent. The writer also must be able to demonstrate an age-appropriate level of maturity in expressing ideas. Less mature forms of writing are characterized by naming and describing, while more mature writing features plot development or discussion of issues or points of view (Nodine et al., 1985; Vallecorsa & Garriss, 1990; Harrell & Vallecorsa, 1987). Word choice is another factor that influences the writer's ability to communicate ideas effectively; careful selection of words helps not only to clarify meaning, but also to create excitement and anticipation. Finally, the writer's general style influences how well ideas are communicated. Although writing styles are fairly personal, effective writing incorporates important style features such as cohesion and use of appropriate text cues that influence overall quality.

The second component shown in Figure 6–12 involves the *mechanics* of written expression. This includes knowledge of basic grammatical rules of language, as well as knowledge of conventions that apply only to the *written* form of language (i.e., spelling, capitalization, and punctuation rules). Inadequate skill in any of these areas will greatly compromise the writer's ability to communicate ideas effectively.

The final component shown in Figure 6–12 involves the *composition process*, which includes a set of cognitively related skills necessary to turn an idea into a written composition; in short, the composition process is concerned with the things writers must do to effectively "pull it all together." As reflected in the figure, the composition process typically begins with prewriting activities in which the writer establishes a purpose and audience, explores prior knowledge of the subject, gathers reference materials, discusses ideas, and so on. The next step in the process involves planning for how the ideas will be organized and developed. The plan is then elaborated in a draft in which the writer takes a "first pass" at getting ideas down on paper. Finally, the writer turns attention to evaluating the draft and identifying where revisions must be made. The processes of revising and evaluating are repeated until the writer is satisfied with the finished product.

Listening comprehension tasks can be used to assess student's understanding of material at higher reading levels.

REFLECTION BOX 6–3

The anecdotal record of Tim's performance suggests he has problems with several aspects of written expression. How would you describe his performance in terms of the information presented in Figure 6–12? What additional information might his teacher want to gather and how might it be obtained?

Using Figure 6–12 as a context for gathering information, the first step in conducting a writing assessment is for the teacher to form an initial impression of the student's writing abilities. One commercially available test that provides a good overview of writing skills and can be used with students from grades 2 through 12 is the *Test of Written Language—2* (Hammill & Larsen, 1996). Students are asked to complete a variety of contrived and spontaneous writing tasks that tap into skills related to ideation and the mechanics of writing. Although the test is not designed to assess abilities related to the composing process, teachers can get insights into this area by observing students as they complete the story writing subtest. Another commercially available test that provides criterion-referenced measures for a variety of writing skills is the *Brigance Diagnostic Inventory of Essential Skills* (1981).

As an alternative to using commercial tests, the teacher might choose to begin the assessment by examining products that are on hand. These should include a sampling of "routine" writing tasks such as homework and independent seat assignments, as well as writing on tests and special assignments. In selecting these items, care should be taken to include products from a full range of subject areas, because performance may vary depending on the subject involved and the nature of the writing task. Examining student work products should incorporate error analysis techniques described in Chapter 5. Figure 6–13 presents a summary of error patterns; it also can be a helpful guide in conducting an error analysis. It shows the types of errors students commonly exhibit when they are having problems with particular aspects of written expression. It

FIGURE 6–13 Guide to Error Patterns in Written Expression

Errors Related to Ideation
- too little or too much written
- poor vocabulary for age
- limited sentence structure variation
- limited use of color words

Errors Related to Cohesion
- ideas poorly organized
- relationship among ideas unclear
- poor use of transition devices/text cues

Errors Related to Grammar
- frequent word usage errors
- misuse of pronouns
- poor subject/verb agreement
- problems involving correct tense

Errors Related to Capitalization and Punctuation
- capitals used where not needed
- capitals omitted when needed
- punctuation used when not needed
- punctuation omitted when needed
- inconsistent use of capitalization and punctuation conventions

Errors Related to Poor Auditory Aspects of Spelling
- syllables and sounds missing
- words strung together
- words separated
- bears no relation to intended word
- extra sounds added

FIGURE 6–13 continued

Errors Related to Visual Aspects of Spelling
- limited use of sound/symbol variants
- selecting wrong sound/symbol variants
- overreliance on phonics
- omitting unheard word parts
- sequence errors

Morphological Rules for Spelling
- errors involve prefixes or suffixes
- errors involve change of root word

Remembering Letter Shapes
- reversals
- mixed use of upper/lower case
- mixed use of manuscript/cursive

Remembering Motor Plans
- numerous erasures
- deep grooves
- overlapping lines
- poor spacing
- irregular size and shape
- deterioration over time
- making letter differently each time

is important to note, however, that the written expression patterns reflected in the figure are endemic to Western (i.e., U.S.) culture. How other cultures relate to the various components of writing shown in the figure can vary. Care should be taken to modify these error patterns accordingly to reflect cultural differences. Figure 6–14 shows how one teacher modified the error pattern guide so it also could be used to summarize assessment findings.

Examinations of student writing products can be enhanced by an interview of the student to confirm findings. This is especially the case when exploring problems related to ideation or the composing process. For instance, a review of Juan's writing products showed that his handwriting was difficult to read, and that his papers were always brief although they had no spelling errors. In a follow-up interview about his writing, Juan reported that he hated writing because handwriting was a great chore for him and he despised making spelling mistakes in his written work; as a result, he chose only words he knew he could spell and he wrote as little as possible. The interview clarified that what might have been considered a problem in expressing ideas was really more a problem with the mechanics of writing.

Student ______________________________ Date ______________

Task(s) ____

Error Category	Performance Summary
Ideation	
Composing Skills	
Auditory Aspects of Spelling	
Visual Aspects of Spelling	
Morphological Rules for Spelling	
Remembering Letter Shapes	
Remembering Motor Plans	

FIGURE 6–14 Summary of Writing Performance

A variety of follow-up probes can be conducted to further pinpoint instructional needs. Criterion-referenced tests and performance tasks can be easily constructed using the procedures outlined earlier in this chapter. King-Sears (1994) also has provided an excellent set of case examples to illustrate how the APPLY model can be used to carry out ongoing curriculum-based assessments in writing. Examples are provided in the areas of letter formation, spelling, sentence writing, and paragraph writing. The task hierarchy presented in Figure 6–15 also can be used to guide construction of teacher-made writing assessments for students who are performing at a variety of skill levels. The teacher begins by identifying the *highest level* at which the target student can perform. This is done by considering the student's typical performance on writing tasks in the classroom. Does the student have enough skill to produce a series of thematically linked paragraphs (i.e., can the student generate a story or theme, even if it is not particularly well written)? If not, is the student capable of producing a series of thematically linked sentences (i.e., can the student write a paragraph)? Assuming paragraph writing is too difficult, is the student at least able to write a series of individual sentences? Or will the assessment have to focus on having the student perform each of the component skills of writing in isolation?

After the teacher decides to assess the student at the level of writing continuous text or single sentences, a decision also must be made as to how much assistance will be given to help structure the task for the student. That is, what sort of stimulus cue, if any, will be provided? The hierarchy presented in Figure 6–15 suggests a number of alternatives that might be considered. Similarly, if the teacher decides that the assessment should focus on having the student demonstrate the component skills of written expression, tasks like the ones shown in Figure 6–16 would be appropriate options.

FIGURE 6–15 Written expression task hierarchy

Note: *From:* Assessment for Instructional Planning in Special Education *(p. 129), by N. Zigmond, A. Vallecorsa, & R. Silverman, 1983, Upper Saddle River, NJ: Prentice Hall. Copyright 1983 by Prentice Hall. Reprinted by permission.*

3. Writing Continuous Text

A. Generate a story (or series of paragraphs)
   1. with no teacher direction
   2. from topic
   3. from story starter
   4. from picture
   5. from sequence of pictures

B. Generate a paragraph
   1. with no teacher direction
   2. from topic
   3 from topic sentences
   4. from picture
   5. from sentence starter

2. Writing Single Sentences

A. Generate a sentence
   1. from topic
   2. from word
   3. from picture
   4. from sentence starter

1. Demonstrating Component Skills of Written Expression

A. Generating ideas in oral language
B. Handwriting
C. Spelling
D. Knowing conventions of print

Writing portfolios also permit ongoing assessment of writing performance, particularly when they include systematic collections of interview (self-reflection) data and results from teacher conferences. Those who are interested in learning more about implementing a portfolio writing assessment system should refer to Graves and Sunstein (1992) which addresses many of the procedural concerns associated with using this approach and provides a good model for those who are just beginning.

ASSESSING BASIC MATH SKILLS

Although students with learning and behavior problems most often have difficulties with the language arts, such students frequently have problems with mathematics, as well. Unfortunately, mathematics disabilities have received considerably less attention than problems involving reading and writing performance (Carnine, 1991; Carpenter, 1985; Fleishner, 1994; Vaughn & Wilson, 1994). Perhaps this is because it is easy to see how reading and writing skills are necessary for success across subject areas in school. The link between mathematics ability and school success is sometimes less obvious. Still, many subject areas require problem-solving, reasoning, and logical thinking, all

Generating ideas

- tell a story
- tell a story in response to a picture or series of pictures
- describe a familiar event or experience

Spelling

- write sentences from dictation
- write individual words representing predictable and unpredictable patterns
- write letters to represent sounds

Handwriting

- write name and known spelling words from dictation
- copy a series of sentences or individual words
- write the alphabet in manuscript and cursive spelling
- write sentences from dictation
- write individual words representing predictable and unpredictable patterns
- write letters to represent sounds

Conventions of Print

- correct capitalization and punctuation errors on a sample paragraph
- correct errors in sample sentences

FIGURE 6–16 Sample tasks for assessing component skills

skills developed in the mathematics curriculum. Other subject areas involve more basic math skills like the ability to understand charts and graphs or to estimate. In addition to being an important component for school success, mathematics skill is becoming increasingly essential for success in the workplace.

According to Rivera and Smith (1997), most students with special needs are not exposed to advanced components of the mathematics curriculum. Therefore, the following discussion on conducting mathematics assessments is limited to the basic mathematics skill areas; more advanced mathematics skills such as those involved in algebra and geometry are not included.

Numerous descriptions in the literature exist that cover the mathematics domain. We have chosen to summarize the basic elements of mathematics in three broad skill categories, shown in Table 6–2. *Computation* involves the manipulation of numbers according to rules to arrive at a predictable answer that would be the same no matter who was doing the calculating. We have further divided computation into three subskill areas. First, children must master a number of readiness skills before they can begin to use numbers to compute or solve problems. They must be able to match one object or symbol with another (one-to-one correspondence) and must have the ability to sort

TABLE 6–2 Elements of Basic Mathematics

Computation	Measurement	Problem Solving
• Readiness one-to-one correspondence classification seriation numeration place value • Basic number facts • Algorithms addition subtraction multiplication division	• Linear • Liquid • Time	• Determining what is needed • Organizing information • Developing an action strategy for solving • Applying correct number computations • Evaluating outcomes

objects based on one or more common properties (classification). They need to be able to order objects depending on the degree to which the object reflects a particular characteristic such as length or height (seriation). Finally, children need to acquire a basic understanding of numbers and the number system (numeration and place value).

The second category of computation skill involves knowledge of basic facts. Described as the most fundamental set of data used in computation (Choate et al., 1995), basic facts are "small problems" committed to memory in much the same way that basic sight words are committed to memory in reading. Both have the effect of increasing fluency and accuracy.

Finally, computation involves mastery of certain algorithms or operational rules to be followed to arrive at answers. Algorithms must be mastered for carrying out the operations of addition, subtraction, multiplication, and division of whole numbers. Students also must learn algorithms for carrying out these operations with fractions and decimals.

The second broad category shown in Table 6–2 involves three types of measurement skill: linear, liquid, and time. Students typically are required to become familiar with a variety of concepts, terms, and measuring instruments associated with each type of measurement. They also must be able to complete computations involving measurement.

The final category shown in Table 6–2 involves problem solving, which might be viewed as the goal of all computation and measurement mathematics instruction. Problem solving is the application of a variety of mathematics skills and knowledge to new or different situations in order to understand "unknowns." We have divided problem-solving into the series of subskills suggested by Choate et al. (1995). These subskills reflect the set of procedures one typically goes through to solve a problem. We believe this framework is useful for its diagnostic value; that is, it helps isolate the source(s) of a student's problem-solving difficulties.

A number of commercially available criterion-referenced tests can be quite helpful in diagnosing mathematics difficulties across a range of grade levels. For example, the *Brigance Diagnostic Comprehensive Inventory of Basic Skills* (Brigance, 1983) has mathematics

Teachers can construct criterion-referenced tests that reflect the curriculum goals and objectives as their class.

subtests covering each of the skill areas shown in Table 6–2 and can be used with students from kindergarten through Grade 9. Its companion test, the *Brigance Diagnostic Inventory of Essential Skills* (Brigance, 1981), stresses functional and applied mathematics skills and is appropriate for students from grades 4 through 12. The *Enright Diagnostic Inventory of Basic Arithmetic Skills* (Enright, 1983), can be used with students from fourth grade through adult. While its focus is somewhat more narrow (it deals exclusively with aspects of computation), it provides detailed error analysis procedures that link directly to instructional objectives. Another option is the *Hudson Education Skills Inventory—Mathematics* (Hudson & Colson, 1989), which can be used with students across all grade levels to assess a broad range of mathematics skills. A computerized version also is available, which generates instructional goals and objectives based on a computer analysis of student performance.

While commercially available tests can provide important assessment information, teacher-made criterion-referenced tests have the added benefit of linking directly to a specific curriculum. Teachers can construct items that reflect goals and objectives that are the focus of instruction in their own classroom. This is especially useful because mathematics curriculum materials vary significantly in the amount of emphasis placed on particular skills and when skills are introduced.

To appreciate this point, let us consider Mrs. Harkins, a math teacher at Brightwood Middle School. Her first-period class of basic math students is working from a curriculum that focuses on functional math skills and places considerable emphasis on developing basic computation skills, particularly consumer-related skills such as budgeting, managing money, computing taxes, and measuring. In contrast, the curriculum for her second-period math class has a focus on developing more advanced computation skills (i.e., completing operations with fractions, decimals, and percentages), solving simple algebraic equations, and multistep problem-solving. If she develops criterion-referenced tests for these two classes, the content of the two tests would need to differ significantly. The steps she would go through to develop the two tests, however, would be the same. She would begin by establishing parameters for the assessment; that is, she would isolate the specific skills to be addressed in each assessment. She would then decide on the number of items to be administered to obtain a fair estimate of the student's abilities and she would establish a criterion or "benchmark" for judging performance as being acceptable or unacceptable. Figure 6–17 shows an example of a criterion-referenced test Mrs. Harkins developed for her second-period class using these procedures.

As an alternative to constructing criterion-referenced tests, Mrs. Harkins could also gather information by systematically examining student work products. These prod-

Math Test

Class: Math (period 2) Date: 5-4-98

Teacher: Harkins

A. Focus: Adding sums of mixed numbers with regrouping, same denominator

8 3/5 + 2 4/5	6 4/7 + 3 6/7	4 2/3 + 9 2/3
3 1/5 + 11 4/5	9 2/3 + 2 2/3	5 5/8 + 12 7/8

B. Focus: Adding sums of mixed numbers, no regrouping, different denominators

5 1/3 + 3 1/2	6 1/4 + 3 1/3	9 1/5 + 7 2/3
6 1/4 + 8 3/8	11 6/10 9 3/8	14 3/5 + 16 3/4

Performance criteria:
Mastery = at least 5 problems correct for the skill category
Non-mastery = fewer than 4 problems correct per skill category
Uncertain mastery = 4 problems correct for the skill category

FIGURE 6–17 Sample Criterion-Referenced Math Test

ucts could include routine class assignments and homework, as well as weekly tests, unit tests, or semester tests.

Regardless of the assessment approach Mrs. Harkins selects, she should use a number of strategies for analyzing performance outcomes in conjunction with the general guidelines for error analysis presented earlier. And she can learn a great deal about the source of a student's math problems by conducting an oral diagnostic interview, either while the student is completing a math assessment task or as a follow-up activity. By asking the student to explain how a problem was solved or the rationale behind a particular answer, the teacher can gain insight into the student's thinking; this helps to identify exactly which skills to teach and how to teach them. Another strategy is to group computation errors into categories based on the *source* of the errors. Figure 6–18 presents a summary of common computation error patterns and provides examples of each type. A more thorough listing of common computational error patterns can be found in Ashlock (1998).

FIGURE 6–18 Summary of Error Types in Computation

Error Type	Examples		
Wrong operation	$\begin{array}{r} 47 \\ -\ 63 \\ \hline 110 \end{array}$	$\begin{array}{r} 82 \\ -\ 19 \\ \hline 101 \end{array}$	
Computation errors	$\begin{array}{r} 64 \\ +\ 12 \\ \hline 77 \end{array}$	$\begin{array}{r} \overset{8}{\not{9}}1 \\ -\ 36 \\ \hline 56 \end{array}$	$\begin{array}{r} 28 \\ \times\ 9 \\ \hline 104 \end{array}$
Faulty algorithm	$\begin{array}{r} 16 \\ +\ 9 \\ \hline 115 \end{array}$	$\begin{array}{r} 34 \\ -\ 18 \\ \hline 24 \end{array}$	$\begin{array}{r} 78 \\ \times\ 12 \\ \hline 716 \end{array}$
Random response	$\begin{array}{r} 34 \\ +\ 12 \\ \hline 93 \end{array}$	$\begin{array}{r} 71 \\ +\ 23 \\ \hline 36 \end{array}$	$\begin{array}{r} 50 \\ -\ 28 \\ \hline 94 \end{array}$
Carelessness	$\begin{array}{r} 6894 \\ +3047 \\ \hline 10941 \end{array}$	$\begin{array}{r} 746 \\ -331 \\ \hline 15 \end{array}$	$\begin{array}{r} 46 \\ \times\ 3 \\ \hline 128 \end{array}$
Not understanding the concept	$\begin{array}{r} 3.2 \\ +\ .17 \\ \hline 49 \end{array}$	$\begin{array}{r} 7\frac{5}{6} \\ -\ 3\frac{1}{3} \\ \hline 4\frac{4}{3} \end{array}$	

As was true for other subject areas discussed earlier in the chapter, a final important component in conducting a mathematics assessment is to summarize performance outcomes in some fashion, making certain that the summary includes a listing of specific skill needs for the student.

ASSESSING STRATEGIC LEARNING BEHAVIORS

ASSUMPTIONS

While success in school certainly depends on adequate abilities in the basic skill areas we have discussed thus far, students also must possess a number of related skills necessary for independent learning. Independent learners are capable of obtaining, organizing, and expressing knowledge effectively. They are able to manage time and resources, gain information from lectures and discussion, monitor and evaluate their own progress, and know when to seek assistance. Independent learners apply a variety of reading comprehension techniques to gain meaning from text, and they use systematic strategies to synthesize, memorize, and retrieve information. In short, independent learners employ "strategic learning behaviors" to acquire and use the information taught in school.

REFLECTION BOX 6–4

Ms. Camp's description of Tim includes several bits of information that suggest he may need to improve his repertoire of strategic learning behaviors. What evidence supports this and how would you go about further exploring the issue?

The regular curriculum gives little attention to helping students develop strategic learning behaviors. This is particularly unfortunate for students with learning and behavior problems who lack many of the academic support skills required in general education settings (Hallahan, Kauffman, & Lloyd, 1999; Lerner, 1997; Mercer, 1997) and won't learn them unless they are explicitly taught.

In the discussion that follows we have divided important strategic learning behaviors into two broad categories: learning strategies and study skills. Although these two terms have been defined a number of ways in the literature, we like the definition used by Wade, Trathen, and Schraw (1990): a wide range of " . . . tactics used together in a purposeful way to accomplish a particular learning task" (p. 147).

LEARNING STRATEGIES

Learning strategies can be thought of as procedures that individuals go through to learn, remember, solve problems, and understand. Learning strategies are the ways individuals approach learning tasks and how they think about planning, executing, and evaluating their performance. In short, learning strategies are the behaviors individuals use to participate in their own learning.

Effective learners employ a variety of learning strategies to direct and control their learning. Examples of learning strategies and how each strategy might be operationalized are provided in Table 6–3. For instance, the strategy of "active processing" is used when the individual employs techniques such as self-talk, self-questioning, and elaboration. Active processing requires the individual to interact with the material to be learned in an ongoing fashion. Similarly, when learners employ devices such as mnemonics, visual images, or color cues in dealing with information, they are providing themselves with memory cues which can be drawn on to help jog memory and aid retrieval.

STUDY SKILLS

Effective learners also employ a variety of study skills to help them gain meaning from textbooks, lectures, and class discussions as well as manage themselves and the wealth of information they are confronted with in each subject area. Figure 6–19 is a commercially available inventory that can be used to gather information on students' use of various study strategies.

Assessment of students' use of learning strategies and study skills also can be accomplished rather easily through teacher-developed tasks and activities. For example, a teacher can gather extensive assessment information on learning strategies by asking students to talk about how they approach and carry out certain types of classroom tasks. Interview questions like the ones shown in Figure 6–20 can help the teacher determine where instruction may be needed. Similarly, systematic observation

TABLE 6–3 Important Learning Strategies

Strategy	Examples
Active processing	Self-talk Self-questioning Collaborating
Memory cues	Mnemonics Visual imagery Color cues
Verbal rehearsal and review	Reciting Paraphrasing
Organization	Grouping Clustering Graphic organizers/diagrams
Evaluation	Predicting Self-checks Reflection

Completed by: ________________ Student: ____________________ Date: ______________

Place the appropriate number (1, 2, or 3) in the box next to each study skill subskill (1-Mastered—regular, appropriate use of skill: 2=Partially Mastered—needs some improvement: 3=Not Mastered—infrequent use of skill).

Reading Rate

- ☐ Skimming
- ☐ Scanning
- ☐ Rapid reading
- ☐ Normal rate
- ☐ Study or careful reading
- ☐ Understands importance of reading rates

Listening

- ☐ Attends to listening activities
- ☐ Applies meaning to verbal messages
- ☐ Filters out auditory distractions
- ☐ Comprehends verbal messages
- ☐ Understands importance of listening skills

Note Taking/Outlining

- ☐ Uses headings/subheadings appropriately
- ☐ Takes brief and clear notes
- ☐ Records essential information
- ☐ Applies skill during writing activities
- ☐ Uses skill during lectures
- ☐ Develops organized outlines
- ☐ Follows consistent note taking format
- ☐ Understands importance of note taking
- ☐ Understands importance of outlining

Report Writing

- ☐ Organizes thoughts in writing
- ☐ Completes written reports from outline
- ☐ Includes only necessary information
- ☐ Uses proper sentence structure
- ☐ Uses proper punctuation
- ☐ Proofreads written assignments
- ☐ States clear introductory statement
- ☐ Includes clear concluding statements
- ☐ Understands importance of writing reports

Oral Presentation

- ☐ Freely participates in oral presentation
- ☐ Oral presentations are well-organized
- ☐ Uses gestures appropriately
- ☐ Speaks clearly
- ☐ Uses proper language when reporting orally
- ☐ Understands importance of oral reporting

Graphic Aids

- ☐ Attends to relevent elements in visual material
- ☐ Uses visuals appropriately in presentations
- ☐ Develops own graphic material
- ☐ Is not confused or distracted by visual material in presentations
- ☐ Understands importance of visual material

Test Taking

- ☐ Studies for tests in an organized way
- ☐ Spends appropriate amount of time studying different topics covered on a test
- ☐ Avoids cramming for tests
- ☐ Organizes narrative responses appropriately
- ☐ Reads and understands directions before answering questions
- ☐ Proofreads responses and checks for errors
- ☐ Identifies and uses clue words in questions
- ☐ Properly records answers

FIGURE 6–19 Sample Study Skills Inventory

- ☐ Saves difficult items until last
- ☐ Eliminates obvious wrong answers
- ☐ Systematically reviews completed tests to determine test-taking or test-studying errors
- ☐ Corrects previous test-taking errors
- ☐ Understands importance of test-taking skills

Library Usage

- ☐ Uses cataloging system (card or computerized) effectively
- ☐ Able to locate library materials
- ☐ Understands organizational layout of library
- ☐ Understands and uses services of media specialist
- ☐ Understands overall functions and purposes of a library
- ☐ Understands importance of library-usage skills

Reference Materials

- ☐ Able to identify components of different reference materials
- ☐ Uses guide words appropriately
- ☐ Consults reference materials when necessary
- ☐ Uses materials appropriately to compute assignments
- ☐ Able to identify different types of reference materials and sources
- ☐ Understands importance of reference materials

Self-Management

- ☐ Monitors own behavior
- ☐ Changes own behavior as necessary
- ☐ Thinks before acting
- ☐ Responsible for own behavior
- ☐ Identifies behaviors that interfere with own learning
- ☐ Understands importance of self-management

Summary of Study Skill Proficiency

Summarize in the chart below the number of Mastered (1), Partially Mastered (2), and Not Mastered (3) study skill subskills. The number next to each study skill represents the total number of subskills for each area.

Study Skill	M	PM	NM	Study Skill	M	PM	NM
Reading Rate—6				Test Taking—13			
Listening—5				Library Usage—6			
Note Taking/Outlining—9				Reference Materials—6			
Report Writing—10				Time Management—9			
Oral Presentation—6				Self-Management—6			
Graphic Aids—5							

Summary Comments:

FIGURE 6–19 continued

Note: *From* Teaching Students with Learning Problems to Use Study Skills: A Teacher's Guide *(pp. 14–16), by J. J. Hoover & J. R. Patton, 1995, Austin, TX: PRO-ED. Copyright 1995 by PRO-ED. Reprinted by permission.*

FIGURE 6–20 Sample Study Skill Interview

1. What do you do when you have a reading assignment for a class? What steps are taken to help you understand and remember what you read?
2. How do you keep track of your assignments?
3. What steps do you follow when you have several homework assignments to complete?
4. What strategies do you use when you have to take notes on a class lecture?
5. How do you plan your time when you have to complete a big project?
6. How do you prepare for tests? Do you take any special steps to help you get ready?
7. What steps do you take to get help when you are having problems in a class?
8. How do you keep track of your progress in a class?

can reveal how a student works through different tasks, which tasks seem most and least problematic for the student, and what the student does when difficulties are encountered. An examination of student work products also can show patterns of specific study skill deficiencies. Perhaps the student's errors tend to involve items covered in class discussion, suggesting possible problems with listening or taking notes. Or they may cluster around items taken from independent reading assignments, suggesting there may be a need to teach the student strategies for understanding and organizing text material. In addition to these possibilities, learning strategies can be assessed using procedures embedded in the Strategies Intervention Model (SIM) introduced in Chapter 3.

MONITORING ACADEMIC PROGRESS

Throughout this chapter we have stressed the importance of summarizing the outcomes of assessment activities as a means of developing a written plan to guide intervention efforts and provide a context for monitoring student progress. In this section we discuss several approaches to monitoring progress that can easily evolve from the assessment summary. Procedures for using graphing techniques were addressed earlier in the chapter and therefore will not be included in this section.

The easiest way to monitor student performance is to keep a written record of objectives that have been successfully mastered. To accomplish this, the teacher might highlight a number of objectives on the assessment summary that will be current instructional priorities or short-term objectives for the student. Or the teacher might list current priorities for the student on an open-ended form like the one shown in Table 6–4. In either case, care should be taken to indicate the date when instruction was initiated and when mastery was achieved. It is also a good idea to show the level of mastery demonstrated and, if possible, attach the student's work product to document performance. This approach is particularly useful in keeping track of a student's progress when instruction must focus on unique remedial skills that no one else in the class is learning. Information from performance summaries can be used to update students' IEPs periodically regarding their mastery of short-term or long-term objectives specified in the IEP document.

TABLE 6–4 Open-Ended Form for Summarizing Current Instructional Priorities

	Skill Area	Instruction Initiated	Mastery Date	Mastery Criterion
1.	Subtraction with regrouping, zeros involved	9/24/98		100%
2.	Reading 15 new sight words	9/21/98	9/30/98	100% (attached)
3.	Capitalizing proper names	9/18/98	10/5/98	100% (attached)
4.	Identifying cause-effect relationships	9/15/98		95%
5.				
6.				
7.				
8.				
9.				
10.				

This method can also be used to track a student's progress through a specific curriculum. For example, Figure 6–21 provides a listing of objectives to be covered in an eighth-grade consumer math class. The teacher pulled these objectives from the scope and sequence information included in the teacher's manual that accompanied the class text. As the target student moves through the curriculum, the teacher keeps a running record of performance. Note that the teacher uses the form to guide subsequent planning for the student. Thus, when it was clear that Kammie was having trouble computing the sales tax for items purchased, her teacher listed two instructional interventions to assist her.

Figure 6–22 presents a progress monitoring form that can be used to track progress through the curriculum for several students at once. Notice the range of information that this fairly simple form provides. It shows that two students, Aprille and Amy, have made excellent progress through the curriculum and are ready to move on to new material or enrichment work. It also shows that three other students need to spend additional time working on some of the objectives listed, and it shows how they could

Student: Kammie

Units covered: 3-5 Consumer Math

Objective:	Date Introduced	Date Mastered	Criterion	Comments
1. Computing sales tax	10/16/98			Consistently misplaces decimal; review procedure and have her use a cue card
2. Identifying best buys based on unit price	10/26/98	11/5/98	95%	
3. Filling out checks to pay bills	11/6/98	11/16/98	100%	
4. Balancing a checkbook				
5. Computing sale price based on percentage markdown				
6. Calculating Internet fees				

FIGURE 6–21 Summary of Progress Through the Math Curriculum

STUDENT

Aprille	Amy	Josh	Turell	Juan	Skill/Date Introduced	Mastery Level
M/O	M/O	M/O	M/O	M/O	Counting by 5s (9/14)	100%
M/O	M/O	RT/O	M/O	RT/O	Basic addition facts to 10 (9/16)	95%
M/C	M/C	M/C	M/C	M/C	Naming coins (9/16)	95%
M/WS	M/WS	M/WS	M/WS	M/WS	Adding 2 digit numbers, no regrouping (9/16)	100%
M/WS	M/WS	RT/WS	RT/WS	RT/WS	Adding 2 digit numbers, with regrouping (9/25)	100%

STATUS
M = mastered
RT = reteach

EVALUATION PROCEDURE
WS = worksheet
T = written test
O = oral test
C = flash card drill

FIGURE 6–22 Summary of Group Progress Through the Curriculum

be grouped for this instruction. In addition, it provides a record of when instruction took place, the criteria for mastery, and the method used to evaluate performance.

Another method of monitoring progress that is becoming increasingly popular involves use of student portfolios. According to McRobbie (1992), portfolios are "purposeful, collaborative, and self-reflective collections of student work" that are generated during the instructional process. Students select materials to be included in the portfolio that they consider examples of their "best work." This provides the teacher with a set of products reflecting student performance at different points in time.

SUMMARY

Effective instruction for students with mild disabilities is closely linked to how well teachers are able to pinpoint student needs. In this chapter we introduced a range of strategies they can use to assess student performance in key basic skill areas. Particular emphasis was placed on several nonstandardized alternative assessment approaches including criterion-referenced assessments, curriculum-based measurements and authentic performance assessments. These approaches are especially useful because they can help teachers determine exactly what their students need to learn and also help them monitor student progress once they begin instruction to address these concerns. Teachers who are adept at using the strategies discussed in this chapter will have a clear sense of the instructional "agenda" for each of their students and a context for judging how well that agenda is being addressed.

FOLLOW-UP ACTIVITIES

1. Develop a list of authentic assessment tasks that could be used to evaluate the written expression skills of a group of fourth-grade students.
2. Tape-record an oral reading sample for a student who is having reading difficulties. Use the information presented in Figure 6–9 and Table 6–1 to analyze the student's performance. Prepare a summary of your findings.
3. Collect several writing samples from a target student. Use the error pattern guide presented in Figure 6–13 to analyze the student's performance. Prepare a summary of your findings.
4. Obtain several samples of a student's performance on computation worksheets. Use the guide presented in Figure 6–18 to analyze the student's error patterns. Prepare a summary of your findings.
5. Interview a student concerning the types of learning strategies the student uses to facilitate mastery of course content. Analyze the student's approach in terms of the categories presented in Table 6–3. What suggestions would you give for expanding the student's approaches?
6. Interview a general education teacher and a special education teacher to learn how they monitor student progress. In particular, find out how these teachers keep track of student progress relative to mastery of IEP objectives. What strengths and weaknesses do you see in their approaches?

7 CHAPTER ACADEMIC ACCOMMODATIONS

KEY WORDS

Curriculum Adaptation Quick Screen
PIRATES
SCORER
T-*note strategy*
KWL
advanced organizers
focus questions
study guides
study skills

OBJECTIVES

After reading this chapter the student will be able to:

1. discuss steps in making effective accommodations.
2. discuss factors to consider in making accommodations.
3. list formats to use when implementing accommodations.
4. delineate ways to evaluate accommodations.
5. list detailed suggestions for making accommodations.
6. provide examples of adaptations in the content areas of social studies, science, written language, and mathematics.
7. discuss study skill strategies, including test taking and note taking.

Mrs. Wannemaker, a fourth-grade teacher, is working with a group of 23 students on a social studies project; students are to work independently, each researching the similarities and differences among the regions of the state of North Carolina. Four of her 23 students are poor readers; two of these have been identified as having learning disabilities. The two students with learning disabilities, Justin and Megan, not only have reading problems but also have difficulty with written language. Two other students in the class have attention deficit hyperactivity disorders (ADHD). The students with ADHD cannot work independently without constant reminders to focus on the task rather than on the physical education class going on outside. Mrs. Wannemaker has always liked the unit on the regions of North Carolina, but this year she knows she will need to make quite a few accommodations and she feels overwhelmed.

Mrs. Wannemaker simply cannot decide which accommodations she should implement at the beginning of the project. For example, she thinks that a study guide with a list of due dates for each section of the project would help all her students, but especially the ones with ADHD who have a hard time staying on task. In addition, if she divided the students into smaller cooperative learning groups it might help those students with special reading needs, but changing the independent research project to a cooperative learning project would require her to change her whole grading system!

Mrs. Wannemaker decides to implement the cooperative learning groups. She assigns one student with reading or learning problems or ADHD to each group, and carefully balances the other three members of each group so that there are both high achievers and low achievers in every group. In this way, she believes that the cooperative learning group members will be able to help each other and everyone will benefit.

Grading the projects has always been difficult for Mrs. Wannemaker, but her system has been to read each individual report and grade it for content, spelling, and presentation (handwriting and neatness). This year there are additional complications. Not only does she have to figure out how to assign a grade fairly to each of the four students in each cooperative learning group, but she knows that in Justin and Megan's groups (the two students with writing disabilities) she may need to provide the option of an oral report. For all of the students, she may need to factor into their grade some measure of their cooperation and effort.

Mrs. Wannemaker begins the class and introduces the project. Her students are enthusiastic. She assigns students to their groups, and after a few moans and groans on their part, she gets them started. She hands out the study guide and reviews the calendar provided for keeping track of due dates. As the students begin to work, she notices that some of the groups are "clicking" and some are not; in one of the groups, all four students are working independently. Mrs. Wannemaker wonders if this grouping accommodation will work, and what other accommodations she should have used.

The purpose of this chapter is to describe strategies and procedures to help teachers adapt and implement the required school curriculum for elementary and secondary students with disabilities who are educated in inclusive general education classrooms. Practical and effective strategies for adapting curricula for students with learning and behavior problems are discussed. Teaching and study strategies are presented in a format that facilitates easy application to the classroom.

The federal requirement that, to the maximum extent appropriate, *all* students, including those with disabilities, be afforded learning opportunities within the mandated school district curriculum, has placed increasing demands upon educators. General and special educators now find themselves trying to develop appropriate adaptations to the general education curriculum. Finding effective educational accommodations that are not excessively time consuming or intrusive continues to be a significant challenge. "Nowhere is the impact of the inclusion movement more pronounced than in the area of curricula and their implementation and adaptation" (Hoover & Patton, 1997, p. 4).

Educators frequently find themselves asking if they should shorten the assignment, extend the time allowed for tests and exams, or lower the grading standards for a student who is having difficulties. These three accommodations are most commonly offered to students with mild disabilities who are served in general education classrooms, but they may not be the most effective. For example, if a student cannot read the test, providing extra time to complete the test is not likely to be particularly helpful. In some cases, well-meaning accommodations may actually impede a student's academic progress.

Providing appropriate accommodations for students with disabilities entails much more than simply selecting from a list of suggested adaptations for various subject areas. It requires planning, assessment of the student's ability and skill, and consideration of resources. It also involves collaboration among all the educators involved with that student. In the following sections we discuss (1) steps to making effective accommodations, (2) factors to consider in making accommodations, (3) formats to use when implementing accommodations, (4) ways to evaluate accommodations, and (5) suggestions for making accommodations. We also suggest specific content area accommodations along with study skill strategies.

STEPS TO MAKING EFFECTIVE ACCOMMODATIONS

Accommodations are most effective when educators design them as an integrated part of the curriculum. Teachers who follow the following steps should find it easier to integrate accommodations into their curriculum:

- Get to know your students and how they learn (e.g., learning styles, strengths and weaknesses, disabilities).
- Determine *what* you will teach and what you want your students to learn and be able to do (e.g., long-term goals and objectives, short-term goals and objectives).
- Decide *how* you will teach (e.g., instructional decisions) (Council for Exceptional Children, 1997).

For example, consider a fourth-grade general education teacher: All her students are of average or above intelligence, but several have been identified through the school district's procedures as having specific learning disabilities in the areas of reading and written language. Most of the students appear to learn best using their visual modality. For this week, the teacher has planned to teach the history of aviation, and in particular, the events leading to the first flight of Orville and Wilbur Wright. She has taught this unit each year—it is one of her favorites—but this year, given the number of students with academic problems in the class, she knows she needs to make some changes. In consultation with the special education teacher in the building, she has decided to change the culminating assignment. In the past, this assignment has been an independent research paper; this year the teacher will use a team project instead. The entire class will be divided into pairs, each student with a disability will be paired with a student who does not have disabilities. Each partner will have an assigned task: One will be responsible for securing all the visuals and the research to support the team project (she gives this job to the students with written language disabilities in each of the pairs). The other team member will be responsible for writing the report on the computer (she assigns this task to the students without the written language disabilities in each team). The teacher believes that the benefit of using this approach is that it does not focus only on the students with disabilities because all students in the class are paired and in each pair, one student has the writing assignment.

This teacher has changed the classroom organization to accommodate students with academic difficulties. Figure 7–1 lists this and other dimensions of the class that could be the focus of accommodations for students with special needs. Accommodations could vary classroom organization, classroom management, methods of presentation, methods of practice, or methods of testing, depending on the needs of individual students.

Hoover and Patton (1997) suggest using a *Curriculum Adaptation Quick Screen* (Figure 7–2) to identify content needs, instructional strategy needs, instructional setting needs, and student behavior needs around which accommodations could be developed. This screening device can be completed by each of the educators involved with a particular student to identify modifications or adaptations that might be needed in various classes.

FACTORS TO CONSIDER IN MAKING ACCOMMODATIONS

The following list contains some of the questions a classroom teacher might want to answer before selecting an accommodation to implement in the classroom:

- Why are you making an accommodation? What educational objectives still need to be accomplished?
- How good are the student's social skills? Do social and communication skills need to be taken into account in selecting an accommodation?
- Does the student want the teacher to use any accommodations? Is the student more comfortable with one kind of accommodation than another?
- How acceptable is one particular accommodation to the student with special needs and to the other students? (Council for Exceptional Children, 1997)

Classroom Organization	Classroom Management	Methods of Presentation	Methods of Practice	Methods of Testing
Vary grouping arrangements • large-group instruction • small-group instruction • individual instruction • peer tutoring • independent self-instructional activities • learning centers Vary methods of instruction • teacher directed • student directed	Vary grading system • homework • tests • class discussion • special projects Vary reinforcement system • praise • notes sent home • grades • free time • special activity • tangibles • progress charts Vary rules • differentiated for some students • explicit/implicit	Vary content • amount to be learned • time to learn new information • conceptual level Vary general structure • advanced organizers • previewing questions • cues, mnemonic devices • provide immediate feedback • involve students actively Vary type • verbal—lecture, discussion • written—tests, worksheets • demonstration • audiovisuals • tape recorders • filmstrips • movies • opaque projectors • transparencies	Vary general structure • amount to be practiced • time for practice • group/individual • teacher directed/independent • items ranging from easy to difficult Vary level of response • copying • recognition • recall with cues • recall without cues Vary type of materials • worksheets • texts • audiovisual equipment	Vary type • verbal • written • demonstration Vary general structure • group/individual • amount to be tested • time for completion Vary level of response • recognition • recall with cues • recall without cues

FIGURE 7–1 Instructional Alternatives for a Mainstream Teacher

Note: *From "Teaching Secondary Learning Disabled Students in the Mainstream" by T. E. Laurie, L. Buchwach, R. Silverman & N. Zigmond.* Learning Disability Quarterly, *1978, 1(4), 68. Copyright 1978 by the Division for Children with Learning Disabilities. Reprinted by permission.*

Educator: ____________ Student: ____________ Subject: ____________

Strategy: ____________

Class setting: ____________

Place a check next to each ability the student possesses for working within the classroom relative to the identified subject, strategy, and setting.

Content Needs

- ❒ Sufficient reading level
- ❒ Necessary prerequisite skills
- ❒ Necessary experiences
- ❒ Sufficient language abilities
- ❒ Sufficient abstract-thinking abilities
- ❒ Interest in subject area material
- ❒ Other:

Instructional Strategy Needs

- ❒ Motivated by strategy used
- ❒ Strategy generates active student participation
- ❒ Acquires information through strategy
- ❒ Understands strategy used
- ❒ Strategy holds student's attention to task
- ❒ Other:

FIGURE 7–2 Curriculum Adaptation Quick Screen

Of course, first and foremost accommodations must make it more possible for students to accomplish the educational objectives of the general education class than they might without the accommodation. For example, an accommodation frequently recommended for a student with a learning disability is to give the student extra time when taking a test. But the student's problem may be difficulty with *reading* the test, not poor test-taking skills; providing extra time for this student might be of little or no support. For this student, the teacher may need to consider reading the questions aloud instead of giving extra time. A second student may not have a reading disability but rather an attention deficit hyperactivity disorder; for this student, extra time may

Instructional Setting Needs

- ❐ Able to attend to task within type of setting used
- ❐ Able to work independently when necessary
- ❐ Possesses appropriate peer interaction skills for type of setting used
- ❐ Acquires information easily through setting used
- ❐ Participates freely in setting
- ❐ Completes assignments within setting used
- ❐ Other:

Student Behaviors

- ❐ Maintains self-control
- ❐ Completes assigned tasks on time
- ❐ Is responsible for own actions
- ❐ Uses effective self-management techniques
- ❐ Uses study and learning strategies effectively
- ❐ Exhibits appropriate behaviors for type of instructional setting used
- ❐ Other

Summary of Curriculum Adaptation Needs

Content ____

____

Instructional strategy ____

____

Instructional setting ____

____

Student behaviors ____

____

FIGURE 7–2 *continued*

be just the right thing. In the same vein, before selecting an accommodation that requires interacting in a group, the teacher may want to make certain the student with disabilities knows how to work cooperatively, will be comfortable working with a group of peers and has adequate expressive language skills and social interaction skills. If working in a group places more of a burden on the student with disabilities than working independently, then this type of grouping accommodation doesn't make sense.

Accommodations should make the student with disabilities feel supported, but some students may not want to use the accommodations that are offered. This is often the case in middle and high school settings where the accommodation requires students to be obviously different than their peers. For example, if a teacher provides extended time to take a test, but the extended time must be taken during recess or lunch, students with disabilities may balk at having to give up their social time to take a test. They would not want to miss the only time in the school day during which it is possible to interact with peers.

Finally, accommodations need to fit into a teacher's routines and procedures. Certain accommodations may simply be too costly in time or money. For example, study guides are useful organizers for students with disabilities and their peers without disabilities, and they are usually appreciated by parents, as well. But many educators do not have the time to prepare appropriate study guides. Some teachers may quickly draft a list of questions to serve as a study guide, but this may not be helpful for the students who do not know where or how to find the answers.

As the general education teacher begins to consider which accommodations to implement, it may be helpful for the special education teacher to assist in completing a summary of accommodation possibilities for each student with disabilities. In Figure 7–3 we have completed such a summary of accommodation needs for Justin. This summary could be shared with all his general education teachers.

FORMATS WHEN IMPLEMENTING ACCOMMODATIONS

Accommodations may be instituted through several formats. For example, classroom teachers may want to change the instructional grouping arrangement, the lesson format, or the goal of their lessons. They may also want to consider a change of teaching style (see Figure 7–4) (Council for Exceptional Children, 1997).

CHANGING GROUPING ARRANGEMENTS

Instructional arrangements range from large-group instruction, cooperative learning groups, and peer partners, to individual instruction and independent seat work (see chapters 4 and 5 for more information on instructional arrangements). Some elements to consider when adapting instructional arrangements are listed in Figure 7–5. For example, a teacher might want to change from a large-grouping arrangement to a cooperative-learning grouping to accommodate students who have difficulty staying on task.

CHANGING LESSON FORMATS

Lesson formats encompass traditional lecture/demonstration/practice, whole-class discussion, games and simulations, and experiential learning. Changing the lesson format to make students more active learners can be a successful accommodation for many students with attention deficit hyperactivity disorders.

Summary of Accommodations

Name: Justin Date: 11-9-98

Grade: 7th Subjects: Social Studies and Science

Current Behavior: Justin does not turn in assignments on time. Justin does not prepare for tests.

Objective: Increase number of assignments turned in on time; and increase test scores

Previous Accommodations Tried: None

Accommodation Strategies:

1. Homework assignments will be written on the front blackboard at the beginning of class each day in large print.
2. Justin's class will be divided into pairs. Each pair of study buddies will be asked to make sure they both have the day's assignment written in their agenda book.
3. A note-taking strategy will be taught to the entire class that facilitates studying for a test without recopying.
4. A daily notebook check will take place to make sure all students (especially Justin) are keeping notes.
5. A partially complete study guide will be provided in class at the beginning of each unit of study. At the conclusion of the unit study buddies will compare their study guides for completeness and correctness. A completed study guide will be available for students.

Teachers Signatures:____________________

Duration of Implementation of Strategies: Nine weeks

Dates for Review:____________________

FIGURE 7–3 Sample Adaptation Needs Form Completed for Justin

REFLECTION BOX 7–1 What factors do you think Mrs. Wannemaker considered in making the accommodations she implemented? What other factors should she consider? What other information should be considered? What factors should be considered for every teacher's class?

CHANGING THE GOALS OF INSTRUCTION

Changing the goals of instruction could include changing the pace of delivery or changing the amount of information that is delivered to students. Or it could mean changing

FIGURE 7–4 Focus in Accommodations

1. Changing the instructional grouping or arrangement
2. Changing the lesson format
3. Changing the goals
4. Changing the teaching style

the sequence of activities, providing more practice opportunities, or providing an array of small tasks for a child to complete in lieu of one large assignment. Changing your teaching style could include providing more prompts, providing more verbal or written instructions, or using more physical guidance. It may also mean instituting more behavior management practices. Selection of any of these alternatives should be guided, of course, by assessment data collected on teacher behavior in the classroom.

EVALUATING ACCOMMODATIONS

Teachers should always evaluate the effectiveness of the accommodations they implement to make certain that the accommodations are achieving their purpose. Questions to consider include the following:

- Does the accommodation increase the student's interactions with classmates?
- Does it improve the student's ability to be an active learner?
- Does it build independent skills?
- Does it make the curriculum relevant to the student's current or future life?
- Does it reduce the abstraction and complexity of the task?
- Does it fit with your teaching style and the student's learning style? (Council for Exceptional Children, 1997)

FIGURE 7–5 Elements to Consider When Adapting Instructional Arrangements

Note: *From* Curriculum Adaptations for Students with Learning and Behavior Problems: Principles and Practice *(p. 44), by J. J. Hoover & J. R. Patton, 1997, Austin, TX: PRO-ED. Copyright 1997 by PRO-ED. Reprinted by permission.*

- Seating arrangements and use of study carrels
- Organization of different learning areas within the classroom
- Grouping arrangements
- Overall organization for delivering different types of instruction
- Flexibility in groupings based on learning experiences provided
- General climate conducive to positive learning, quality time on-task, and effective interactions

Frequently, modifications and accommodations are put in place with no evaluation procedure or plan to determine their success. Sometimes educators can evaluate the success of a particular modification by reviewing the student's grades before and after the modification is implemented. However, grades do not address outcomes such as increasing the student's interactions with classmates or improving the student's ability to be an active learner. It is easier to evaluate the success of a particular modification if at the initiation of the modification all parties involved (i.e., parents, educators, and student) decide on the goals for the use of the modification. The form in Figure 7–6 can be used at the time that the modification or accommodation is put in place and reviewed regularly. These reviews provide quick assessments of the success of the modification(s) and also indicate whether adjustments should be made.

It is critical that educators provide modifications appropriate for an individual student's academic and behavioral needs *and* that they regularly evaluate the effective-

Name of student: ______________________________

Date modifications began: ______________________________

Class modifications to be used: ______________________________

Date modifications are reviewed: ______________________________

Strengths and Weaknesses of Student

Strengths	Weaknesses
____________________	____________________
____________________	____________________
____________________	____________________
____________________	____________________

List of Objectives of Modifications

____

____

____

____

List of Modifications

____

____

____

____

FIGURE 7–6 Modification Evaluation Guide

ness of such modifications. Periodic and systematic evaluation can inform educators if the modifications are no longer appropriate socially, or are no longer needed for academic reasons. Regular evaluation can also inform educators of the need to adjust the accommodations. For example, the daily review of a student's agenda book instituted to ensure that homework assignments were being written down might be adjusted to a weekly review based on the student's increased success at appropriately recording daily homework assignments.

SUGGESTIONS FOR MAKING ACCOMMODATIONS

In this section, we provide suggestions for making accommodations in your classroom. First are several general accommodations that are appropriate across the curriculum. Second are study-skill strategies or teaching strategies intended to improve students' study habits. Then come suggestions for accommodations in specific content areas. The general accommodation strategies are highlighted under the following contexts: (1) participation factors, (2) textual elements, (3) assignment completion components, and (4) influence of instructions (Council for Exceptional Children, 1997). The study skills section includes suggestions for test-taking modifications and note-taking strategies. The final section includes suggestions for accommodations in mathematics, science, and social studies.

GENERAL ACCOMMODATION STRATEGIES

This section discusses general accommodations educators can make to (1) increase students' class participation, (2) facilitate students' understanding of their textbooks, (3) increase students' completion of assignments, and (4) increase the power of teacher instructions.

PARTICIPATION FACTORS. Frequently teachers want to increase class participation of students with or without disabilities during large-group instructional periods. To accomplish this, the teacher might introduce one of the following activities: "think, pair, and share"; KWL (know, want-to-know, learned); or "free-write, free-tell" (Council for Exceptional Children, 1997). In a "think, pair, and share" activity, the teacher poses questions to the class about the topic, asks students to think about the answers, then has each student find a partner. Each partner team shares responses to the question and one student from each team reports back to the teacher when the class gets back together. When using a "KWL" procedure, the teacher asks the class to brainstorm together what *they already know* about the topic; the students' responses are written on the board or on an overhead transparency projected on a screen. Then the students are asked what they *want to know* about the topic. After the lesson is completed, the students again join to discuss what they have *learned* about the topic and compare it with the lists made previously. KWL can be incorporated into the beginning and end of any unit. Teachers also can have students travel to charts posted around the room and write or draw their current knowledge about the subject on appropriate charts; later these charts can be used as easy references or study guides when students prepare for the test on the unit.

A "free-write, free-tell" activity encourages students to write down any aspect of the lesson that was confusing to them or about which they had questions. For example, after a discussion on the history of flight, the teacher might ask students to stop and write down what they have learned and any questions they still have. The teacher might also use a free-write activity in conjunction with note taking. First, the students are asked to take notes using a three-column format. In the first column they are to write the main ideas, vocabulary words, or the major themes. In the second column they write the supportive ideas, the definition of the words, and the minor themes. The third column is reserved for questions they might have concerning the topics recorded in the first two columns. Figure 7–7 is an example of a blank form on which three-column notes can be taken.

Increasing students' participation in the learning process increases students' time on-task; the more time students spend on-task the more likely learning will take place. The previous examples are but three activities that can increase participation. Many more examples can be found in Polloway & Patton (1997) *Strategies for Teaching Learners with Special Needs*.

TEXTUAL ELEMENTS. Easily implemented teaching accommodations can be provided using advanced organizers. Examples include focus questions, study guides, preteaching of vocabulary words, providing a videotape for prior knowledge viewing, teaching textbook or chapter structure, or providing a partial outline. Each of these examples are briefly explained here:

Focus questions. Focus questions provided before a lesson encourage the students to reflect on the topic of the lesson. For example, in a pre-algebra class the focus question might consist of a math puzzle projected to a screen from the overhead. As the students enter the room they are given five minutes to find the answer to the math puzzle. To complete the puzzle students must understand the mathematical concepts

Main ideas Vocabulary words Major themes	Supportive ideas Definitions of the words Minor themes	Questions

FIGURE 7–7 Three-Column Format for Note Taking

discussed and practiced in class the previous day. This puzzle, therefore, prepares the students for the next step in the sequence, which is the topic of today's lesson.

Study guides. Study guides allow the students to actively record their knowledge. Study guides highlight the important information that will be needed for the upcoming test, and may be constructed in one of several formats. Teachers may pair questions on a study guide with the page numbers in the text on which the answers can be found. Or study guides can provide open spaces after each major point to allow students to fill in the answers as they listen to a lecture. Study guides also can be completed by pairs of students working together. To construct a study guide, the teacher should develop an outline of the chapter or lecture but leave blank spaces that force the students to become actively involved in inserting the missing information. The teacher should allow time for review when students have completed the study guide, otherwise students who completed the study guide incorrectly may memorize the wrong information. In addition, study guides should be given to the class at least one week before the test, so students have time to complete them and use them to study from.

Preteaching vocabulary words. As subject-matter content becomes more complex, teachers may need to preteach vocabulary words. This can be done as a game or as a whole-class activity. Teachers can have students make "power cards"—index cards with a vocabulary word written on one side and the definition written on the other. For example, if the new social studies chapter on the Middle Ages contains several new words including some unusual proper names, the teacher may want to have students learn the new words before reading the chapter. Many textbooks highlight new vocabulary either at the beginning of the chapter or in bold print throughout the chapter. Students could make power cards of the new vocabulary and, in pairs, drill each other on the definitions. Preteaching new vocabulary this way can enhance the level of discussion on the chapter once the reading of the book or the lecture is introduced.

Video viewing. Presenting a video on the topic to be discussed is a popular way to introduce a new topic. The National Geographic Society and Public Broadcasting Service both provide videos that can be used for previewing content. Video rental stores may also be a resource for appropriate videos.

Teaching textbook structure. Educators should frequently review textbook structure (headings, subheadings, differing print, introductory and summary paragraphs) with their students. Beginning a lesson by reading the summary paragraphs of the text, or reviewing the end-of-chapter questions helps students prepare for the new topic to be discussed. It gives them a framework for the information they will get when they later read the chapter from the beginning. To encourage active reading of a textbook, the teacher might pair students off and have each student read one paragraph in turn, then cover it and paraphrase the main point or the most important piece of information to the partner. After completion, the partner could read the next paragraph and complete the same tasks. For more competent readers, a whole page might be read at one time instead of just one paragraph.

Partial outline. A partial outline of important information that can be completed while reading, allows students to actively read the text material. Encouraging students to stop and review or write about what they have read benefits students who are easily distracted. The partial outline also allows the teacher to quickly assess each student's progress through the reading assignment.

In summary, many accommodations can be implemented to help students become more actively involved in learning. These organizers are particularly useful because they can be implemented easily for one student or for the entire class.

SEQUENCING ASSIGNMENTS FOR COMPLETION. Teachers may also find it useful to modify the sequence of the material covered or the sequence of assignments given for review. Educators can break up long-term tasks into smaller, more easily attainable steps, and assign due dates to each step. This not only provides a schedule for students but also helps them learn to break a long-term task into manageable parts. For example, requiring students to write their autobiography is a terrific written language assignment. However, the teacher would not want to encourage students to write 10 chapters in one night. Having students do the task in pieces allows the teacher to monitor students' progress, provide timely feedback, and encourage students to complete a small amount of the work each week.

Educators can also provide examples and specific steps to accomplish each task. Teachers who frequently assign similar projects year after year should keep copies of the best of these projects and use them as examples for next year's class. Providing a visual sample of what the task should look like at completion helps students who have difficulty generating such a mental picture on their own. Educators can also provide a list of the tasks required or post the requirements and dates necessary to complete each assignment. Many students work more successfully when they see a list of the tasks they need to complete and can check off the parts as they are accomplished. This technique also trains students to manage their time.

Other easily implemented accommodations may include frequent checking that assignments are written in the homework book, or arranging for students to have "study buddies" who will make sure the assignments are written in their buddies' agenda books and that all necessary materials for homework have been placed in their buddies' backpacks. The advantage of the buddy system is that students can work together to remind each other, freeing the teacher from this tedious task.

REFLECTION BOX 7–2

In Chapter 6 we met Tim, a student in Ms. Camp's class. Based on her description of Tim's performance it would seem that he might benefit from several of the strategies discussed in the previous section. Which of these techniques might be appropriate for Tim?

GIVING INSTRUCTIONS. Giving instructions to students is a critical skill for teachers to learn. Some students may need to *hear* instructions and others may need to *see* instructions to completely understand what is required of them. When students with disabilities are in the classroom, it is always safest to try to provide both a visual list of instructions and an auditory version. It is useful to get the student's attention before giving instructions, using alerting cues such as turning the lights on and off or raising your hand. Raising your voice or shouting, "Eyes on me, please!" is not usually advisable. Nonverbal cues obtain the desired result without raising the noise level of the class.

Teachers should practice giving directions one at a time. Many educators give several directions in a single string and are disappointed when a student completes only the first step. Some students with mild disabilities can process only one instruction at a time. If it is important for the rest of the class to enumerate the entire set of instructions for the next activity, the teacher should write the instructions on the chalkboard or the overhead projector, or distribute a photocopied list to students. This way, the instructions will remain visible after they have been spoken. If no printed copy of the instructions is available, the teacher may need to find a way to quietly repeat the directions to some students after speaking the list to the entire class. You may have to check for understanding by having these students repeat the directions.

Getting a student's attention and asking him to repeat the instructions to the group is helpful for all the students in the class.

Always place *general* methods of operation and expectations on charts displayed around the room or on sheets in the students' notebooks. Homework should always be written in the same place on the chalkboard. Assignments should always be turned in to the same box placed at the front of the class. Students are less likely to misunderstand directions or miss a homework assignment if routines are standardized.

GRADING ALTERNATIVES. Alternative grading for students with mild disabilities is often an extremely useful accommodation. Grades are an important and required form of student evaluations, integral to the education process. Grades serve a variety of purposes: They communicate accomplishment or achievement, can motivate students to put forth more effort, link home and school in assessments of student progress, give students a sense of success, and so on. For many students with disabilities, however, good grades derived from a standard grading system are out of range. For these students, grades are only discouraging: They do not motivate effort, they do not communicate accurate levels of student achievement, and they do not give students a feeling of accomplishment. For these students, alternative grading systems can be developed and implemented, but only if the purpose of the grades is made very clear to teachers, parents, and students.

One teacher may want to use a pass/fail system instead of the multilevel grading system to reduce the pressures of competition and the embarrassment of rankings of student performance. Another teacher may want to use more than one grade to communicate to parents both achievement and effort. A third teacher may want to involve students themselves in developing a grading scale and may develop a grading contract with each student in which both student and teacher agree on the quantity and quality of work that will constitute a particular letter grade. Whatever the system selected, teachers should supplement letter or numeric grades with oral and written descriptive information distributed to parents, the student, and the student's future teachers.

When a general education teacher and a special education teacher share responsibilities for grading their students, as in a co-taught class, it is important that both teachers be involved in assigning grades. To facilitate this process, teachers should do the following:

- Communicate often about student progress.
- Make certain both teachers are aware of the students' level of functioning and strengths and weaknesses.
- Strive for consistency across the two teachers in the adaptations to tests that will be used (oral examinations or taping of responses to tests).
- Develop a mutually agreed-on alternative grading system that both teachers can explain and justify.

SPECIFIC ACADEMIC ACCOMMODATION STRATEGIES

Teachers are often asked to provide academic accommodations for students with mild disabilities. In the sections below we discuss strategies for reading comprehension, written language, and study skills.

READING COMPREHENSION. Comprehension is the ultimate goal of the reading process. Many students with mild disabilities have difficulty comprehending what they read. One way to improve reading comprehension is to get students to be more active readers. Several strategies have been developed to teach students to be active readers and they are not difficult to implement in a general classroom. One example is the paraphrasing strategy introduced by Schumaker, Denton, & Deshler (1984) that teaches students to read a paragraph and ask themselves a few questions. As with many strategies that come out of the Kansas Strategies Intervention Model, the paraphrasing strategy employs a mnemonic to help students learn and apply the strategy.

R–**R***ead a paragraph.*
A–**A***sk yourself "What are the main ideas and details in this paragraph?"*
P–**P***ut the main idea and details into your own words.*

Semantic mapping may also assist students in reading comprehension. Students use a mapping procedure to organize the main ideas and details of a passage or chapter. Another strategy is an adaptation of the SQ3R method, and is called the "multipass strategy" by Schumaker, Deshler, Alley, & Denton (1982). The multipass strategy teaches students to make three passes through a content subject chapter, first to familiarize themselves with the main ideas and organization of the passage, second to gain specific information, and finally to test themselves on the chapter material.

WRITTEN LANGUAGE. Written language deficiencies present serious problems for students with mild disabilities because students in general education classes are expected to use their writing skills across all academic areas. Strategies that structure students' thinking and encourage students to follow a step-by-step sequence to produce written texts can be very helpful. For example, the University of Kansas researchers have suggested a cognitive strategy such as TOWER structures that teach students to follow a sequence of steps to produce an acceptable written product. TOWER steps include the following:

T–**T***hink*
O–**O***rder ideas*
W–**W***rite*
E–**E***dit*
R–**R***ewrite*

Another related strategy for writing theme papers has been suggested by Ellis and Lenz (1987), and is remembered by the acronym DEFENDS.

D–**D***ecide on your exact position*
E–**E***xamine the reasons for your position*
F–**F***orm a list of points that explain each reason*
E–**E***xpose your position in the first sentence*
N–**N***ote each reason and supporting points*

D–**D***rive home the position in the last sentence*
S–**S***earch for errors and correct*

An error-monitoring strategy developed by Schumaker et al. (1985) called COPS helps students detect and correct errors in their written products.

C–*Have I* **C***apitalized the first word in the sentence and proper names?*
O–*How is the* **O***verall appearance?*
P–*Have I used end* **P***unctuation, commas, and semicolons correctly?*
S–*Do the words look as if they are* **S***pelled correctly?*

Once students have learned the COPS strategy, they can be taught to apply it in the Edit step of the TOWER strategy.

REFLECTION BOX 7–3

Both Justin and Megan in Mrs. Wannemaker's class seem to be good candidates for academic accommodations. What areas do you think such accommodations should focus on?

STUDY SKILLS. Educators know that students who use effective study skills perform better in school. Effective study skills are critical to school success at every level: elementary, secondary, or postsecondary (Hoover, 1990). Yet, few educators explicitly teach students to employ study skills; they expect students to apply them without instruction. Students who need this explicit instruction most are those with mild disabilities—many of whom have documented deficiencies in study skills (Polloway & Patton, 1997; Smith & Dowdy, 1989; Strichart & Mangrum, 1993; Strichart, Mangrum, & Iannuzzi, 1998).

Study skills are defined as support skills students must employ to effectively and efficiently process, organize, integrate, and evaluate oral and written information in the process of learning. Efficient use of study skills becomes more important as facts and concepts become more complex. Inefficient study skills at the second- and third-grade levels may not cause too much difficulty because the material to be learned is not very abstract or complex. By the middle school years, however, deficiencies in study skills begin to take their toll. In this section we discuss three critical study skills: (1) time management, (2) note taking, and (3) test taking.

Time management skills. Under most conditions, students with mild disabilities require more time to complete assignments and to master the curriculum. Part of the problem may be that they take longer to commit information to memory. But part of the problem may also be that they have never been taught how to manage time effectively, and they do not master scheduling time on their own. Alley and Deshler (1979) believe that students with disabilities fall into one of two groups: Some students are "confusion squared" and "go with the flow"; other students are minute-to-minute planners. Both types are nonproductive and do not use their time wisely.

To accommodate these time management problems, teachers might show students how to use a semester calendar, a weekly planner, and a daily agenda. The semester calendar allows students to record due dates for long-term projects and regular exams. Students can break assignments into shorter segments and note due dates for each part on the calendar. In addition, students can mark school holidays and special school events. Such a long-term calendar allows students to plan ahead and monitor their progress. Teachers should keep a copy of the semester calendar, and students should keep a copy at home.

The weekly planner provides a more detailed account of a student's assignments. The daily boxes should be larger than on the semester calendar and provide for an hourly (or per-period) notation of commitments. Students should review their semester calendar each weekend and add the next week's entries to the weekly planner. Assignments given in class should be entered on the weekly planner. After-school activities such as soccer practice, part-time employment, scouts, or church activities also should be added to the weekly planner.

The daily organizer is the most detailed of the three. Students should review their weekly planners each morning and make notes about the day ahead. There should be a space at the bottom of the daily organizer for special "stuff" that may need attention (e.g., go to office supply store for more computer paper). The daily organizer should be

Listing assignments on the board and reviewing them with students helps the students to fill in their own planners at their own pace.

a "list of things I need to do today." Students should be taught to write all their entries in pencil and to review their list regularly. Many computer software programs provide blank calendars, to-do lists, and daily organizers. Students who are trained to use these time-management tools can be helped to structure their daily routines.

Using a notebook as an organizational tool is also an aid to time management skills. Notebooks help students keep track of assignments and stay organized. The notebook should be large enough to be missed if it is not in the backpack. It should also have folder pockets on the front and back covers. The front cover should hold all materials that are due that day. The back cover should hold any materials required for homework that night. The weekly planner and daily organizer should be kept in the front of the notebook. Colored dividers can be used to keep notes and handouts for each subject separate. A zippered pouch can hold extra pencils, rulers, calculators, and so on. Teachers might suggest that each student put something of value into their notebook. The premise is that if a "valuable" item is in the notebook, the student is less likely to lose the notebook. One section of the notebook could be set aside for student self-recording of assignment and test grades for each subject. By recording their own grades students may find they are less surprised by their final grade at report-card time.

Note-taking strategies. Note taking requires students to document major ideas and details for later use, and to classify and organize information as they are writing. Note taking is a complex task. Students with mild disabilities frequently have difficulty understanding and processing auditory information (Lerner, 1997); many have difficulty attending to the most important ideas in a lecture. In addition, many students with mild disabilities have difficulty with written language; for many students, making sense of their notes is difficult because of their illegible writing and incorrect spelling (Suritsky & Hughes, 1997).

Because note taking is such a complex skill and so difficult for many students, teachers in general education classrooms often must decide whether to spend time teaching note-taking skills or to focus their energies on providing accommodations for note taking deficiencies (Suritsky & Hughes, 1997). When the decision is to teach note taking, a particularly helpful strategy that is relatively easy to teach is called the "T-Note Strategy" (Davis & Clark, 1991). Students are taught to draw a line down the middle of the page vertically and cross the line at the top, forming a "T". On the right side of the "T" students write main ideas, vocabulary words, diagrams, or an "H" if the teacher gave a handout. On the left side of the page students write the minor parts of main ideas, definitions of vocabulary words, labels for the diagrams, and the title of the handout. Spaces are skipped between each idea or vocabulary word. The information to be remembered becomes "chunked" and thus, easier to remember. In addition, students can easily fold the paper in half vertically to test themselves on the content. Finally, a heading and a page number are added to the top of each page.

Accommodations for students who have difficulty with note taking may include having students tape-record lectures then augment any notes taken online with note taking on repeated listenings. Or teachers may provide partially completed lecture/text outlines or study guides to facilitate note taking. Finally, students who cannot write may be provided with a peer note taker who uses carbon paper, or photocopies of notes taken by a peer or prepared by the teacher.

Ideally, these accommodations should help students with mild disabilities improve their own note taking skills. If students do not have severe aural or motor problems, there are significant benefits to learning a system that works for them over teaching them to rely on an accommodation approach. Figure 7–8 provides 10 tips for teaching study skills; Fender (1990, 1996) make available reproducible materials effective for training students to use effective study skills.

Test-taking skills. In school, students demonstrate their mastery of information by taking tests. In many classes, however, students with disabilities learn what is required of them, but fail to demonstrate their understanding when given a test because they are "no good at taking tests." They lack a sense of test-wiseness (Hughes, 1997; Scruggs & Mastropieri, 1988; Veit & Scruggs, 1986). They are at a disadvantage relative to other students who have equal knowledge but more effective test-taking skills. Furthermore, the deficiencies in test-taking skills lead to fear of taking tests. Anxiety rises as each test draws closer. Poor test-taking skills and high anxiety work against the student with disabilities ever being able to demonstrate mastery.

Tests should determine if students have learned new concepts and their application; they should not measure primarily whether students understand how to take tests. If tests are to provide feedback to students and teachers on how successful they have been in learning and teaching, students must be skilled at how to take the tests. For

1. Introduce simple variations of the different study skills in the early grades.
2. Gradually increase to the more complex elements associated with each study skill as students progress through the grades.
3. Identify specific goals and objectives for a study-skills program before implementing the program.
4. Let students' individual strengths and weaknesses guide decision making concerning what study skills to emphasize at any particular time.
5. Know what motivates students to use different study skills and emphasize these motivations in program implementation.
6. Explain and demonstrate the proper use of each study skill.
7. Expect students to use different study skills appropriately through guided practice and planned learning experiences.
8. Provide continued opportunity for practicing study-skill usage to assist students in acquiring and maintaining mastery of the skills.
9. Facilitate the regular use of study skills in natural classroom settings as the need arises in different subject areas.
10. Assist students in generalizing acquired study skills through an emphasis on more complex use of the skills once initial mastery of the basic study skills has been achieved.

FIGURE 7–8 Ten Tips to Teaching Study Skills

students with mild disabilities, this means explicit instruction in how to prepare for and take tests. This instruction should include the study skills described here that help students prepare for an upcoming test, as well as test-taking skills for reading and following directions, thinking through questions before writing the answers, allocating time for all parts of the test, and proofreading and checking answers. To assist students with test preparation it is helpful to teach them to keep track of upcoming tests using an assignment book. In addition, previewing knowledge test formats with the students and encouraging them to use the study guide can help students prepare. For test taking, the PIRATES strategy provided in Figure 7–9 has been found to be helpful for students with learning disabilities (Hughes, Ruhl, Deshler, & Schumaker, 1993). Another test-taking strategy developed by Carman and Adams (1972) is SCORER:

S–**S***chedule your time*
C–**C***lue words*
O–**O***mit difficult items*
R–**R***ead carefully*
E–**E***stimate your answers*
R–**R***eview your work*

In addition to teaching test-taking strategies, educators may want to offer alternative forms of tests (e.g., oral, essay, short answer, multiple choice, fill in the blank) to some students with mild disabilities. Offering alternative test *settings* may also be helpful (testing the student in the special education resource room instead of in the general education classroom); often students with mild disabilities are distracted by the rest of the students taking the test. A second accommodation is to offer extra time;

Offering alternative test-taking settings is especially helpful for students with attention deficit disorders.

FIGURE 7–9 *Note:* From *Memory and Test-Taking Strategies* by C. A. Hughes, in D. D. Deshler, E. S. Ellis, & B. K. Lenz (Eds.)., *Teaching Adolescents with Learning Disabilities,* 2nd ed. (pp. 209–266), 1997, Denver, CO: Love.

Step 1:	**P**repare to succeed Put your name and PIRATES on the test. Allot time and order to sections. Say affirmations. Start within 2 minutes.
Step 2:	**I**nspect the instructions. Read instructions carefully. Underline what to do and where to respond. Notice special requirements.
Step 3:	**R**ead, remember, reduce.
Step 4:	**A**nswer or abandon.
Step 5:	**T**urn back.
Step 6:	**E**stimate. Avoid absolutes. Choose the longest or most detailed choice. Eliminate similar choices.
Step 7:	**S**urvey.

this can lower some students' anxiety and allow them to concentrate on the topic of the test rather than on the clock. If the purpose of the test is to determine what the student has learned, the method used to find that out should not be important. Some test modifications do require more teacher time (e.g., giving an oral test to each student versus giving a paper-and-pencil multiple-choice test to the entire class). However, some students require such modifications to demonstrate their mastery.

Educators should also use clear, readable, and uncluttered test forms. Handwritten tests should be used only as a last resort. Computer-generated formatting should be used whenever possible. Educators should also format test items so that students can follow the item sequence easily. If a student has difficulty responding in writing, it may be useful to provide a scribe or voice-activated software used on a personal computer. Allowing students to take tests on computers is becoming common. Word processing software systems allow students to spell-check their final product. Keep in mind the student should be given the opportunity to practice any test modifications before the actual test.

ACCOMMODATIONS FOR SPECIFIC CONTENT AREA SUBJECTS

Accommodations in the content area subjects of mathematics, social studies, science, and written language are provided in Figures 7–10, 7–11, 7–12, and 7–13. These sug-

When teaching math, *teachers should move toward a strand design* rather than teaching chapter by chapter. In strand design, the instructor will work with students on several ongoing topics. Instead of a single objective for one day, the students will tackle 2–3 topics, doing only a little each day, and gradually building up over several days. For example, in a unit on problem solving, the teacher would also give the students some basic computation problems and problems on fractions. To ensure students are not overwhelmed, new information would be presented in only one area; the other areas would be reviewed. Some advantages to this system is that in addition to moving us away from "drilling overkill" on one skill, the strand method also helps to keep students attention fresh.

In math lessons, *students should have a high rate of success.* Pace instruction carefully so that students are experiencing success the majority of the time.

Make sure you include judicious review in your planning—enough initial practice for students to master a new concept, as well as repeated opportunities to practice over several days. Then, gradually increase the time between practice opportunities.

Give students mixed practice sets. Once a problem or concept is introduced and students are doing well, give them mixed practice sets in which problems of different types are mixed together. When students are only given blocked practice sets (problems of same type), they don't need to attend to signs, which hurts them on tests. Be careful not to mix the problem types too soon, but when the students are ready, integrate what you have just taught them with that they have done before.

Teach problem solving strategies. Look for strategies that work for the widest range of examples. For example, when teaching how to find the volume of a 3-dimensional object, build on the concept of area rather than having students memorize separate formula for each object. Thus, students would learn that to find the volume of a wedge, rectangular prism, or cylinder, they could use the same formula: the area of the base times the height. To find the volume of a pyramid or cone, students would use the formula, the area of the base times 1⁄3 the height. With this method, students not only memorize fewer formulas, they also have a conceptual link on which to base their understanding.

Use mediated scaffolding or guided practice to help students move from text examples to working independently. Initially, coach students step by step, and have lots of questions and answers. Gradually fade out your support as you work with the students through several examples. For example, when finding the perimeter of an object, say: "Look at first figure. Remember perimeter is length around whole figure. What kind of problem is this? Right, addition. How many sides does the object have? So, how many numbers will be in your addition problem? Don't forget, you have five numbers to add. Now work the problem." As the students become more proficient, fade out some of these questions.

Teach one way to solve a problem. Find a generalized strategy that works consistently for a particular problem type and stick with it. Then give students practice and guidance until they master the process. It is not necessarily a good idea to use manipulatives, at least to introduce a concept. Work with the conceptual analysis first. Often kids are distracted by other features of the task when using manipulatives. Instead, use semiconcrete objects like diagrams to show students a range of examples and how the concept works.

FIGURE 7–10 Adaptations for Math
Note: Courtesy of Bernie Kelly

Provide many examples for a concept and many "nonexamples." Reduce the number of vocabulary words in a science text to those that are crucial to understanding.

For the vocabulary you teach, teach it well. Give many examples and nonexamples to show when the concept fits and when it doesn't. For example, for conduction to occur, objects must touch. Students could be asked if conduction will occur between objects of different temperatures that are touching. Here, the answer is yes because the objects have different temperatures and are touching. The teacher should also give examples that don't have those features.

Show physical examples or draw pictures to illustrate concepts as much as possible.

Give students concept maps. In science, teachers often need to provide concept maps rather than have students design their own, because the students may have difficulty determining how concepts are related. One popular method to eliminate misconceptions is to use cognitive dissonance—present a situation and have students identify what is wrong. For example, students might think large objects sink and small objects float. With this method, the teacher would show the students large objects that float and small objects that sink. However, a lot of students operate with probability, and won't change their expectations regarding the rule—even when they are shown otherwise. Therefore, when you show them the example, tell them the rule!!!

If the course has a textbook, read the text orally and ask a lot of interspersed questions frequently.

Choose a well-designed curriculum where things are integrated and build on each other.

Initially, give students a lot of teacher guidance, then have them continue to use that skill until they don't need the teacher coaching or guidance. Sometimes in science, we want students to learn through self-discovery. However, students may not have the skills for self-discovery. If that is the case, we must give them help and then fade the assistance out.

FIGURE 7–11 Accommodations for Science
Note: Courtesy of Bonnie Grossen

gestions for content-area modifications were written by colleagues in the field of special education and are provided on the web site for the Council for Exceptional Children (see www.cec.sped.org/nw-menil.htm). The following may also be helpful resources for content subject accommodations: (1) Camine, Caros, Crawford, Hollenbeck, & Harniss; 1996; (2) Harniss, Hollenbeck, Crawford, & Camine; 1994; and (3) Miller, Crawford, Hamiss, Hollenbeck, & Camine; 1997.

REFLECTION BOX 7–4

In Chapter 5 we introduced you to Carlos, a student who was having problems in Ms. Pope's social studies class. Ms. Pope's description of Carlos' classroom performance suggests that he might respond well if she were to make adaptations in her instructional arrangement. What changes are likely to be helpful for Carlos?

SUMMARY

The current practices of inclusion and collaboration present a variety of challenges to general and special educators in their efforts to meet individual student's academic and learning needs. In this chapter, we discussed steps that can be taken to provide appropriate modifications and accommodations for students with mild disabilities so they can be successful in the general education setting. Suggestions were given for implementing specific content area accommodations as well as for teaching specific study strategies. Ideally, general educators will become proficient in providing and evaluating appropriate modifications based on careful study of each student's strengths and weaknesses.

The following are some common problems students with disabilities encounter in social studies classes and suggestions for accommodations that teachers can implement to help overcome the difficulty.

Problem 1

A large portion of history/social studies instruction is organized around a textbook. Students who have difficulty accessing information from text will gain less information from the reading of the text than other students.

Solution. Have students read orally from the text in large groups or in smaller cooperative settings. This ensures that two things happen. First the teacher can monitor to be sure all students read the text (i.e., have the opportunity to learn). Second, students with reading disabilities will be more likely to access textual information by listening to others read. We have successfully implemented oral reading up to the 8th grade. (Note: All students should have the opportunity to read aloud, especially those who struggle with reading; however, slower readers may read fewer sentences than other students in a given time period.)

Problem 2

The history and social studies content areas are "information dense." Students must not only learn and retain large amounts of complex, interrelated information, but also use that information in sophisticated ways.

Solution 1. Teach for depth rather than breadth by selecting the most important information and organizing that information in ways that make sense for the content area you are teaching. For example, much of history can be organized within a problem–solution–effect text structure. Groups of people or individuals have problems (usually economic or people's rights), they try to solve these problems in some way, and there is an effect that follows. The effect may be a solution to the initial problem and/or may create a new problem.

FIGURE 7–12 Adaptations for Social Studies
Note: Courtesy of Mark Harniss

Another "big idea" in history is the factors that effect group success. Students can be taught to analyze the likelihood of a group's success in an endeavor by evaluating the group's (a) resources, (b) capability, (c) leadership, and (d) motivation. These factors of group success allow students to evaluate why a group was successful or predict whether a group will be successful. These organizational structures should be explicitly taught and students should be shown how to apply them to the content generated by the text (see scaffolding below).

Solution 2. Provide extensive scaffolding for your students. Scaffolding is a teaching procedure in which a teacher initially provides high levels of structure and support to naive students, but over time reduces the structure and support until students are able to perform independently. For example, in history and social studies, students might initially be given graphic organizers in which content information has already been added. Later, students might fill in graphic organizers with teacher support. Eventually, students would fill them in by themselves. Scaffolding can also be textual. Initially, students should be shown how to adequately answer complex questions (e.g., compare/contrast or casual structures). Next, they would answer questions with teacher support and prompting, and finally by themselves.

Solution 3. Provide thoughtfully planned review opportunities. Textbooks provide extremely limited opportunities for review; frequently at the end of each chapter. Teachers should plan review that is sufficient (i.e., adequate to initially learn the content information), distributed (i.e., integrated over time so students don't learn something and then forget it), cumulative (i.e., new information should build upon previously learned information), and varied (i.e., once information is learned in one context it should be eventually applied in another context). Only important information should be placed into the review cycle. If it is important enough to teach, then it should be important enough to remember. If your instruction is clearly defined, then what to review will be clear as well.

FIGURE 7–12 *continued*

FOLLOW-UP ACTIVITIES

1. Select a chapter from a content subject text and prepare a study guide for the chapter. Make sure to design the guide in such a way that it will require active student participation.
2. Obtain a sample test from a content subject teacher. Modify the test so it includes a liberal number of items that do not require extensive written responses.
3. Prepare an example of "T-Notes" for a chapter from a content subject textbook.
4. Visit the web site for the Council for Exceptional Children to obtain additional ideas for making accommodations in the area of social studies and science.
5. Interview a teacher using the "*Curriculum Adaptation Quick Screen*" to identify modification or adaptations needed to meet a target student's learning and behavior needs. Be prepared to describe both the student and the current instructional practices in the classroom.

Think Sheets

Think sheets provide a way for students to visually process what they need to do. Think sheets are working sheets that help students plan their compositions, and they make it easy for students to see what it is they have to work on. Because think sheets are more visually spatial than traditional outlines, it is easier for students to see the whole project as well as how each part fits into the whole. For stories, students would first write their ideas for characters, setting, etc. If students are writing a persuasive paper, they would write their statement of belief, the reasons for their belief, and the facts to support their belief on their think sheet.

Mnemonic Devices for the Writing Process

Mnemonic devices can help students remember the steps involved in the writing process. Some examples include: POWER = plan, organize, write, edit, and rewrite; TREE (for persuasive paper) = Choose your Topic, list your Reasons, Explain your reasons, write your Ending—the restatement of your statement belief (Topic, Reasons, Explain, Ending).

Writing Fluency

Use Invented Spelling. When students don't know how to spell a word: They spell as much as they can, underline it, and keep going. At a stopping point, they raise their hand and the teacher gives them the correct spelling. (Note: While this technique helps with writing fluency, teachers should not depend on it to improve student spelling. To improve spelling, students need a good spelling program in which they are taught how to spell the high-frequency words they have trouble with. Allow students to write on the computer, but teach them keyboarding skills. That way their attention is not focused on typing but on the thought process for writing.) Put key vocabulary words on the board so that students can copy them easily when they need to use the words.

The Editing Process

Proofreading. Teach students the COPS rule. First, look for capitals; second, overall appearance; third, punctuation; and fourth, spelling. Having students work in groups or pairs is a good strategy for helping them learn about audience awareness in their writing. This technique can help students put themselves in the point of view of their reader, and develop perspective of needs of the reader. The writer reads the first draft to the group or to a partner, who listens and comments on content using the following format:

I hear ____________. The listener tells the reader what she thinks is the gist or main idea of the story. This feedback lets the writer know if he or she has communicated the main ideas.
I like ____________. Here the listener tells the writer what he likes about the piece, which is a good opportunity for positive reinforcement.
I want to know ____________. With response, the listener helps identify holes or gaps in the story. This technique avoids criticism while giving the writer valuable feedback.

Self-Evaluation

Have students use a scoring card for their writing in which they can determine whether they have included all the necessary components in their work. For example, if students are writing factual paragraphs, their scoring card might include: Does the paragraph have more than one sentence? Does the paragraph have a topic sentence? Do all the sentences relate to the topic? Do all the sentences tell facts, not opinions? When students reread the composition, they can circle yes or no for each question. If they circle no, the students can go back and correct their error.

FIGURE 7–13 Adaptations to Help Students Master the Writing Process

CHAPTER 8 EVALUATING BEHAVIOR PROBLEMS

KEY WORDS

psychosocial concerns
behavioral excesses
physiological factors
inappropriate controls
attention deficit hyperactivity disorder
inappropriate responses to self
"mistaken goals" of misbehavior
inappropriate contingencies
behavioral deficits
baseline estimate

OBJECTIVES

After reading this chapter you should be able to:

1. describe the role academic deficiencies and ineffective instructional practices play in explaining many behavior problems.
2. identify common sources of behavior problems.
3. provide examples of commercially available assessment tools that can be used to evaluate student behavior.
4. develop effective teacher-made assessment tools for evaluating behavior.
5. use results from behavioral assessment to develop an intervention plan.
6. describe several strategies for monitoring effectiveness of behavioral interventions.

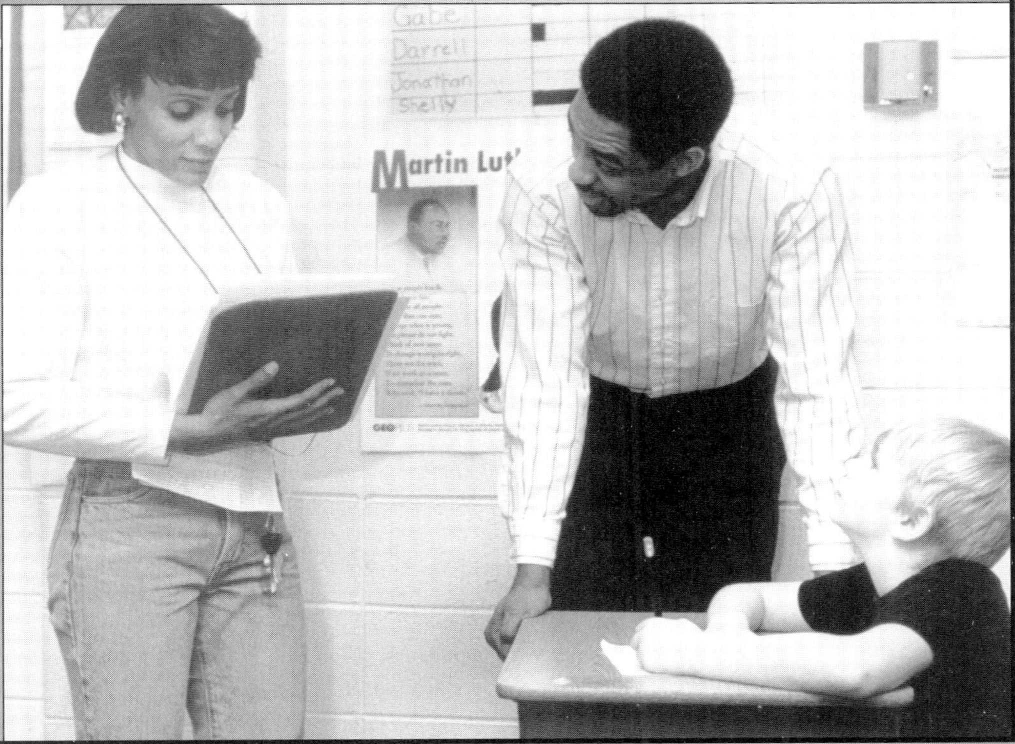
Gabe
Darrell
Jonathan
Shelly
Martin Lut

Angela Cobb has been a special education teacher at Buxton Elementary School for seven years. She has enjoyed her experiences there and has come to be known as one of the school's most effective teachers. So it was no surprise when Mr. Santos, the fourth-grade teacher, turned to Ms. Cobb for assistance in dealing with Zachary Walter, a student whose disruptive behavior was creating real problems in Mr. Santos' class.

According to Mr. Santos, Zachary usually started each day without incident, but within the first half-hour or so of class he would begin to misbehave. His misbehaviors generally started with Zachary fidgeting in his seat and playing with items on his desk. Then he would start talking to those around him, calling out, and leaving his seat. Mr. Santos usually responded to these behaviors by reminding Zachary of the class rules and redirecting him to whatever task was at hand. This usually worked, but only for a few minutes.

Mr. Santos reported that Zachary's behavior would usually grow increasingly worse as the day progressed. The misbehavior seemed to be most pronounced during group spelling lessons and when Zachary was supposed to be completing independent seat assignments in reading. He also indicated that Zachary frequently ran into problems during small-group reading instruction, which was surprising to Mr. Santos because Zachary was one of only five students working directly with the teacher. According to Mr. Santos, "Most students are on their best behavior when they're sitting directly under the watchful eye of their teacher. But not Zachary!"

When asked by Ms. Cobb to describe in greater detail what happens when Zachary misbehaves during reading group, Mr. Santos responded that it usually begins when he has the students take turns reading from their reading text.

He added, "Zachary calls out words when it's not his turn to read and often makes derogatory statements to other students, such as, 'That's not right. How can you miss such an easy word?' or 'Even my little sister would know that word!' When it's Zachary's turn to read he rushes through the material and makes frequent errors. This starts a chain-reaction because I have to stop and correct him and he hates being corrected so he usually makes a smart comment or two, and then I have to correct him again. The same sort of thing happens when we work on answering comprehension questions. Zachary jumps in with answers when it's not his turn. When it is his turn, he blurts out a response almost without thinking. Half the time he's not even on the same question as everyone else because he's rushed ahead to the next item. As I'm sure you can imagine, this totally disrupts the reading group and is frustrating to me and the other students."

Ms. Cobb agreed this sounded like a frustrating situation and promised to help Mr. Santos come up with an effective way to deal with the problem. She suggested that the logical next step would be for her to gather some additional information to help her study the problem more systematically. She planned to begin this process the next day.

In Chapter 6 we discussed approaches to evaluating academic performance in a number of key subject areas. This chapter focuses on another critical concern for teaching students with disabilities in general education settings: evaluating *behavior*. In addressing this concern we will show how the same strategies we introduced for gathering information on classroom environments and academic skills (i.e., asking, observing, and examining) can be used to evaluate student behavior.

UNDERSTANDING BEHAVIOR PROBLEMS

INSTRUCTIONAL ISSUES

There is no question that misbehavior can have a serious effect on student learning. Misbehavior creates disruptions in the flow of classroom activities and thus interferes not only with the learning of the student who is misbehaving, but also with the learning of the class as a whole. When behavior problems occur routinely, they set the tone for the class and greatly influence classroom climate. To get a sense of just how true this is, talk to any teacher who has had to deal with a student who exhibited ongoing behavior problems. That teacher is likely to tell you that until the student's behavior was successfully brought under control, the student played a major role in determining how each day would unfold. Or as one teacher put it, "I hate to admit it, but I was always a little bit pleased when Devon was absent. I knew this meant things would go much smoother for the day and we would get so much more accomplished." To avoid this situation, teachers must learn how to address classroom behavior problems.

To effectively manage behavior problems, the teacher must learn to view student misbehavior within the larger context of the classroom setting and the instructional program. Classrooms vary significantly with respect to physical arrangement, daily routines, and general climate, all of which can have an important effect on student performance and student behavior (Evans, Evans, & Mercer, 1986). As we showed in Chapter 5, classrooms can also differ in terms of instructional factors related to curriculum, instructional materials, instructional delivery, and evaluation procedures. Often student misbehavior is linked directly to the instructional program being used. When instruction fails to focus on the "right stuff" for an individual student, or when a mismatch exists between how instruction is delivered and how the student learns best, the student is likely to have a difficult time succeeding in the class. It is easy to see how this might cause the student to become frustrated and could result in misbehavior. Indeed, the literature suggests that when effective instructional practices are used, teachers have fewer discipline problems in their classrooms (Emmer & Evertson, 1994 ; Kindsvatter, Wilen, & Ishler, 1988; Walker & Walker, 1991).

REFLECTION BOX 8–1

Classroom and instructional variables can play an important role in explaining many behavior problems. This is certainly an issue Ms. Cobb will want to explore in gathering information to understand Zachary's behavior problems. What do you think she should plan to look for during her inquiry?

Figure 8–1 presents an overview of some common instructional variables that can contribute to behavior problems (Foster-Johnson & Dunlap, 1993). Because variables such as these are frequently the source of misbehavior, we recommend that they be among the first to be explored in analyzing behavior problems, particularly because most of them are under the immediate control of the teacher and can be easily modified. According to Kauffman, Mostert, Trent, and Hallahan (1998), the most productive way for teachers to deal with behavior management problems is to view them as *instructional* problems. When viewed this way, the most important consideration for teachers becomes how to arrange the classroom environment and the instructional program to avoid misbehavior and to *teach* appropriate behavior.

Given that instructional variables help to explain behavior problems, a critical first step in dealing with such problems is to determine whether the problem is related primarily to classroom setting or to instructional issues. A good starting point for exploring this issue would be to use the framework presented in Figure 8–1 as a guide or checklist for identifying potential problem areas in the classroom. Items on the list can be turned into a series of questions to be answered using the target classroom as a context. Respondents might include the classroom teacher, the special educator, or both working together.

Kauffman et al. (1998) suggest that the following questions also can guide teachers in determining the likely source of the behavior problem:

- How relevant to or functional in the student's life is the curriculum?
- Do I have the option of teaching something more relevant and functional?

FIGURE 8–1 Instructional Variables that Can Lead to Misbehavior

Note: *From* Teaching Students with Special Needs in Inclusive Settings *(2nd ed., p. 161), by T. E. Smith, E. A. Polloway, J. R. Patton, and C. A. Dowdy, 1998, Boston: Allyn & Bacon. Copyright 1998 by Allyn & Bacon. Reprinted with permission.*

Variables Linked to Classroom Environment

- High noise level
- Poor seating arrangement
- High levels of stimulation or activity
- Frequent disruptions
- Inadequate structure or rules
- Inconsistent expectations

Variables Linked to Curriculum and Instruction

- Unpredictable schedule
- Inadequate availability of assistance
- Unclear directions
- Materials that are visually confusing or cluttered
- Activities that are too difficult
- Activities that are too lengthy
- Activities that are highly repetitive
- Few opportunities for student input
- Few variations in the mode of instruction

- To what extent could I individualize instruction?
- How successfully is this student or group performing in the curriculum?
- Am I using an approach to teaching that provides too little structure, too much direction, too little positive feedback, or too much criticism?
- How frequently do my students have an opportunity to respond to academic tasks?
- What percentage of the time are my students actually actively engaged in learning?
- How and how much could I change the teaching strategies I use? (p. 6).

If it appears that a behavior problem is indeed related to instructional variables, interventions to address the problem will need to focus on the types of concerns discussed in Chapters 5 and 6. If student misbehavior does not appear to be related to instructional variables, then intervention efforts will need to emphasize strategies described in this chapter and also in Chapter 9.

COMMON CAUSES OF BEHAVIOR PROBLEMS

Even if classroom environment and instructional factors are eliminated as causes of misbehavior, a variety of other sources might be contributing to classroom behavior problems. Some of these are complex, difficult to understand, and not easily controlled by a teacher. Others are fairly uncomplicated and rather easy to control. Effective management of problem behaviors requires an understanding of these other common sources of misbehavior. This can help the teacher separate surface misbehaviors from more significant behavior problems that may require therapeutic interventions outside the classroom. It also provides an essential context for collecting and interpreting assessment data. In the discussion that follows we address some of the more common causes of behavior problems. Numerous sources are available that provide a much more detailed discussion of this topic (See, for example, Levin & Nolan, 1996, or Kauffman et al., 1998).

ENVIRONMENTAL AND PSYCHOSOCIAL CONCERNS. Student misbehavior is often directly related to environmental problems, that is, significant problems at home. A student may lack adequate food or clothing, or may live in substandard housing. Supervision or consistent routines may be lacking at home. Perhaps the approach to discipline used in the home is inappropriate, either because too few rules or limits have been established or because misbehavior is handled in ways that are overly punitive. Or it may be that the dynamics of the family as a whole are dysfunctional. Problems such as these can translate into misbehavior in the classroom. A teacher may not be able to change the negative conditions existing in a student's home, but it is, nevertheless, important for the teacher to understand these conditions and take them into account when developing a plan to address student misbehavior.

A second source of student misbehavior may involve **psychosocial concerns,** including a student's values, motivation to learn, and task preferences (Burden, 1995). Obviously, these factors will affect the sorts of activities and assignments a student is interested in—and when the focus of a classroom does not match well with a student's values, motivation, and preferences, the result is often inattentiveness and dis-

Many students with attention deficit disorders have high levels of motor activity.

tractibility. In many cases, this in turn leads to behavior that can disrupt the academic activities of the entire class.

PHYSIOLOGICAL CONCERNS. Student misbehavior also can derive from a host of **physiological factors**. These may involve fairly obvious conditions such as chronic illnesses or physical and sensory disabilities, or they might not be so apparent. Health problems such as allergies, reactions to drugs or medications, and nutritional deficiencies also can have a negative effect on students' classroom behavior and their ability to participate in instructional activities. It is important to remember, however, that although teachers may not be able to control these physiological factors, they can minimize the effect of such factors by taking them into account in planning instructional programs for the student.

One physiological problem of note is the neurologically based condition referred to as **attention deficit hyperactivity disorder** (ADHD). Attention deficit hyperactivity disorders are considered to be associated with dysfunction in the areas of the brain that control motor activity and attention. ADHD is characterized by high levels of seemingly nonpurposeful motor activity hyperactivity and difficulty sustaining attention. ADHD is also characterized by a tendency to respond to stimuli quickly and without reflection (a condition referred to as impulsivity). Youngsters who have ADHD are not likely to follow directions well, work independently, take turns, or move quietly from one task to another. Structured classroom activities, such as participating in a discussion or completing a group drill-and-practice activity are likely to be problematic—yet unstructured class activities may prove equally difficult. A detailed discussion of ADHD and strategies for addressing this problem in the classroom are outside the scope of this textbook, but a number of excellent sources provide extensive information on these topics. Two that are especially helpful are Levine (1990) and Rief (1993).

REFLECTION BOX 8–2

A number of psychosocial and physiological factors can contribute to behavior problems in the classroom. Is there any evidence in the description of Zachary's behavior that suggests psychosocial or physiological factors might be involved? How would you follow up on this concern?

MISTAKEN IDEAS ABOUT MISBEHAVIOR. Another way of understanding the causes of student misbehavior is to consider the misbehavior from the standpoint of the purpose it serves. According to Dreikus, Grunwalk, and Pepper (1982), all behavior is purposeful. It would follow therefore, that to deal appropriately with student misbehavior, teachers need to figure out the purposes behind the behavior. Dreikus suggests that like all social beings, students want to be accepted. When students misbehave, it is often because they have **"mistaken goals" of misbehavior** and believe the behavior will get them the recognition and acceptance they want. Well-behaved students have discovered that one way to gain recognition and acceptance is by following rules and completing work successfully. Students who do not feel capable of obtaining recognition through these channels or have not been successful in earlier attempts, may do just the opposite to be recognized. These students seek acceptance through behaviors that, while annoying, provide them with a sense of identity and belonging.

Dreikus et al. (1982) have identified four "mistaken goals" that characterize the misbehavior of many students. These are (1) seeking attention from either teacher or peers, (2) exerting power or control over a situation, (3) seeking revenge or getting even, and (4) hiding inadequacy by refusing to participate. Once a teacher understands the underlying goal of a student's misbehavior, an appropriate plan for dealing with the behavior can be developed.

REFLECTION BOX 8–3

Which of the "mistaken goals" of behavior might Zachary be exhibiting? What additional information would you plan to gather to help you verify this concern?

Student misbehavior can be related to more than one factor; behavior problems are not necessarily linked to a single cause. Kauffman et al. (1998) suggest that teachers begin the process of dealing with behavior problems by first trying to identify the principal explanation for the student misbehavior. Teachers should ask, "Although a variety of things may be contributing to this student's misbehavior, what do I think is the *key* contributing factor?" The answer will have important implications for how the teacher proceeds and the extent to which the teacher gets involved in addressing the problem. Some causes of behavior problems, such as biological factors or conditions in the home, will be beyond the teacher's direct control, but the teacher still has an important role to play in alerting other professionals who may need to become involved (e.g., health-care providers, social workers, counselors, and so on). Other causes of behavior problems, particularly psychological variables or factors within the classroom environment, offer the greatest opportunity for teacher control.

CONSIDERING DEGREES OF SEVERITY

In addition to understanding the sources of behavior problems, effective management of such problems also requires an appreciation of their severity. Misbehaviors can range from mild to severe; the degree of severity associated with a problem should influence the response to it.

According to Evans, Evans, and Schmid (1989), several factors should be considered in evaluating the severity of misbehavior. These include appropriateness, magnitude, intent, and the extent to which a behavior differs from what is expected in a particular setting. The need for intervention and the comprehensiveness of that intervention are determined by the severity of the problem. Indeed, anyone who has spent time in a classroom knows that nearly all students are guilty from time to time of not doing what they are supposed to be doing, but such "lapses" do not constitute significant behavior problems and can be handled in a fairly straightforward manner. Teachers may choose to ignore those minor misbehaviors, or the "intervention" may involve little more than redirecting the student. When a student's misbehavior is more persistent or pronounced, however, a more structured plan to deal with the problem will have to be developed.

Table 8–1 describes a continuum of misbehaviors in terms of three broad categories of severity. This information can be used as a context for considering the degree of response called for in a particular situation.

REFLECTION BOX 8–4

Zachary's behavior is clearly creating a problem for Mr. Santos. How severe a problem do you think it is in terms of the continuum presented in Table 8–1?

TABLE 8–1 Continuum of Misbehavior: Examples of Mild, Moderate, and Severe Misbehavior

Mild Misbehavior	Moderate Misbehavior	Severe Misbehavior
Minor defacing of school property or property of others	Unauthorized leaving of class	Defacing or damaging school property or property of others
Talking back	Abusive conduct towards others	Theft, possession, or sale of another's property
Talking without raising hand	Noncompliance	Truancy
Getting out of seat	Smoking or using tobacco in class	Being under the influence of alcohol or narcotics
Disrupting others	Cutting class	Selling, giving, or delivering alcohol, narcotics, or weapons to another person
Sleeping in class	Cheating, plagiarizing, or lying	Assault or verbal abuse of the teacher
Tardiness	Using profanity, vulgar language, or obscene gestures	Assault of other students
Throwing objects	Fighting	Incorrigible conduct, noncompliance
Eating in class		Sexual misconduct
Making disruptive sounds		Coercion

Note: *From* Effective Teaching Methods *(3rd ed., p. 24), by G. D. Borich, 1998, Upper Saddle River, NJ: Merrill/Prentice Hall. Copyright 1998 by Prentice Hall. Adapted by permission.*

ASSESSING BEHAVIOR PROBLEMS

ANALYSIS OF ANTECEDENTS AND CONSEQUENCES

As we pointed out in Chapters 5 and 6, the first step toward developing an academic intervention plan is to gather diagnostic information that helps clarify the nature of the problem. In those chapters, we suggested that teachers begin the assessment by broadly surveying suspected problem areas, then using survey information as a guide to help pinpoint the problem. This same approach is useful in dealing with misbehavior, although behavior problems are sometimes more difficult to understand than academic problems and solutions rely even more heavily on *precise* analysis. This approach—survey first, then go more deeply—can help a teacher distinguish between surface misbehaviors and more serious behavior problems, and can provide a systematic framework for analyzing the more serious problems.

In Chapter 6 we emphasized that to effectively evaluate an academic problem the teacher should begin by considering what elements constitute that academic domain. We begin the same way in evaluating behavior problems. Kauffman et al. (1998) have suggested a number of elements that constitute the domain of behavior problems (i.e., areas in which information needs to be gathered for the teacher to understand a behavior problem). These have been summarized in Figure 8–2. The first element is definition—the teacher must define the problem behavior to be evaluated. This may seem like a relatively easy task, but it can be problematic. Often students will display an array of inappropriate behaviors, some of which might overlap (e.g., talking to other students while moving around the classroom without permission). Care must be taken to describe which target behavior will be the focus of the assessment, and to define the target behavior as explicitly as possible in terms that are both observable and measurable. For example, indicating that the evaluation will focus on "Joe's disruptions during class time" is far too vague because the term *disruptions* is subject to a range of interpretations. Specifying particular disruptive behaviors such as "calling out without raising his hand" or "leaving his seat without permission," leaves little room for confusion as to when the behavior occurs.

The next two elements in Figure 8–2 involve the factors that precede or follow misbehaviors (antecedents and consequences). It is important for the teacher to gather information that describes the context in which the misbehavior typically occurs. The teacher needs to explore antecedent patterns of events that might predict when, where, and under what conditions the misbehavior is most likely and least likely to occur. In addition, the teacher should gather information about what happens as a result of the misbehavior, what the consequences are, and how the student seems to benefit from the misbehavior. Teachers should keep one note of caution in mind, however, when gathering information about the consequences of misbehavior. Often the "payoff" for the student may not be readily apparent or may involve something that others might view as negative or punishing. Consider Tim, for example, who verbally challenges his teacher regularly and is frequently sent to the principal's office as a punishment. After carefully considering this pattern of behavior, Tim's teacher realized that what she considered to be a "punishment" for Tim (being sent to the office) was actually something he found attractive; Tim's trips to the principal's office allowed him to get out of doing classwork and gave him an opportunity to eavesdrop on what was happening in the school's main office, a bustling center of activity. For Tim, these two positives far outweighed the punitive value of any lecture the principal might deliver before sending him back to class.

The next element in Figure 8–2 that should be addressed in gathering assessment data is the extent to which the target misbehavior is associated with a chain of events

FIGURE 8–2 Factors to Consider in Analyzing Behavior Problems

Definition: What is the behavior of interest?

Antecedents: What events or conditions precede the behavior?

Consequences: What are the consequences of the behavior?

Event chains: Is the behavior linked to a chain of events?

Escalation: Are there events causing misbehavior to escalate?

in which antecedents and consequences interact with each other in sequence. One example involves Leah, an eighth-grade student who frequently makes inappropriate comments during her social studies class. In attempting to determine the cause of Leah's misbehavior, Ms. Shelton, the social studies teacher, realized that Leah's tendency to make comments was most pronounced when students were taking turns reading aloud from the social studies textbook. When Leah was called on to take a turn, she frequently responded by making a wisecrack. Others in the class would laugh at such comments, which typically resulted in Ms. Shelton redirecting the group, reprimanding Leah, and calling on another student. Leah would continue to call out wisecracks for the remainder of the class period. At first Ms. Shelton thought Leah's continued misbehavior was in response to her reprimand, but after studying the problem further she realized that something quite different was going on. It became clear that the triggering event for Leah's misbehavior was her being asked to read aloud. The consequence of Leah's wisecrack was twofold. She (1) received considerable positive attention from her peers in the form of laughter, and (2) did not have to read from the textbook. Once these two things happened, they in turn became triggering events (or antecedents) for subsequent misbehaviors; that is, they set the stage for Leah to continue to wisecrack to keep getting attention from her peers and avoid all invitations to read aloud.

The final element shown in Figure 8–2 is the extent to which the misbehavior is characterized by an escalating pattern of aversiveness. According to Kauffman et al. (1998), behavior problems may begin because some antecedent is aversive (i.e., something the student would like to avoid). The behavior problem is an attempt by the student to control the situation; the response by the teacher is an attempt to regain control over the student. Each uses increasingly powerful negative consequences. For instance, a student is engaging in a particularly disruptive behavior and receives some form of punishment from his teacher. This leads the student to increase (rather than decrease) the level of misbehavior in an attempt to maintain control of the situation. The teacher, in turn, responds by increasing the severity of punishment. A cycle is established with each party intensifying their responses in an attempt to emerge as the "winner."

ASSESSMENT TOOLS

Information useful in assessing behavior problems can be gathered in a variety of ways, although the basic tools used in assessing behavior problems will involve the same strategies that have been discussed in previous chapters (asking, observing, and examining). Tools range from screening instruments to highly detailed assessment systems and include commercially available or teacher-made materials. According to Kauffman et al. (1998), survey or screening-type assessments often can provide all the information a teacher needs to deal successfully with mild behavior problems. More serious problems will almost always require additional diagnostic assessments, and often, additional personnel involved in the assessment.

One popular method for gathering preliminary information on behavior problems is to use a *behavioral* checklist or rating scale, which asks respondents from various groups (e.g., teachers, parents, peers, the students themselves) to provide their perceptions of the target student's behavior. These behavioral checklists or rating scales are different from the *observation* checklists and rating scales described in Chapter 5. Those observation checklists and rating scales provide direct information about the presence, frequency, and intensity of target behaviors based on examination of behaviors as they occur within a specific timeframe. Behavioral checklists and rating scales used for behavior screenings produce indirect information by asking others to provide *impressions* of behavior patterns based on their observations and experiences with the student over time.

It is not difficult to construct a behavioral checklist or rating scale. It is simply a matter of identifying the field of behaviors on which you would like to gather information, including behaviors derived solely from the teacher's experience, or pulled from various source materials. For example, one special education teacher referred to a textbook from a college methods class and found a behavioral continuum that described behaviors associated with various classroom situations. She developed the rating scale shown in Figure 8–3 by listing the behaviors identified in her textbook and providing a numerical scale for capturing respondents' perceptions. The left side of the scale describes a series of "appropriate" classroom behaviors while the right side of the scale lists "inappropriate" behaviors. Respondents mark the scale by indicating where the target student's behavior falls relative to these two anchor points. Analysis of the rankings provides a quick overview of areas which are problematic for the student. The example shown in Figure 8–3 indicates that the target student's problems primarily involve issues related to staying on task and completing her work.

Other examples of teacher-made checklists and rating scales that can guide you in creating your own instrument can be found in Chapter 5. Examples of several commercially available instruments are presented in Table 8–2. In addition to these measures, there also are a number of rating scales that deal primarily with behaviors associated with attention deficit hyperactivity disorder and hyperactivity, such as the *Teacher Questionnaire* and the *Parent Questionnaire* developed by Conners (1969).

Another method for gathering preliminary information about a behavior problem is to conduct interviews with the target student and the student's teachers, peers, and parents. Of course, effective interviewing is not simply a matter of sitting down with a respondent and having a conversation. Thought must be given to the specific questions that will be posed or, at the very least, the topic areas that will be explored. According to Kanfer and Grimm (1977), interview questions and topics should include the following:

- The extent to which the individual demonstrates **behavioral deficits** such as limited understanding of what constitutes appropriate behavior, poor knowledge of social skills, limited skill in self-monitoring, and unresponsiveness to common reinforcers.
- The presence of **behavioral excesses,** such as anxiety and the need for high levels of activity or novelty.
- The extent to which **inappropriate controls** within the environment may be a factor such as limited opportunities for the student to practice appropriate behavior or ineffective classroom organization and management procedures.
- The extent to which the student demonstrates **inappropriate responses to self** such as misinterpretation of one's abilities and unrealistic expectations or goals.

- Evidence of **inappropriate contingencies** such as lack of reinforcement for desired behavior, reinforcement for inappropriate behavior, or random reinforcement.

One final note of caution if the target student will be the respondent when using checklists, rating scales, or interviews. Because these methods involve self-report and focus on a negative concern (i.e., misbehavior), it is possible that the student will not

Respondent: C.C. Richardson

Target Student: K. Haynes

Date: 4-2-99

Please rate the student on each of the items listed below based on your experiences with the student. Each item represents a continuum that ranges from an appropriate behavior listed on the left side to an inappropriate behavior listed on the right side. Your ratings indicate where on this continuum the student's behavior typically falls. Put a check next to any item you think you cannot accurately assess.

Appropriate Behavior						Inappropriate Behavior
Begins tasks promptly	1	2	3	4	(5)	Begins tasks only after being reminded
Attends to task	1	2	3	(4)	5	Does not attend to task
Completes task	1	2	3	(4)	5	Fails to complete task
Follows directions	1	(2)	3	4	5	Does not follow directions
Completes neat work	1	(2)	3	4	5	Does careless or sloppy work
Remains in seat	1	2	3	(4)	5	Is out of seat
Speaks when appropriate	1	2	(3)	4	5	Interrupts others
Talks with permission	1	2	(3)	4	5	Talks out of turn
Tells the truth	(1)	2	3	4	5	Does not tell the truth
Speaks appropriately	(1)	2	3	4	5	Uses abusive language
Interacts with others	1	(2)	3	4	5	Withdraws from others
Participates without constant reassurance	1	(2)	3	4	5	Requires constant reassurance
Makes realistic statements about self	(1)	2	3	4	5	Makes self-deprecating comments
Cries at appropriate times	(1)	2	3	4	5	Cries at inappropriate times
Engages in appropriate age play	(1)	2	3	4	5	Engages in inappropriate age play

FIGURE 8–3 Teacher-Made Rating Scale

Appropriate Behavior						Inappropriate Behavior
Initiates contact with others	1	(2)	3	4	5	Fails to initiate contact with others
Initiates contact with group	(1)	2	3	4	5	Fails to engage in group activities
Is persistent	1	2	3	4	(5)	Gives up easily
Shares with others	(1)	2	3	4	5	Refuses to share with others
Appearance of mood fits setting	(1)	2	3	4	5	Appearance of mood does not fit setting
Is ill with apparent cause	(1)	2	3	4	5	Claims illness without apparent physical cause
Accepts consequences of behavior	1	(2)	3	4	5	Runs away
Cooperates with others	(1)	2	3	4	5	Is uncooperative
Follows class and school rules	1	(2)	3	4	5	Is disorderly in class and school
Resolves problems without violence	1	(2)	3	4	5	Is aggressive
Respects property	(1)	2	3	4	5	Destroys property
Resolves problems appropriately	1	(2)	3	4	5	Exhibits temper tantrums
Takes things with permission	1	(2)	3	4	5	Steals
Completes own work	1	(2)	3	4	5	Cheats

FIGURE 8–3 *continued*

Note: *From* Behavior and Instructional Management: An Ecological Approach *(p. 22), by W. H. Evans, S. S. Evans, and R. E. Schmidt, 1989, Boston: Allyn & Bacon. Copyright 1989 by Allyn & Bacon. Adapted by permission.*

be totally candid, choosing instead to provide misleading or even inaccurate information. As a result it is a good idea to get verification of the information provided by the student from at least one other source.

Another approach to gathering information about behavior problems is through *direct observation*. Several approaches to direct observation were presented in Chapter 5. The methods ranged from simple and general to highly structured and focused. Obviously, if the goal of the assessment is to obtain *preliminary* information about a problem behavior, the best choice would be a method that will provide a general impression of the problem and help define its parameters. Once such information has been obtained, more highly structured observations can be conducted as necessary. Structured observations are also useful for following up on information obtained from checklists, rating scales, and interviews. For example, Figure 8–4 shows a set of questions which might be explored through a teacher interview. These same questions might, in turn, guide direct observation of the student in various situations using the case-study technique described in Chapter 5. If the problem needs to be explored further, information obtained from the interview and the preliminary observation can be used to develop a more structured observation plan.

TABLE 8–2 Selected Behavioral Checklists and Rating Scales

Instrument	Characteristics
Behavior Rating Profile–2 (Brown & Hammill, 1990)	• A battery of six subtests or components: Teacher Rating Scale, Student Rating Scales (home, school, and peer) and Sociogram. • Each component can be used independently or combination. Norms for ages 6 through 18. • Classification of student's behavior as within the "normal" range or within a "deviant" range.
Test of Early Socioemotional Development (Hresko & Brown, 1984)	• An extension of the BRP for younger children, ages 3 through 7. • Four components: Student Rating Scale, Teacher Rating Scale, Parent Rating Scale, and Sociogram.
Social–Emotional Dimension Scale (Hutton & Roberts, 1986)	• A school-based rating scale • For students 5 years through 18 years. • Identifies risk related to six types of problem behavior: avoidance of peer interaction, aggressive interaction, avoidance of teacher interaction, inappropriate behavior, depressive reaction, and physical/fear reaction.
Child Behavior Checklist (Achenbach & Edelbrock, 1981, 1984)	• Available in both parent's report and teacher's report forms. • Can be used with students ages 6 through 16. • Relates items to problem factors such as: social withdrawal, anxious, unpopular, obsessive–compulsive, immature, self-destructive, hyperactive, and aggressive.
Behavior Evaluation Scale 2 (McCarney & Leigh, 1990)	• Yields behavioral information from the teacher about students in kindergarten through twelfth grade • Five subscales: learning problems, interpersonal difficulties, inappropriate behavior, unhappiness/depression, and physical symptoms/fears.
Revised Behavior Problem Checklist (Quay & Peterson, 1987)	• Distinguishes among behavior not observed, observed but mild, and observed and severe. • Used for students in kindergarten through eighth grade • Can be completed by parents, teachers, or anyone familiar with the student. • Problem behaviors are classified as (1) conduct disorders, (2) personality disorders, (3) inadequacy or immaturity, and (4) subcultural (socialized) delinquency.

If information will be collected using observation, careful planning is important. While it is true that teachers are constantly observing student behavior, such observations usually are not systematic enough to provide much more than general impressions. To obtain the type of information needed for program planning, a sound observation plan must be developed. Procedures that can be followed to develop such a plan are outlined below:

FIGURE 8–4 Questions to Guide an Interview or Direct Observation

Note: *From* Characteristics of Behavior Disorders of Children and Youth *(6th ed., p. 173), by J. M. Kauffman, 1997, Upper Saddle River, NJ: Merrill/Prentice Hall. Copyright 1997 by Prentice Hall. Reprinted with permission.*

- In what settings (home, school, math class, or playground) is the problem behavior or behavioral deficit exhibited?
- With what frequency, duration, or force does the behavior occur in various settings?
- What happens immediately before the behavior occurs? What seems to set the occasion for the misbehavior?
- What happens immediately after the behavior occurs that may strengthen or weaken it?
- What other inappropriate responses are observed?
- What appropriate behavior could be taught or strengthened to lessen the problem behavior?
- What does the student's behavior communicate to others?

1. *Define the behavior.* Carefully define the target behavior in terms that are both observable and measurable.
2. *Select a measurement system.* Select a measurement system that will capture the specific behavior defined in Step 1. Measurement approaches discussed in Chapter 5 ranged from observer checklists and rating scales to more structured time-based and event-based recording systems. Figure 8–5 can help guide selection of an appropriate observation system. The left portion of Figure 8–5 describes possible measurement options when the goal of the observation is related to determining *how often* a behavior occurs. The right portion is concerned with strategies to use when the main concern involves determining *how*

Checking with parents can help determine if the problem behavior is school specific.

long a behavior lasts. Other factors to consider in selecting a measurement system include the amount of time needed to implement the system; the availability of others who can help; and the extent to which detailed observation data is needed to understand the problem. It is important to remember that some observation systems can be time consuming, especially if the teacher is the only person available for gathering the data. Sabornie and deBettencourt (1997) advise teachers to use measurement systems that are accurate and provide sufficient information to guide program planning, but that are as simple as possible to use. When it does appear that a detailed measurement system is the appropriate choice, we recommend that special and general educators work together to implement the system.

REFLECTION BOX 8–5

Mr. Santos described a range of inappropriate behaviors that Zachary demonstrated on a regular basis. Imagine you are going to observe his reading group. What behavior(s) would you want to focus on and how might you measure the behavior?

3. *Develop an observation schedule.* First, determine how often observations will occur. According to Lewis and Doorlag (1999), factors that should be considered in

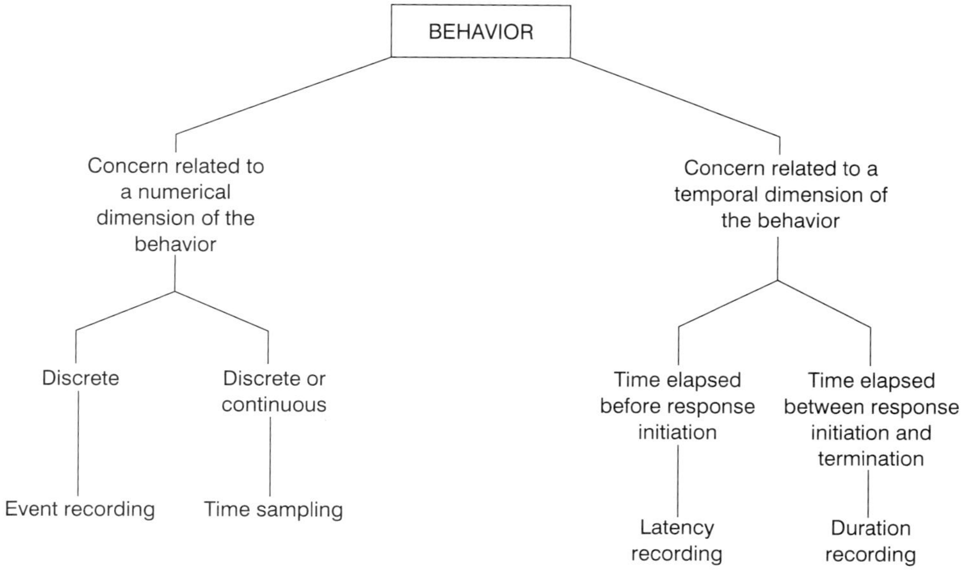

FIGURE 8–5 Procedures for Observing Behavior

Note: *From:* Applied Behavior Analysis for Teachers *(5th ed., p. 127), by P. A. Alberto and A. C. Troutman, 1999, Upper Saddle River, NJ: Merrill/Prentice Hall. Copyright 1999 by Prentice Hall. Adapted with permission.*

making this decision include availability of the target student and the availability of the observer. As a rule, observations should occur frequently to provide an accurate assessment of problem behaviors, but each observation need not be lengthy. Regardless of what type of measurement system is being used, it has been suggested that a minimum of five observations be conducted to provide an accurate baseline estimate of the behavior against which the effects of subsequent intervention efforts can be compared.

Second, determine the context in which observations will take place. Wherever possible, observation schedules should be structured to take into account the times of day and situations when the misbehavior is most likely to occur. A teacher may know, for example, that Joey's disruptive outbursts are more pronounced in the afternoon, especially during math and science class. It would make good sense for the observation schedule to focus heavily on these class times.

4. *Design a data-collection form.* Develop a form that will permit easy recording of what is seen. Obviously, the design of such a form will be closely tied to the type of measurement system being used. For example, a teacher who is planning to gather information using a simple event-based measurement system to see how often a behavior occurs, might prepare a form like the one shown in Figure 8–6. It provides space to record instances of the target behavior over the course of three class periods and can be used to monitor the behavior of several students at one time. The teacher might want to use an event-based system focusing on smaller units of time to get a better feel not only for how often during class time but also for *when* misbehavior occurred. In this case the teacher might use a more elaborate recording form like the one shown in Figure 8–7. It is designed to keep

Date: 9/14/98 Target Behavior: Calling Out

STUDENT	CLASS/TIME Reading (9-9:40)	Spelling (10-10:30)	Math (11:15-11:45)
Joey M.	𝍸 𝍸 𝍸 |	𝍸 𝍸 |||	𝍸 ||
Sandra G.	|||	𝍸 ||	𝍸 𝍸

FIGURE 8–6 Sample Recording Form for an Event-Based Observation System

Observer: S. Gordon

Student: Dewey H.

Target Class: Reading

Target Behavior: Calling out without raising hand

Date: 9/14/98 Start: 9:00 End: 9:45	Interval 5 |	Interval 10 |||	Interval 15 O	Interval 20 ||	Interval 25 卌	Interval 30 卌 |	Interval 35 卌	Interval 40 ||	Interval 45 O	Interval 50
Date: 9/16/98 Start: 9:00 End: 9:45	Interval 5 ||	Interval 10 ||	Interval 15 |	Interval 20 |	Interval 25 ||||	Interval 30 卌	Interval 35 ||||	Interval 40 |	Interval 45 |	Interval 50
Date: Start: End:	Interval ___	Interval ___	Interval ___	Interval ___	Interval ___	Interval ___	Interval ___	Interval ___	Interval ___	Interval ___
Date: Start: End:	Interval ___	Interval ___	Interval ___	Interval ___	Interval ___	Interval ___	Interval ___	Interval ___	Interval ___	Interval ___
Date: Start: End:	Interval ___	Interval ___	Interval ___	Interval ___	Interval ___	Interval ___	Interval ___	Interval ___	Interval ___	Interval ___

FIGURE 8–7 Sample Recording Form for an Event-Based Observation System with 5-Minute Intervals

track of the number of misbehaviors observed during 5-minute intervals across a class period. The form in Figure 8–7 shows that this student tends to begin class without too many problems, but the misbehavior escalates as class proceeds.

Figure 8–8 shows an example of a recording form for a duration measurement system. It provides space in the first column for the teacher to indicate the date of the observation, with additional space provided in the next two columns for the teacher to note when the target behavior was initiated and when it ended. At the conclusion of the observation, the teacher uses the final column on the form to indicate the duration of the target behavior. A similar form for a latency measurement system is presented in Figure 8–9. It provides space for the teacher to note when the triggering cue was given (in this case, a verbal reminder for the student to sit down) and when the response to the cue occurred.

5. *Develop a form for charting or graphing outcomes.* For data gathered through observation to be most meaningful, it should be summarized on a chart or graph. The chart or graph provides a "picture" of the student's performance over time and a context for making instructional decisions. Specific guidelines for charting and graphing academic outcome data were presented in Chapter 6; they can be applied to behavioral outcomes as well.

INTERPRETING ASSESSMENT DATA

It should be clear by now that the process of assessing behavior problems involves more than the collection of data from a variety of sources. As information is gathered it must be systematically analyzed in much the same fashion as one would analyze outcomes from an academic assessment. In both cases, the teacher is looking for pat-

Student Kelly Observer Mr. Walters

Behavior Time spent collecting reading materials

Date	**Time**		**Duration**
	Response initiation	**Response termination**	
9/16/98	10:05	10:07	2 min.
	10:15	10:21	6 min.
9/17/98	10:00	10:04	4 min.
	10:13	10:16	3 min.

FIGURE 8–8 Duration Recording Data Sheet

Student *Geri* Observer *Mr. Rice*

Behavior *Time elapsed before taking seat*

Date	Time		Latency
	Delivery of cue	Response time	
3/12/99	9:02	9:05	3 min.
	9:12	9:13	1 min.
	9:18	9:20	2 min.
	(9:20 – Reading	group with teacher)	

FIGURE 8–9 Latency Recording Data Sheet

terns that point to certain possibilities and eliminate others. Both types of assessment call for the teacher to form an impression or hypothesis as to the source of the problem and to test out this belief by gathering additional information as necessary.

Regardless of what type of assessment tool is used to gather information, it is helpful to summarize the findings in a way that will facilitate understanding of the problem and formulating a hypothesis. An example of a form that can serve this purpose is presented in Figure 8–10. Notice that the form has been organized around the critical categories of information likely to be explored through various means. The form provides space for recording the most important findings of the assessment activities. It can be used to record key impressions of probable cause of the problem and to outline steps that should be taken to confirm these impressions. The value of a form like the one shown is that it provides a single vehicle for consolidating information that may have been recorded in a number of separate locations.

SUMMARY

Behavior problems can have a serious effect on the academic achievement of students who misbehave, as well as on others in the class. In this chapter, we showed that some misbehaviors are primarily related to instructional issues, and that when instruction is carefully tailored to meet student needs, misbehavior is often no longer a concern.

We also emphasized the importance of understanding the range of noninstructional factors that can contribute to student misbehaviors. These included a variety of con-

FIGURE 8–10 Summary Form for Analyzing a Behavior Problem

Student: Leah P.

Behavior: Making inappropriate comments/"wisecracks"

Antecedents

Students participate in round-robin reading activity
Teacher calls on Leah to take a turn

Consequences

Classmates laugh, activity interrupted
Teacher reprimands, redirects group, calls on another student

Chains of Events

Oral reading leads to wisecrack
Wisecrack leads to laughter and not having to take a turn

Follow-up Procedures

Explore what happens when students are allowed to volunteer to read instead of being called on. Does wisecracking continue?

cerns related to environmental and psychosocial factors, physiological factors, and misguided goals. Guidelines were presented for conducting behavioral assessments that stressed the need to move from broad survey-type assessments to more highly structured assessments, particularly in situations involving complex behavior problems. Guidelines were also presented for interpreting assessment data and developing intervention plans.

Although not all causes of behavior problems are under a teacher's immediate control, many sources of misbehavior can be rather easily modified—provided the teacher knows what to look for and how to use this information to develop sound intervention plans.

FOLLOW-UP ACTIVITIES

1. Interview a teacher about a student who is misbehaving in class. Based on that interview, create a list of things you would want to examine further in a classroom observation.
2. Develop an observation procedure that would allow you to assess a student's tendency to call out in class without raising a hand. Your procedure should include all five steps discussed in this chapter.

3. Interview a teacher about a student who is misbehaving in class. Based on that interview create a list of steps you would take to determine if the problem is primarily related to classroom setting or instructional issues.
4. Assume you are working with Mr. Santos to find a way of dealing with Zachary's behavior problems. Create a list of interview questions that would help you explore the source(s) of Zachary's difficulties.
5. Volunteer to help a teacher study a behavior problem by gathering observation data for the teacher. Begin by jointly identifying the problem behavior you will be targeting. Then develop a procedure for observing the behavior and recording the outcomes. You should complete a minimum of three observations using this procedure. Results from the observations should be charted, analyzed, and shared with the classroom teacher.

CHAPTER 9 BEHAVIOR MANAGEMENT STRATEGIES

KEY TERMS

Good Behavior Game
interdependent group-management procedures
Group Timeout Ribbon
cognitive behavior management
group token systems

OBJECTIVES

After reading this chapter the student will be able to:

1. outline strategies for promoting positive behavior with groups of students, including students with disabilities.
2. describe the steps to implement several group behavior management strategies in a general education classroom.
3. identify strategies to help students manage their own behavior.
4. describe strategies to help develop effective communication between home and school.

As Mr. Evans, the seventh-grade teacher at Canter School, looked over the list of students he had been assigned this year he realized he had a very diverse group. He was a little upset! He did not want to spend most of each day monitoring student behavior. He preferred to teach—especially the new information he picked up at a science workshop during the summer. He wanted his students to manage their own behavior and be accountable for their work, but he knew that before that could happen, he would need to start by implementing many management procedures.

Mr. Evans was scheduled to co-teach with Ms. Rice, the seventh-grade team's special education teacher, for a double science period—second and third periods. He feared that the large size and diversity of the class would keep the students from being able to pull together to accomplish his science goals. Ms. Rice also noticed that Billy was in that class. Sixth-grade teachers had all talked about Billy the previous year: He was frequently off-task and encouraged any student seated next to him to act inappropriately. Mr. Evans wondered whether he would have to set up a special behavior management system just for Billy. The year had not even begun and he already dreaded it. On the first day of classes, he asked to meet with Ms. Rice to talk about group-management techniques.

The purpose of this chapter is to offer guidelines for managing student behavior by actively, carefully, and creatively applying approaches to classroom management. Suggestions will be given on how to implement several management procedures and how to monitor the success of these procedures. Procedures for group management, self-management, and home-school management are discussed. Together, these procedures provide a strong foundation for teachers to collaboratively and effectively promote a positive classroom climate.

All teachers spend a good part of each day monitoring student behavior. As part of this routine, teachers should also be actively monitoring their own behavior—that is, they should be reflecting on whether they have chosen the most effective classroom management procedures for each situation and class. Effective classroom management techniques increase all students' learning, but especially the learning of students with cognitive, learning, and behavior difficulties. To assist in monitoring their own management procedures, teachers can ask a co-teacher or colleague to observe their use of classroom management techniques. Then the two teachers can work together to design the most effective procedures for creating a positive classroom environment.

In many classrooms, positive behaviors can be promoted by implementing whole-group strategies. In other situations, self-management or home-school management strategies are more appropriate. When to implement and how to begin using effective whole-group, self-management, and home-school strategies are described in the following sections.

GROUP MANAGEMENT TECHNIQUES

When a behavior problem is common to several students in the class, an appropriate intervention strategy is an **interdependent group-management procedure** (Hayes, 1976). In this strategy, a predetermined contingency is applied to the entire class based on appropriate behavior demonstrated by the entire class. Potential contingencies or reinforcers for appropriate group behavior include free time, class parties, class trips, class games, visits to the playground, or special privileges (e.g.,"hat days"). Interdependent group-management procedures promote positive behaviors among all students in the class. Procedures to choose from include **group token systems, the Good Behavior Game,** and the **Group Timeout Ribbon** procedure.

GROUP TOKEN SYSTEMS

In a **group token system** (Kazdin, 1977), the group is given a predetermined number of tokens, which are placed in full view of students and within easy reach of the teacher (Salend, 1997). Tokens can be checkers, colored strips of paper, marks on the chalkboard, or play money. The tokens should not be easily counterfeited; the teacher doesn't want to give students an opportunity to undermine the system. Once tokens have been given to the group, one token is removed from the pile each time any student in the group displays behavior that has been previously defined as inappropriate. If any tokens remain at the end of a predetermined time, the agreed on reinforcement is delivered to the entire group.

When beginning this kind of management system, the teacher should want to guarantee initial success; one way to do that is to start each time period with a large number of tokens allocated to the group, then gradually reduce the number of tokens initially given.

A group token system can be used by the teacher to promote positive behaviors among all students in the class.

A token economy is another group token system that can be used to manage the behavior of a whole class. In this technique, students earn individual privileges and other rewards for displaying desired classroom behaviors. To implement a token economy system, take the following steps:

1. Clearly identify the behaviors for which students will receive tokens. A small number of behaviors should be specified and defined in observable terms (e.g., keeping hands to oneself, bringing to class all needed equipment). Post the list in a prominent spot in the classroom. Students can be involved in the selection of the behaviors.
2. Select a "token" to use—points, poker chips, play money, or checks on a card. Select a token that is not easily counterfeited and that students will not play with or lose.
3. Assign a value to each behavior. Some behaviors can be worth more points or tokens than others.
4. Determine the rewards the students can earn. Selection of the rewards will vary depending on the age and interests of the students and different rewards will be earned with different numbers of tokens. The number of tokens needed for each reward should be clearly posted in the classroom. Be sure that at least one reward is available for the minimum number of tokens that can be earned. For example, if a student is caught exhibiting good behavior once and earns one token, there should be at least one reward available for that one token earned. Figure 9–1 illustrates a token economy menu.
5. Explain the token system to the students. Demonstrate the system with several examples, and make sure students understand it. Explain to the students the predetermined time span during which the tokens will be used (e.g., during math class).

FIGURE 9–1 Token Economy Menu

Note: *From* Including Students with Special Needs: A Practical Guide for Classroom Teachers *(p. 417), by M. Friend and W. Bursuch, 1996, Boston: Allyn & Bacon. Copyright 1996 by Allyn & Bacon. Adapted by permission.*

Reward List

Item		Points Needed
1.	10 minutes free time	10
2.	15 minutes of computer time	50
3.	5 stickers each	50
4.	A cartoon pencil each	75
5.	Lunch in classroom with friends	100
6.	A book	125
7.	Helping first-grader in art for a specified time	150
8.	Discount movie pass	150
9.	Lunch, at a pizza restaurant with a teacher, principal, or other adult	300

10 points can be earned each day.

6. Establish a clear and systematic manner in which the students can exchange their tokens for rewards. Teachers can set up a weekly auction at which students would bid on items using the currency earned. Teachers may allow students to borrow tokens from one another, although this needs to be closely monitored for abuse.

To make a token economy work effectively, a teacher needs to be flexible and to adjust the system as needs arise. Token systems afford teachers a number of advantages (Polloway & Patton, 1997). Tokens are flexible reinforcement that can be awarded frequently and consistently. Furthermore, token systems not only enhance the smooth running of a classroom, they can also enhance students' learning of academic concepts related to banking, government, retail shopping, and communications.

THE GOOD BEHAVIOR GAME

The **Good Behavior Game** is regarded as a powerful strategy for increasing positive behaviors in the classroom (Barrish, Saunders, & Wolf, 1969). In this game, the class is divided into two competing teams, the competition revolving around good behavior. It is important, however, to make sure that the competition itself does not become the major focus of the game. The procedure includes the following steps:

1. Divide the class into two teams. Each sits on one side of the classroom and competes against the other to display the greatest number of positive behaviors (or the least number of negative behaviors) during a class period or other predetermined time during the day.
2. Describe the target behaviors. If the purpose is to decrease the number of negative behaviors, target behaviors such as out-of-seat behavior would be modeled and explained. If positive behaviors are targeted, examples such as promptly putting materials away or remembering to put papers in correct folders would be explained. Several examples and nonexamples would be provided. Do not make the behavior list too lengthy; students will forget which behaviors are on the list and the teacher will have difficulty monitoring all the behaviors.
3. Set a time period each day for the game to be played, for example, in social studies class. Do not make the time period too long or directly after an active period, like lunch or recess. Also, do not try to implement the Good Behavior Game during a teacher-directed lesson (e.g., a lecture) because it will be too difficult to manage; rather, use it during independent seatwork or student group activity time, when you have more flexibility to observe behavior and assign tokens.
4. Let students know when you notice a target behavior being displayed. Tell the person displaying the behavior, and tally a point—against that person's team if the focus is on negative target behaviors, or in favor of that person's team if the focus is on positive, appropriate behaviors. Mark tallies in full view of all students.
5. At the end of the time period, tally the points and announce which team has won.
6. Give the winning team a reward. To maintain interest, vary the rewards that can be earned.

Teachers can have teams earn points toward a larger reward to be given at the end of the day or week. Encouraging positive behavior rather than noting negative behavior makes this a stronger procedure. One advantage of the Good Behavior Game is that it provides positive behavior models to children who need models to perform appropriately.

> **REFLECTION BOX 9–1**
>
> **Use of a procedure like the Good Behavior Game can be an effective way to improve student behavior classwide. Because it uses a team format, however, this procedure can have drawbacks. What do you think are the limitations of this method and how would you adjust the procedure to address these concerns?**

GROUP TIMEOUT RIBBON

The Group Timeout Ribbon (Salend & Gordon, 1987) uses a ribbon, or a ribbon-substitute such as a piece of colored paper or a piece of string, placed in the classroom within the teacher's reach and where all students can see it. When the students in the class are behaving appropriately, the ribbon remains in view and tokens are dispensed to the students. If a student misbehaves, the ribbon is removed for 1 to 5 minutes, during which time students lose the opportunity to receive tokens (Salend, 1997). When the group has behaved appropriately for the predetermined number of minutes, the ribbon is returned and once again tokens can be earned. If students continue acting inappropriately, the time the ribbon is removed is extended. To use the Group Timeout Ribbon in your class, you should follow these steps:

1. Determine the type of ribbon you will use.
2. Define the behaviors you will consider to be "misbehavior." Do not make this list too long, as the students may not remember all of them.
3. Explain the game to students and model appropriate and inappropriate behaviors.
4. Make sure a clock with a minute hand is in clear sight of both the teacher and the students.
5. Select a predetermined time during the day when the game will be played. Do not make the time period too long in the beginning. Determine the length of the time period during which the ribbon will be removed if an inappropriate behavior occurs.
6. Make a token reward list and post it in a prominent spot in the classroom. Determine the length of time during which tokens can be exchanged for the rewards.

The Group Timeout Ribbon encourages the entire class to display positive behaviors. If one or two students are consistently misbehaving, peer pressure may encourage them to change it. However, to avoid making this student a scapegoat, the teacher must be certain that the misbehavior is not physiologically based, and that the appropriate behaviors are within the student's repertoire.

The advantage of implementing a group-management system is that the teacher can encourage positive cooperative behaviors in the whole group. But to use group-management systems effectively requires not only careful planning but also a willingness on the part of the teacher to make adjustments when necessary.

REFLECTION BOX 9–2

The Group Timeout Ribbon procedure is designed to reward students based on the performance of the group as a whole. It is based on the presumption that all students will work hard to contribute to the good of the group, either by monitoring their own behavior or by assisting others who may need help. While this can be an effective behavior management approach, the procedure can have drawbacks, particularly when some members of the group evidence significant behavior problems. What might be some of the limitations of this method and how would you adjust the procedure to address these concerns?

SELF-MANAGEMENT TECHNIQUES

Another set of techniques to encourage positive behavior involves having individual students take an active role in managing and monitoring their own behavior. These self-management strategies are referred to as **cognitive behavior management** strategies. These strategies teach students to monitor their own cognitive behavior, judge its appropriateness, and change the behavior, if necessary (Meichenbaum, 1977). Cognitive behavior management strategies encourage students to be their own coaches. Cognitive behavior management strategies can be useful in a variety of school settings and outside the school, as well. They have the capacity to produce dramatic improvements in students' behavior, and because they help students shift to an internal locus of control, the changes in behaviors associated with this approach seem more likely to persist and generalize both to other situations and to other behaviors.

A number of self-management systems can be used to help students manage their own classroom conduct. Three types are most commonly used: (1) self-monitoring, (2) self-reinforcement, and (3) self-evaluation. In self-monitoring, the student is taught to be alert to the occurrence of a specific behavior (e.g., inattention to task) and to record when it happens. The student then determines whether a change is needed and makes the change in behavior as necessary.

To begin instruction in self-monitoring, the teacher must be sure that the student can accurately describe and recognize the targeted behavior. The teacher can describe the appropriate behavior and model both the desirable behavior and contrasting examples of undesirable behavior. In addition, the student should demonstrate both the appropriate and inappropriate behaviors. The next step is to develop a method for the student to self-record. A sheet of paper with a picture of the appropriate behavior can be used with young children. Under the picture can be two columns, one for yes (meaning "I was performing the right behavior") and another for no (meaning "I was not performing the right behavior"). Atop the picture can be a question such as, "Am I paying attention?" (see Figure 9–2 for an example of a self-monitoring sheet). For older students, a simple tally sheet can be devised and put on a card that can be placed on the student's desk. At the end of a specified time period, the card can be slipped back into the student's pocket. Initially, a self-monitoring tape that cues the student to self-assess is helpful; the tape consists of prerecorded tones (e.g., piano notes) that sound at random intervals. A multichannel programmable kitchen timer could be substituted for the tape. The tape is turned on to provide an audio cue at random intervals throughout the period designated for self-monitoring. When the tone sounds, the student stops and asks, "Was I paying attention?" The student then places a check in the appropriate column. The student then returns to work until the next tone sounds and the self-monitoring procedure is repeated.

When students' level of on-task behavior has increased to a stable level, the teacher may begin to wean them away from the tape. The students can continue to be praised for progress in performing the desired behavior and instructed to self-record whenever they think about behavior rather than at the sound of the tone. Later, the students could be told to praise themselves rather than self-recording the judgment. If the level of performance drops to an undesirable level at any time during this weaning process, reinstate the most recent component to be removed until performance has returned to an appropriate level. The weaning process works best if it is gradual.

Two recommendations need to be made on the applicability of self-monitoring procedures. First, research suggests that self-monitoring is not applicable to situations involving new learning (Hallahan & Sapona, 1983). The ideal setting for implementing self-monitoring procedures is during seatwork when a student is completing review or practicing independent activities. Second, research suggests only limited success in self-regulating a behavior that has little or no value to the individual (Kanfer & Gaelick, 1986). The value that an individual attaches to the target behavior may directly affect self-monitoring outcomes (Reid, 1996).

The second type of cognitive behavior management strategies used frequently in classrooms are self-reinforcement procedures. In this approach, students self-evaluate, then judge whether they have earned a reward (Friend & Bursuck, 1996). For example, students who receive a perfect score on an assignment or test can give themselves 10 points; a less-than-perfect score might earn 5 points. Students who accumulate 50 points or more can choose a reward from the reinforcement menu posted in the class.

Teaching students to self-evaluate assists them in developing an awareness of what is required of them. Students can be taught to self-monitor, reflect, predict, and transfer skills as they attempt to study and evaluate the tasks given to them. Teachers should demonstrate the proper ways to check answers, monitor behavior, reflect on results, and transfer skills to new situations. As students get older they are expected to learn at home,

Date ______________________

Was I Paying Attention?

	YES	NO
1		
2		
3		
4		
5		
6		
7		
8		
9		
10		
11		
12		
13		
14		
15		
16		
17		
18		
19		
20		

	YES	NO
21		
22		
23		
24		
25		
26		
27		
28		
29		
30		
31		
32		
33		
34		
35		
36		
37		
38		
39		
40		

FIGURE 9–2 Self-Monitoring Sheet

Note: *From* Improving Attention Through Self-Monitoring *(App. B), by D. P. Hallahan, J. W. Lloyd, & L. Stoller, 1982, Charlottesville, VA: University of Virginia Learning Disabilities Research Institute. Copyright 1982 by University of Virginia Learning Disabilities Research Institute. Adapted by permission.*

in school, and in the workplace with less support; teaching self-evaluation will assist them in setting goals independently and in monitoring their achievement of these goals.

Teaching students to use cognitive behavior management strategies involves three main steps (see Figure 9–3 for guidelines on how to teach students to use cognitive behavior management).

Teaching students to self-evaluate assists them in developing an awareness of what is required of them.

REFLECTION BOX 9–3

What advantages do you think Mr. Evans would gain by using cognitive behavior management methods instead of the group-management strategies discussed in the previous section? Are there times when one approach would be a better option than the other?

HOME-SCHOOL MANAGEMENT TECHNIQUES

An important component in any ongoing management program is coordination between home and school. To become a truly effective manager of behavior, the teacher must cultivate skills in working with parents (Kauffman, Mostert, Trent & Hallahan, 1998). Parents can provide valuable support for teachers' efforts. However, teachers must take the lead in establishing and maintaining positive working relationships with parents. Collaboration between the school and family in the decision-making processes involving the student's program was formally established with the passage of Public Law 94-142 in 1975, and continues today under IDEA (Gartland, 1993). But communication must not stop once the annual IEP is signed. Instead, teachers

FIGURE 9–3 Teaching Cognitive Behavior Management Strategies

Note: *From* Including Students with Special Needs: A Practical Guide for Classroom Teachers *(p. 432), by M. Friend & W. Bursuck, 1996, Boston: Allyn & Bacon. Copyright 1996 by Allyn & Bacon. Adapted by permission.*

Generally, teaching CBM strategies to a student with special needs has three main steps.

1. ***Discuss the strategy with the student and present a rationale for its use.*** If you cannot clarify for the student what the strategy is or how it works, the student might not be a good candidate for CBM. To check student understanding, ask the student to explain the approach back to you.
2. ***Model for the student what you expect.*** For example, you might use an old sample of the student's work and walk through the strategy you plan to use. Alternatively, you might use a brief role-play to demonstrate to the student how to self-monitor behavior and record it.
3. ***Provide practice and feedback.*** For this step, the teacher rewards the student for correctly using the approach until the student is confident enough to use the approach without such support. If you are teaching a student to use CBM, use reinforcers with the student until he or she has mastered the strategy. Even after mastery, it is helpful to reward the student periodically for successfully self-managing behavior. This step can be enhanced by helping the student develop a personal reinforcement menu so rewards are meaningful. Parents and colleagues can sometimes assist in implementing this step.

might begin each school year surveying parents to determine their preferences regarding communication. That will alert parents to the importance you place on maintaining communication channels between home and school. Figure 9–4 provides an example of a home-school communication preference inventory.

Several procedures facilitate communication between parents and teachers: the telephone, the note sent home, and the parent conference. Each of these is discussed in the following sections.

THE TELEPHONE

Telephone communication requires minimal time and effort, especially if you can get in the habit of having brief conversations. Some teachers use a recording on their home telephone answering machine to keep parents up to date with the progress of the class (Heward & Chapman, 1981). Some teachers provide their home telephone number for evening calls within a designated period of time (e.g., "Please call between 9:00 and 9:30 P.M.). Regular phone calls from the teacher can help keep parents aware of their child's progress in behavior as well as in academics. Regardless of the outcome of the conversation, teachers should always end the telephone call by thanking the parent for the time spent talking with them.

To ensure that your child is receiving the best possible educational program, it is important that there be ongoing communication between your family and school professionals. It is our experience that families have different preferences for what kinds of information will be shared. In addition, families have different preferences regarding how and how often such information will be transmitted. The purpose of this inventory is to determine your preferences for communicating with the professionals in our program.

Listed below are a number of examples of types of information that can be shared. There are also a number of examples of strategies or methods that can be used to share this information.

In the box immediately to the right of each item, please rate your level of interest:

put "0" if it has no interest to you at all
put "1" if the information has a low priority for you
put "2" if the information has a medium priority for you
put "3" if the information has a high priority for you

Next, please tell us how often you would like to share information:

put a "√" under "never" if you are not interested at all
put a "√" under "occasionally" if you would like to share the information 3-5 times per year
put a "√" under "regularly" if you would like to share the information 2-3 times per month
put a "√" in the appropriate box under "frequently" to indicate whether you would like to share the information weekly or daily

For example, Mr. Christopher filled out the first item this way:

	Priority	Never	Occasionally	Regularly	Frequently	
					Weekly	Daily
Special accomplishments	3	☐	☐	☐	√	☐

Mr. Christopher's answer tell us that it is important for school professionals and his family to share his son's special accomplishments and that he would like to communicate weekly about such accomplishments.

Please indicate your preferences on the following chart.

Type of information I would like shared between home and school

	Priority	Never	Occasionally	Regularly	Frequently	
					Weekly	Daily
Special accomplishments	☐	☐	☐	☐	☐	☐
Special activities (e.g., going to the park, going swimming, visiting grandma)	☐	☐	☐	☐	☐	☐
Progress toward educational goal/grades	☐	☐	☐	☐	☐	☐
Toileting habits	☐	☐	☐	☐	☐	☐

FIGURE 9–4 Home-School Communication Preference Inventory

	Priority	Never	Occasionally	Regularly	Frequently Weekly	Frequently Daily
Eating habits	☐	☐	☐	☐	☐	☐
Sleeping/napping habits	☐	☐	☐	☐	☐	☐
Behaviors	☐	☐	☐	☐	☐	☐
Other (please specify)						
______________________	☐	☐	☐	☐	☐	☐
______________________	☐	☐	☐	☐	☐	☐
______________________	☐	☐	☐	☐	☐	☐
______________________	☐	☐	☐	☐	☐	☐
Home-School Communication Strategies						
Home visits	☐	☐	☐	☐	☐	☐
Informal school visits	☐	☐	☐	☐	☐	☐
Individual conferences	☐	☐	☐	☐	☐	☐
Group conferences	☐	☐	☐	☐	☐	☐
Telephone calls	☐	☐	☐	☐	☐	☐
Log books, notes	☐	☐	☐	☐	☐	☐
Newsletters	☐	☐	☐	☐	☐	☐
Audiotapes	☐	☐	☐	☐	☐	☐
Report cards	☐	☐	☐	☐	☐	☐
Other (please specify)						
______________________	☐	☐	☐	☐	☐	☐
______________________	☐	☐	☐	☐	☐	☐
______________________	☐	☐	☐	☐	☐	☐
______________________	☐	☐	☐	☐	☐	☐

FIGURE 9–4 continued

Note: *From* Families, Professionals, and Exceptionality: A Special Partnership *(pp. 142–143), by A. P. Turnbull & H. R. Turnbull III, 1997, Upper Saddle River, NJ: Merrill/Prentice Hall. Copyright 1986 by Merrill/Prentice Hall. Adapted by permission.*

Another use of the telephone is to organize a telephone tree. Telephone trees are efficient ways to get information to all parents of students in a class. The teacher calls one parent, and that parent calls two or three other parents, each of whom call two or three more, and so on. Telephone trees are frequently used in team sports and most parents are familiar with the procedures.

WRITTEN COMMUNICATIONS

Some parents prefer written communications to telephone calls. Notes can be one-way (teacher to parent, such as a progress report or good behavior award sent home by the teacher, or parent to teacher, such as a note informing the teacher of a change in medications or an important incident in the family) or two-way (as in a daily notebook or log that travels back and forth between school and home). Daily correspondences have the advantage of providing continuous monitoring of home and school activities. Their disadvantage is the amount of time involved in maintaining them for both the parents and the teacher. Weekly or periodic reports may be much more manageable ways to disseminate essential information to parents. Newsletters can also be used when the same information can be or needs to be distributed to parents of all students in the class. Teachers can enlist parent volunteers to assist in the production of a newsletter; students can also help. All these systems can be tailored to address a child's behavior or academic achievement in the class.

PARENT CONFERENCES

Perhaps the most common way to communicate with parents is through the parent conference. Because conferences bring parents and teachers face to face, they are among the most effective methods to facilitate productive partnerships. Conferences can have a significant effect on student performance, particularly if they occur more frequently than at the beginning and end of the school year.

There are two types of conferences: planned and unplanned. Planned conferences have three phases: (1) preconference planning, (2) conference, and (3) postconference review. During the preconference planning, parents are notified about the conference in a written note. Parents need to know the purpose of the meeting (the agenda), the date and time, the expected length, and the location. If parents need to prepare for the conference, materials should be sent home for them to read well ahead of the date of the meeting. Teachers should prepare for the conference by reviewing the student's record, assessing the student's progress, and noting areas of concern. They should also gather specific examples of the student's work and other materials that help to explain the student's program (e.g., textbooks, curriculum-based tests, and so on). The teacher might also prepare an outline for the meeting, including the items to be discussed and a list of other professionals who may need to be invited. If others will be coming to the conference, it would be helpful for the teacher to inform them of their role during the conference. The agenda is important, not only because it alerts participants about the topics to be covered but also because it serves to structure and sequence topics in the conference. The agenda should be flexible, however, to accommodate last-minute additions and changes. Figure 9–5 shows an outline for preparing a conference agenda.

During the conference, the teacher should establish an atmosphere that enhances communication among the parents and the educators. The meeting might begin with a preview of the agenda, clarifying the purpose and the role of each participant. The teacher might acknowledge appreciation to the parents and staff for their interest and attendance and encourage all parties to take an active role in the meeting. Parents should be invited to share information by using open-ended questions and demonstrating an interest in their responses in both verbal (e.g., saying "uh-huh," reflecting back to the parent what was just said) and nonverbal ways (e.g., maintaining eye contact and open posture). Information should be shared using jargon-free language and the conference should begin with some positive comments about the student's progress, providing specific examples. All participants should be aware of and responsive to the effect of what is being said on the parents.

After the conference, if the student was not present, the teacher should spend some time reviewing the meeting with the student. Also, the outcome of the conference should be shared with other professionals involved in the student's program. Notes from the conference should be recorded and filed as soon after the conference as possible so details are not forgotten. Such items as the time, location, participants, agenda topics, nature of the interactions, and decisions made should be included in those notes.

Unplanned or impromptu conferences or meetings are a different matter. Before they come up, teachers need to consider what sorts of meetings are acceptable and what sorts are not, given the other demands on the teachers' time and energy. For example, one teacher may decide that telephone calls at home on weeknights are acceptable, but impromptu conferences at the grocery store are not. A second may not want to talk on the home telephone, but may be willing to be interrupted by a parent stopping by during the school day. Teachers must set their parameters, then seek support from the school administration early in the school year. The administration should inform parents of your preferences both orally and in written form to avoid any misunderstandings. Other professionals in the building can provide suggestions on how to deflect meetings that a teacher does not want to have. Most important, a teacher must stay organized! Well-organized files, data sheets, and permanent records can make the difference between disastrous and successful unplanned conferences. It is also helpful to have on hand an up-to-date file of community resources and other helpful agencies.

"Although teachers and parents readily acknowledge the importance of schools and homes working together, there are a number of barriers to home–school collaboration" (Ysseldyke & Algozzine, 1995 p. 487); some of these are listed in Figure 9–6. Teachers need to work to overcome barriers to home-school communication by using some of the strategies discussed in the above sections. A successful parent–teacher partnership provides benefits for the professional, the parents, and most important, the child.

Conference Outline

Date 2-15-99 Time 4:30–5:00

Student's Name Jeremy Wright

Parents' Name(s) Barbara and Tom

Teacher's Name Tim G.

Other Staff Present None

Objectives for Conference: (1) Show graph of J's reading progress, (2) find out about spelling program, (3) get parents' ideas: intervention for difficulties on playground/in gym, (4) share list of books of leisure reading.

Student's Strengths
- good worker academically, wants to learn
- excited about progress in reading fluency

Area(s) Where Improvement is Needed:
- continue w/spelling at home
- arguments & fighting w/other kids

Questions to Ask Parents:
- Interactions w/friends while playing in neighborhood?
- How would they feel about f'dback from classmates re: playground/gym behavior?
- Consequences?

Parent's Responses/Comments:
- very pleased w/reading – want to build on it
- wondering how long w/in-home spelling?
- willing to give rewards at home: playground/gym

Examples of Student's Work/Interactions:
- graph of corrects/error per min: reading
- weekly pre- & post-test scores: spelling

Current Programs and Strategies Used by Teacher:
- reading: silent read, two 1-min time trials, self-charting comprehension practice
- spelling: practice w/tape recorder, self-checking

Suggestions for Parents:
- continue spelling games (invite friends)
- show interest in/play fantasy games (Dung. & Dragons) w/J

Suggestions from Parents:
- Try using some high-interest spelling words (e.g., joust, castle)
- Matt & Amin could help with playground/gym program

Follow-up Activities: (Agreed to in conf)

Parents:
- Continue to play spelling game 2 nights per week
- Take J to library for adventure books

Teacher:
- Ask J for high-interest words & use 3-4 in his weekly list.
- Develop peer intervention strategy w/Matt, Amin & J (group contingency?)

Date Called for Follow-up and Outcome: Feb. 26 (Friday)

FIGURE 9–5 Parent-Teacher Conference Agenda Outline

Note: *From* Exceptional Children *(p. 605), by W. L. Heward, 1996, Upper Saddle River, NJ: Merrill/Prentice-Hall. Copyright 1996 Merrill/Prentice Hall. Reprinted by permission.*

FIGURE 9–6 Barriers to Effective Home–School Collaboration

- Parents and teachers have negative stereotypes of each other.
- Parents feel intimidated by the number of professionals and the unfamiliar terminology.
- Parents believe teachers know what is best and do not want to be co-participants in their child's educational program
- Teachers sometimes do not make the time to meet with parents and fully explain the student's program.
- School meetings may conflict with parent's work schedule.
- Teachers and parents may have different values and may come from different cultural backgrounds.
- Parents may not come to school because they cannot afford to take time from work or pay for child care.
- Teachers and parents may blame each other for the student's failure.

SUMMARY

This chapter offered guidelines in managing student behavior. Suggestions included group management, self-management, and home-school management strategies. Together these procedures provide a strong foundation for teachers to collaboratively and effectively maintain a positive classroom climate.

FOLLOW-UP ACTIVITIES

1. Develop a list of possible rewards for students in a third-grade, seventh-grade, and tenth-grade class. Be prepared to discuss the strategy you followed in developing your lists.
2. Interview an elementary-level teacher concerning techniques that teacher uses to manage student behavior. Complete a second interview with either a middle-grade or high school teacher. Make sure to have each teacher talk about the strengths and weaknesses of the methods they use, especially in terms of logistical issues. Be prepared to discuss your findings.
3. Review at least two data-based articles dealing with the use of self-management strategies in classroom contexts. Prepare a summary that shows what happened when this approach was used. Make sure to include in your summary any implementation strategies suggested in the articles.

4. Interview two teachers in your school concerning strategies they use to communicate with parents. Be prepared to discuss the strengths and weaknesses of each approach, particularly with respect to specific improvements that could be made.
5. Interview an elementary-level teacher concerning strategies used to manage student behavior. Develop a plan which shows how you would modify this procedure for use with students at the middle-grade or high school level.

REFERENCES

Achenbach, T. M., & Edelbrock, C. S. (1981). Behavior problems and competencies reported by parents of normal and disturbed children aged four through sixteen. *Monographs of the Society for Research in Child Development*, 46 (1, Serial No. 188).

Achenbach, T. M., & Edelbrock, C. S. (1984). *Child behavior checklist—Teacher's reports*. Burlington, VT: University Associates in Psychiatry.

Adler, A. (1964). *Social interest: A challenge to mankind*. New York: Capricorn Books.

Alberto, P. A., & Troutman, A. C. (1999). *Applied behavior analysis for teachers* (5th ed.). Upper Saddle River, NJ: Merrill/Prentice Hall.

Alley, G. R., & Deshler, D. D. (1979). *Teaching the learning disabled adolescent: Strategies and methods*. Denver: Love Publishing.

Anderson, L. W., & Burns, R. B. (1989). *Research in classrooms*. Oxford: Pergamon Press.

Argyris, C. (1964). *Integrating the individual and the organization*. New York: Wiley.

Arter, J. A., & Spandel, V. (1991). *Using portfolios of student work in instruction and assessment*. Portland, OR: Northwest Regional Education Laboratory.

Ashlock, R. B. (1998). *Error patterns in computation: A semi-programmed approach*. (7th ed.). Upper Saddle River, NJ: Merrill/Prentice Hall.

Babcock, N. L., & Pryzwansky, W. B. (1983). Models of consultation: Preferences of educational professionals at five stages of service. *Journal of School Psychology*, 21, 359–366.

Baker, J., & Zigmond, N. (1990). Are regular education classes equipped to accommodate students with learning disabilities? *Exceptional Children*, 56, 515–526.

Ball, E., & Blachman, B. (1991). Does phoneme segmentation training in kindergarten make a difference in early word recognition and developmental spelling? *Reading Research Quarterly*, 26, 49–86.

Barrish, H. H., Saunders, M., & Wolf, M. M. (1969). Good Behavior Game: Effects of individual contingencies for group consequences on disruptive behavior in a classroom. *Journal of Applied Behavior Analysis*, 2, 119–124.

Bateman, B. D., & Chard, D. J. (1995). Legal demands and constraints on placement decisions, In J. M. Kauffman, J. W. Lloyd, D. P. Hallahan, & T. A. Astuto (Eds.), *Issues in Education Placement: Students with emotional and behavioral disorders*, (pp. 285–316). Hillsdale, NJ: Erlbaum.

Bauwens, J., & Hourcade, J. J. (1995). *Cooperative teaching: Rebuilding the schoolhouse for all students*. Austin, TX: PRO–ED.

Bauwens, J., Hourcade, J. J. , & Friend, M. (1989). Cooperative teaching: A model for general and special education integration. *Remedial and Special Education*, 10(2), 17–22.

Berdine, W. H., & Cegelka, P. T. (1995). Collaborative consultation: A key to effective educational delivery. In P. T. Cegelka & W. H. Berdine (Eds.), *Effective instruction for students with learning difficulties* (pp. 19–46). Boston: Allyn & Bacon.

Bergan, J. R., & Tombari, M. L. (1976). Consultant skill and efficiency and the implementation and outcomes of consultation. *Journal of School Psychology*, 14(1), 3–14.

Berliner, D. (1987). But do they understand? In V. Richardson-Koehler (Ed.), *Educator's handbook: A research perspective* (pp. 259–295). New York: Longman.

Bloom, L., & Lahey, M. (1978). *Language development and language disorders*. New York: Wiley.

Borich, G. D. (1996). *Effective teaching methods* (3rd ed.). Upper Saddle River, NJ: Merrill/Prentice Hall.

Bos, C. S., & Vaughn, S. (1998). *Strategies for teaching students with learning and behavior problems* (4th ed.). Boston: Allyn & Bacon.
Brigance, A. H. (1977). BRIGANCE *diagnostic inventory of basic skills*. North Billerica, MA: Curriculum Associates.
Brigance, A. H. (1981). BRIGANCE *diagnostic inventory of essential skills*. North Billerica, MA: Curriculum Associates.
Brigance, A. H. (1983). BRIGANCE *diagnostic comprehensive inventory of basic skills student booklet*. North Billerica, MA: Curriculum Associates.
Brophy, J. E., & Good, T. L. (1986). Teacher behavior and student achievement. In M. L. Wittock (Ed.), *Handbook of research on teaching* (3rd ed., pp. 328–375). Upper Saddle River, NJ: Merrill/Prentice Hall.
Brown v. Board of Education, 347 U.S. 483 (1954).
Brown, L. L., & Hammill, D. D. (1990). *Behavior rating profile—2*. Austin, TX: PRO-ED.
Bruner, J. S. (1975). From communication to language: A psychological perspective. *Cognition*, 3, 255–287.
Burden, P. R. (1995). *Classroom management and discipline: Methods to facilitate cooperation and instruction*. White Plains, NY: Longman.
Caplan, G. (1970). *The theory and practice of mental health consultation*. New York: Basic Books.
Carman, R. A., & Adams, W. R. (1972). *Study skills: A student's guide for survival*. New York: Wiley.
Carnine, D. (1991). Reforming mathematics instruction: The role of curriculum materials. *Journal of Behavioral Education*, 1, 37–57.
Carnine, D. W., Caros, J., Crawford, D., Hollenbeck, K., & Harniss, M. K. (1996). Designing effective United States history curricula for all students. In J. Brophy (Ed.), *Advances in research on teaching, Vol. 6., Teaching and learning history.* (pp. 207–256). Greenwich, CT: JAI Press.
Carnine, D., Silbert, J., & Kameenui, E. J. (1997). *Direct instruction reading* (3rd ed.). Upper Saddle River, NJ: Merrill/Prentice Hall.
Carpenter, R. (1985). Mathematics instruction in resource rooms: Instruction time and teacher competence. *Learning Disability Quarterly*, 8, 95–100.
Cegelka, P. T., & Berdine, W. H. (1995). *Effective instruction for students with learning difficulties*. Boston: Allyn & Bacon.
Chesler, M. A., Bryant, B. I. Jr., & Crowfoot, J. E. (1981). *Consultation in schools: Inevitable conflict, partisanship, and advocacy.* In M. J. Curtis & J. E. Zins (Eds.). *The theory and practice of school consultation*. Springfield, IL: Charles E. Thomas.
Choate, J. S., Enright, B. E., Miller, L. J., Poteet, J. A., & Rakes, T. A. (1995). *Curriculum-based assessment and programming* (3rd ed.). Boston: Allyn & Bacon.
Christenson, S. L., Ysseldyke, J. E., & Thurlow, M. L. (1989). Critical instructional factors for students with mild handicaps: An integrative review. *Remedial and Special Education*, 10(5), 21–31.
Coates, R. D. (1989). The regular education initiative and opinions of regular classroom teachers. *Journal of Learning Disabilities*, 22, 532–536.
Coleman, J. (1966). *Equality of educational opportunity.* Washington, DC: Government Printing Office.
Conners, C. K. (1969). A teacher rating scale for use in drug studies with children. *American Journal of Psychiatry*, 126, 884–888.
Connoley, J. C., & Impara, J. C. (Eds.). (1995). *The twelfth mental measurements yearbook*. Lincoln, NE: Buros Institute.
Conoley, J. C., & Conoley, C. W. (1982). *School consultation: A guide in practice and training.* New York: Pergamon Press.
Cook, L., & Friend, M. (1995). Co-teaching guidelines for creating effective practices. *Focus on Exceptional Children*, 20(3), 1–12.

Cooke, N. L., Heron, T. E., & Heward, W. L. (1983). *Peer tutoring: Implementing classwide programs in the primary grades*. Columbus, OH: Special Press.
Cooper, J. D., Warncke, E. W., & Shipman, D. A. (1988). *The what and how of reading instruction*. Upper Saddle River, NJ: Merrill/Prentice Hall.
Cornwall, A. (1992). The relationship of phonological awareness, rapid naming, and verbal memory to severe reading and spelling disability. *Journal of Learning Disabilities, 25*, 532–538.
Council for Exceptional Children. (1997). Effective accommodations for students with exceptionalities, CEC *Today*, 4(3), 1, 9, 15. Reston, VA: Author.
Davis, A., & Clark, E. G. (1991). *T-Notes and other study skills* (4th ed.) Metamora, IL: Author.
Deno, E. (1970). Special education as developmental capital. *Exceptional Children, 37*, 229–237.
Deno, S. L. (1985). Curriculum-based measurement: The emerging alternative. *Exceptional Children, 52*, 219–232.
Deno, S., Marston, D., & Mirkin, P. (1982). Valid measurement procedures for continuous evaluation of written expression. *Exceptional Children, 48*, 368–371.
Deshler, D. D., Ellis, E. S., & Lenz, B. K. (1996). *Teaching adolescents with learning disabilities: Strategies and methods* (2nd ed.). Denver: Love Publishing.
Dettmer, P., Thurston, L. P., & Dyck, N. (1993). *Consultation, collaboration, and teamwork for students with special needs*. Boston: Allyn & Bacon.
Doboer, A. (1995). *Working together: The art of consulting and communicating*. Longmond, CO: Sopris West.
Doren, M. (1973). *Doren diagnostic reading list of word recognition skills* (2nd ed.). Circle Pines, MN: American Guidance Service.
Doyle, W. (1983). Academic work. *Review of Educational Research, 53*, 159–199.
Dreikurs, R., Grunwald, B., & Pepper, F. (1982). *Maintaining sanity in the classroom*. New York: Harper & Row.
Dunn, L. M. (1968). Special education for the mildly retarded—Is much of it justifiable? *Exceptional Children, 35*, 5–22.
Durrell, D. D., & Catterson, J. H. (1980). *Durrell analysis of reading difficulty* (3rd ed.). San Antonio, TX: Psychological Corp.
Education Amendments of 1974, PL 93-380. 88 Stat. 580
Education for All Handicapped Children Act of 1975, 20 U.S.C. § 1401 *et seq*.
Education of the Handicapped Act Amendments of 1983, PL 98-199.
Elementary and Secondary Education Act, amended by PL 89-750. Sec 161 [Title VI], 80 Stat. 1204 (1966).
Ellett, L. (1993). Instructional practices in mainstreamed secondary classrooms. *Journal of Learning Disabilities, 26*, 57–64.
Ellis, E. S., & Lenz, B. K. (1987). A component analysis of effective learning strategies for LD students. *Learning Disabilities Focus*, 2(2), 94–107.
Ellis, E. S., & Lenz, B. K. (1996). Perspectives on instruction in learning strategies. In D. D. Deshler, E. S. Ellis, & B. K. Lenz (Eds.), *Teaching adolescents with learning disabilities: Strategies and methods* (2nd ed., pp. 9–60). Denver: Love Publishing.
Ellis, E. S., Lenz, B. K., & Sabornie, E. J. (1987). Generalization and adaptation of learning strategies to natural environments: Part 2—Research into practice. *Remedial and Special Education*, 8(2), 6–24.
Emmer, E. T., Evertson, C. M., Sanford, J. P., Clements, B. S., & Worsham, M. E. (1989). *Classroom management for secondary teachers* (2nd ed.). Upper Saddle River: NJ: Merrill/Prentice Hall.
Englert, C. S., & Thomas, C. C. (1987). Sensitivity to text structure in reading and writing: A comparison between learning disabled and non-learning disabled students. *Learning Disabilities Quarterly*, 10, 93–105.

Englert, C. S., Tarrant, K. L., & Mariage, T. V. (1992). Defining and redefining instructional practice in special education: Perspectives on good teaching. *Teacher Education and Special Education*, 15, 62–87.

Englert, C. S., Raphael, T. E., Fear, K. L., & Anderson, L. M. (1988). Students' metacognitive knowledge about how to write informational texts. *Learning Disability Quarterly*, 11, 18–46.

Enright, B. E. (1983). *Enright diagnostic inventory of basic arithmetic skills*. North Billerica, MA: Curriculum Associates.

Evans, S. S., Evans, W. H., & Mercer, C. D. (1986). *Assessment for instruction*. Boston: Allyn & Bacon.

Evans, W. H., Evans, S. S., & Schmidt, R. E. (1989). *Behavior and instructional management: An ecological approach*. Boston: Allyn & Bacon.

Fender, G. (1990). *Learning to learn: Strengthening study skills and brain power.* Nashville, TN: Incentive Publications.

Fender, G. (1996). *Teaching for learning success*. Nashville, TN: Incentive Publications.

Fleischner, J. E. (1994). Diagnosis and assessment of mathematics learning disabilities. In G. R. Lyon (Ed.), *Frames of reference for the assessment of learning disabilities* (pp. 441–458). Baltimore: Paul Brookes.

Foster, G. G., Ysseldyke, J. E., & Reese, J. H. (1975). I wouldn't have seen it if I hadn't believed it. *Exceptional Children*, 41, 469–473.

Foster-Johnson, L., & Dunlap, G. (1993). Using functional assessment to develop effective, individualized interventions for challenging behaviors. *Teaching Exceptional Children*, 25(3), 44–50.

Friend, M., & Bursuck, W. (1996). *Including students with special needs: A practical guide for classroom teachers*. Boston: Allyn & Bacon.

Friend, M., & Cook, L. (1990). Collaboration as a predictor for success in school reform. *Journal of Educational and Psychological Consultation*, 1, 69–86.

Friend, M., & Cook, L. (1996). *Interactions: Collaboration skills for school professionals* (2nd ed.). New York: Longman.

Fuchs, D., and Fuchs, L. (1995). "What's 'special' about special education?" *Phi Delta Kappan*, 76, 522–530.

Fuchs, D., & Fuchs, L. S. (1995). Special education can work. In J. M. Kauffman, J. W. Lloyd, D. P. Hallahan, & T. A. Astuto (Eds.). *Issues in Educational Placement* (pp. 363–377). Hillsdale, NJ: Erlbaum.

Fuchs, L. S., & Fuchs, D. (1986). Curriculum-based assessment of progress toward long- and short-term goals. *The Journal of Special Education*, 20, 69–82.

Gagne, R. M. (1985). *The conditions of learning and theory of instruction* (4th ed.). New York: Holt, Rinehart, & Winston.

Gallessich, J. (1982). *The professional and practice of consultation*. San Francisco: Jossey-Bass.

Gartland, D. (1993). Teacher-parent partnerships: Effective communication strategies. *LD Forum*, 18(3), 40–42.

Gartner, A., & Lipsky, D. K. (1987). Beyond special education: Toward a quality system for all students. *Harvard Educational Review*, 57, 367–395.

Gartner, A., & Lipsky, D. K. (1989). *The yoke of special education: How to break it*. Washington, DC: National Center on Education and the Economy.

Gates, A. I., McKillop, A. S., & Horowitz, R. (1981). *Gates-McKillop-Horowitz reading diagnostic tests* (2nd ed.). New York: Teachers College Press.

Gelfand, D. M., & Hartmann, D. P. (1984). *Child behavior analysis and therapy* (2nd ed.), New York: Pergamon Press.

Gerber, M. M. (1984). Investigations of orthographic problem-solving ability in learning disabled and normally achieving students. *Learning Disability Quarterly*, 7, 157–164.

Gerber, M. M., & Hall, R. J. (1987). Information processing approaches to studying spelling deficiencies. *Journal of Learning Disabilities*, 20, 34–42.

Gerber, P., & Reiff, H. (Eds.). (1994). *Learning disabilities in adulthood: Persisting problems and evolving issues*. Boston: Butterworth–Heinemann.

Germann, G., & Tindal, G. (1985). An application of curriculum-based assessment: The use of direct and repeated measurement. *Exceptional Children, 52*, 244–265.

Gersten, R. M., & Jimenez, R. T. (1998). *Promoting learning for culturally and linguistically diverse students: Classroom applications from contemporary research*. Boston: Wadsworth.

Graden, J. L., Casey, A., & Christenson, S. (1985). Implementing a prereferral intervention system: Part I: The Model. *Exceptional Children, 51*, 377–384.

Graham, S., Boyer-Schick, K., & Tippets, E. (1989). The validity of the handwriting scale from the Test of Written Language. *Journal of Education Research, 82*, 166–171.

Graham, S., & Harris, K. (1993). Teaching writing strategies to students with learning disabilities: Issues and recommendations. In L. Meltzer (Ed.), *Strategy assessment and instruction for students with learning disabilities: From theory to practice* (pp. 271–292). Austin, TX: PRO-ED.

Graham, S., Harris, K. R., MacArthur, C. A., & Schwartz, S. (1991). Writing and writing instruction for students with learning disabilities: Review of a research program. *Learning Disability Quarterly, 14*, 89–115.

Grassen, B., & Carnine, D. (1992). Translating research on text structure into classroom practice. *Teaching Exceptional Children, 24*(4), 48–53.

Graves, D. G., & Sunstein, B. S. (Eds.). (1992). *Portfolio portraits*. Portsmouth, NH: Heinemann.

Greenbaum, C. R. (1987). *The Spellmaster Assessment and Teaching System*. Austin, TX: PRO-ED.

Hallahan, D. P., & Sapona, R. (1983). Self-monitoring of attention with learning disabled children: Past research and current issues. *Journal of Learning Disabilities, 15*, 616–620.

Hallahan, D. P., Lloyd, J. W., & Stoller, L. (1982). *Improving attention through self-monitoring*. Charlottesville, VA: University of Virginia Learning Disabilities Research Institute.

Hallahan, D. P., Kauffman, J. M., & Lloyd, J. W. (1999). *Introduction to learning disabilities* (2nd ed.). Boston: Allyn & Bacon.

Hammill, D. D., & Larsen, S. C. (1996). *Test of written language—3*. Austin, TX: PRO-ED.

Handicapped Children's Protection Act of 1986. 20 U.S.C. § 1401 *et seq*.

Harniss, M. K., Hollenbeck, K. L., Crawford, D. B., & Camine, D. (1994). Content organization and instructional design issues in the development of history texts. *Learning Disability Quarterly, 17*, 235–248.

Harrell, J., & Vallecorsa, A. (1987, September). Characteristics of learning disabled students' written compositions. *National Middle School Association Research Annual*, 76–86.

Harris, A. J., & Sipay, E. R. (1990). *How to increase reading ability: A guide to developmental and remedial methods* (9th ed.). New York: Longman.

Harris, K. R., & Graham, S. (1992). *Helping young writers master the craft: Strategy instruction and self-regulation of the writing process*. Cambridge, MA: Brookline.

Hayes, L. A. (1976). The use of group contingencies for behavioral control: A review. *Psychological Bulletin, 83*, 628–648.

Heilman, A. W., Blair, T. R., & Rupley, W. H. (1998). *Principles and practices of teaching reading* (8th ed.). Upper Saddle River, NJ: Merrill/Prentice Hall.

Henderson, A. T., Marburger, C. L., & Ooms. T. (1986). *Beyond the bake sale: An educator's guide to working with parents*. Washington, DC: National Committee for Citizens in Education.

Heron, T. E., & Harris, K. C. (1993). *The educational consultant: Helping professionals, parents, and mainstreamed students* (3rd ed.). Austin, TX: PRO–ED.

Heward, W. L. (1996). *Exceptional Children* (5th ed.). Upper Saddle River, NJ: Merrill/Prentice Hall.

Heward, W. L., & Chapman, J. E. (1981). Improving parent–teacher communication through recorded telephone messages: Systematic replication in a special education classroom. *Journal of Special Education Technology, 4*, 11–19.

Hoover, J. J., & Patton, J. R. (1997). *Curriculum adaptations for students with learning and behavior problems: Principles and practices* (2nd ed.). Austin, TX: PRO-ED.

Hoover, J. J. & Patton, J. R. (1995). *Teaching students with learning problems to use study skills: A teachers' guide*. Austin, TX: PRO-ED.

Hresko, W. P., & Brown, L. L. (1984). *Test of early socioemotional development*. Austin, TX: PRO-ED.

Hudson, F. G., & Colson, S. E. (1989). *Hudson education skills inventory—mathematics*. Austin, TX: PRO-ED.

Hughes, C. A. (1997). Memory and test-taking strategies. In D. D. Deshler, E. S. Ellis, & B. K. Lenz (Eds.), *Teaching adolescents with learning disabilities* (2nd ed., pp. 209–266). Denver: Love Publishing.

Hughes, C. A., Ruhl, K. L., Deshler, D. D., & Schumaker, J. B. (1993). Test-taking strategy instruction for adolescents with emotional and behavioral disorders. *Journal of Emotional and Behavioral Disorders*, 1, 189–198.

Hutton, J. B., & Roberts, T. G. (1986). *Social-emotional dimension scale: A measure of school behavior.* Austin, TX: PRO-ED.

Idol, L. (1987). A critical thinking map to improve content area comprehension of peer readers. *Learning Disability Quarterly*, 10, 214–229.

Idol, L., Nevin, A., Paolucci–Whitcomb, P. P. (1994). *Collaborative consultation* (2nd ed.). Austin, TX: PRO–ED.

Idol, L., & West, J. F. (1987). Consultation in special education (Part II): Training and practice. *Journal of Learning Disabilities*, 20, 474–494.

Idol–Maestas, L. (1983). *Special educator's consultation handbook*. Rockville, MD: Aspen.

Idol-Maestas, L., Lloyd, S., & Lilly, M. S. (1981). Implementation of a noncategorical approach to direct service and teacher education. *Exceptional Children*, 48, 213–219.

Idol–Maestas, L., & Ritter, S. (1985). A follow-up study of resource/consulting teachers: Factors that facilitate and inhibit teacher consultation. *Teacher Education and Special Education*, 8, 121–131.

Imber-Black, E. (1988). *Families and larger systems*. New York: Guilford.

Individuals with Disabilities Act Amendments of 1997, PL 105-17.

Individuals with Disabilities Education Act of 1990, 20 U.S.C. §1401 *et seq*.

Jenkins, J. R., & Jenkins, L. (1985). Peer tutoring in elementary and secondary programs. *Focus on Exceptional Children*, 17(6), 1–12.

Johnson, D. W. (1996). *Reaching out: Interpersonal effectiveness and self-actualization* (6th ed.). Boston: Allyn & Bacon.

Johnson, D. W., & Johnson, R. T. (1986). Mainstreaming and cooperative learning strategies. *Exceptional Children*, 52, 553–561.

Johnson, L. J., Pugach, M. C., & Hammittee, D. J. (1988). Barriers to effective special education consultation. *Remedial and Special Education*, 9(6), 41–47.

Jones, B. F., Palincsar, A. S., Ogle, D. S., & Carr, E. G. (1987). *Strategic teaching and learning: Cognitive instruction in the content areas*. Washington DC: Association of Supervision and Curriculum Development.

Kameenui, E. J. (1993). Diverse learners and the tyranny of time: Don't fix the leaky roof. *Reading Teacher*, 20, 376–383.

Kameenui, E. J., & Simmons, D. C. (1990). *Designing instructional strategies: The prevention of academic learning problems*. Upper Saddle River, NJ: Merrill/Prentice Hall.

Kanfer, F. H., & Gaelick, L. (1986). Self-management methods. In F. H. Kanfer & A. P. Goldstein (Eds.), *Helping people change: A textbook of methods* (3rd ed., pp. 283-345). Tarrytown, NY: Pergamon.

Kanfer, F. H., & Grimm, L. G. (1977). Behavioral analysis: Selecting target behaviors in the interview. *Behavior Modification*, 1, 7–28.

Kauffman, J. M. (1997). *Characteristics of emotional and behavioral disorders of children and youth* (6th ed.). Upper Saddle River, NJ: Merrill/Prentice Hall.

Kauffman, J. M., Mostert, M. P., Trent, S. C., & Hallahan, D. P. (1998). *Managing classroom behavior: A reflective case-based approach*. (2nd ed.). Boston: Allyn & Bacon.
Kazdin, A. E. (1977). *The token economy: A review and evaluation*. New York: Plenum.
Kindsvatter, R., Wilen, W., & Ishler, M. (1988). *Dynamics of effective teaching*. New York: Longman.
King-Sears, M. E. (1994). *Curriculum-based assessment in special education*. San Diego, CA: Singular Publishing Group.
Knackendoffel, E. A. (1996). Collaborative teaming in the secondary school. In D. D. Deshler, E. S. Ellis, & B. K. Lenz (Eds.), *Teaching adolescents with learning disabilities: Strategies and methods* (2nd ed., pp. 579–616). Denver: Love Publishing.
Kurprius, D. (1978). Consultative theory and process: An integrated model. *Personnel and Guidance Journal*, 56, 335–338.
Laughlon, J., & Morris, N. T. (1989). Story grammar knowledge of learning disabled students. *Learning Disabilities Research*, 4, 87–95.
Laurie, T. E., Buchwach, L., Silverman, R., & Zigmond, N. (1978). Teaching secondary learning disabled students in the mainstream. *Learning Disability Quarterly*, 1(4), 62–72
Leinhardt, G., Zigmond, N., & Cooley, W. W. (1981). Reading instruction and its effects. *American Educational Research Journal*, 18, 343–366.
Lemlech, J. K. (1988). *Classroom management methods and techniques for elementary and secondary teachers*. (2nd ed.). Prospect Heights, IL: Waveland Press, Inc.
Lerner, J. (1997). *Learning disabilities: Theories, diagnosis, and teaching strategies* (7th ed.). New York: Houghton Mifflin.
Levin, J., & Nolan, J. F. (1996). *Principles of classroom management: A professional decision-making model* (2nd ed.). Boston: Allyn & Bacon.
Levine, M. D. (1990). *Keeping a head in school: A student's book about learning abilities and learning disorders*. Cambridge, MA: Educators Publishing Service.
Lewis, R. B., & Doorlag, D. H. (1999). *Teaching special students in the mainstream* (5th ed.). Upper Saddle River, NJ: Merrill/Prentice Hall.
Lieberman, L. M. (1985). Special education and regular education: A merger made in heaven? *Exceptional Children*, 51, 513–516.
Lilly, M. S. (1986, October). The relationship between general and special education: A new face on an old issue. *Counterpoint*, 6(1).
Lippitt, G. L. (1969). *Organizational renewal*. New York: Appleton Century Crofts.
Lyon, G. R. (1995). *Learning disabilities*. In E. Marsh & R. Barkley (Eds.), *Childhood psychopathology* (pp. 283–242). New York: Guilford Press.
Madden, N. A., & Slavin, R. E. (1983). Mainstreaming students with mild handicaps: Academic and social outcomes. *Review of Educational Research*, 53, 519–569.
Maeroff, G. I. (1988). *The empowerment of teachers: Overcoming the crisis of confidence*. New York: Teachers College Press.
Maheady, L., Sacca, M. K., & Harper, G. F. (1988). Classwide peer tutoring with mildly handicapped high school students. *Exceptional Children*, 55, 52–59.
Mann, V. (1991). Language problems: A key to early reading problems. In B. Y. L. Wong (Ed.), *Learning about learning disabilities* (pp. 129–162). San Diego: Academic Press.
Mastropieri, M. A., & Scruggs, T. E. (1994). *Effective instruction for special education*. (2nd ed.). Austin, TX: PRO-ED.
Mathes, P. G., Fuchs, D., Fuchs, L., Henley, A. M., & Sanders, A. (1994). Increasing strategic reading practice with Peabody Classwide Peer Tutoring. *Learning Disabilities Research and Practice*, 9, 44–48.
McCarney, S. B., & Leigh, J. E. (1990). *Behavior evaluation scale—2*. Columbia, MO: Hawthorne Educational Services.

McNamara, J. R., & Diehl, L. A. (1974). Behavioral consultation with a Head Start program. *Journal of Community Psychology, 2*, 352–357.

McRobbie, J. (1992). *Using portfolios to assess student performance* (Knowledge Brief #9). California: Far West Laboratory for Educational Research and Development.

Meichenbaum, D. (1977). *Cognitive behavior modification: An integrative approach*. New York: Plenum.

Mercer, C. D. (1997). *Students with learning disabilities* (5th ed.). Upper Saddle River, NJ: Merrill/Prentice Hall.

Mercer, C. D., & Mercer, A. R. (1998). *Teaching students with learning problems* (5th ed.). Upper Saddle River, NJ: Merrill/Prentice Hall.

Mesinger, J. F. (1985). Commentary on "A rationale for the merger of special and regular education" or, is it now time for the lamb to lie down with the lion? *Exceptional Children, 51*, 510–512.

Meyer, C. A. (1992). What's the difference between authentic and performance assessment? *Educational Leadership, 49*(8), 39–40.

Meyers, J., Parson, R. D., & Martin, R. (1979). *Mental health consultation in the schools*. San Francisco: Jossey-Bass.

Miller S. E., Leinhardt G., & Zigmond, N. (1988). Influencing engagement through accommodation: An ethnographic study of at-risk students. *American Educational Research Journal, 25*, 465–488.

Miller, S., Crawford, C., Harniss, M. K., Hollenbeck, K., & Carnine, D. W. (1997). Effective strategies for teaching social studies. In E. Kameenui & D. Carnine (Eds.), *Effective teaching strategies that accommodate diverse learners* (pp. 139–160). Upper Saddle River, NJ: Merrill/Prentice Hall.

National Association of State Boards of Education. (1992). *Winners all: A call for inclusive schools*. Alexandria, VA: Author.

Nodine, B. F., Barenbaum, E., & Newcomer, P. (1985). Story composition by learning disabled, reading disabled and normal children. *Learning Disability Quarterly, 8*, 167–179.

Nowacek, E. J. (1992). Professionals talk about teaching together: Interview with five collaborating teachers. *Intervention in School and Clinic, 27*, 262–276.

O'Connor, P. D., Stuck, G. B., & Wyne, M. D. (1983). Effects of a short-term interaction resource room program on task orientation and achievement. *Journal of Special Education, 13*, 375–385.

Olson, J. L., & Platt, J. M. (1996). *Teaching children and adolescents with special needs* (2nd ed.). Upper Saddle River, NJ: Merrill/Prentice Hall.

Owens, R. E., Jr. (1992). *Language development: An introduction* (3rd ed.). Upper Saddle River, NJ: Merrill/Prentice Hall.

Partanen, J. N. (1993). *Academic experiences of secondary students in special education and regular education classes*, unpublished doctoral dissertation. University of Pittsburgh, Pittsburgh, PA.

Polloway, E. A., & Patton, J. R. (1997). *Strategies for teaching learners with special needs* (6th ed.). Upper Saddle River, NJ: Merrill/Prentice-Hall.

Poteet, J. A., Choate, J. S., & Stewart, S. (1996). Performance assessment and special education: Practices and prospects. In E. L. Meyen, G. A. Vergason, & R. J. Whelan (Eds.), *Strategies for teaching exceptional children in inclusive settings* (pp. 209–242). Denver: Love Publishing.

Prillaman, D. (1981). Acceptance of learning disabled students in the mainstream environment: A failure to replicate. *Journal of Learning Disabilities, 14*, 344–346.

Pugach, M. C., & Johnson, L. J. (1995). Teacher's and students' views of team teaching of general education and learning disabled students in two fifth grade classes. *The Elementary School Journal, 95*, 279–295.

Pugach, M. C., & Johnson, L. J. (1995). *Collaborative practitioners: Collaborative schools*. Denver: Love Publishing.

Pugach, M. C., & Wesson, C. (1995). Teachers' and students' views of team teaching of general education and learning disabled students in two fifth grade classes. *Elementary School Journal, 95*, 279–295.

Quay, H. C., & Peterson, D. R. (1987). *Revised behavior problem checklist*. Odessa, FL: Psychology Assessment Resource.

Rehabilitation Act of 1973. (1973). 29 U.S.C. § 794.

Reid, R. (1996). Research in self-monitoring with students with learning disabilities: The present, the prospects, the pitfalls. *Journal of Learning Disabilities*, 29, 317–331.

Reynolds, M. C., Wang, M. C., & Walberg, H. J. (1987). The necessary restructuring of special and regular education. *Exceptional Children*, 53, 391–398.

Rief, S. F. (1993). *How to reach and teach ADD/ADHD children*. West Nyack, NY: The Center for Applied Research in Education.

Rivera, D. P., & Smith, D. D. (1997). *Teaching students with learning and behavior problems* (3rd ed.). Boston: Allyn & Bacon.

Rodgers, C. R. (1959). A theory of therapy, personality, and interpersonal relationships, as developed in the client-centered framework. In S. Koch (Ed.), *Psychology: A study of science: Vol. II Formulations of the personal and social concept*. New York: McGraw Hill.

Rosenberg, M. S., O'Shea, L., & O'Shea, D. J. (1991). *Student teacher to master teacher: A handbook for preservice and beginning teachers of students with mild and moderate handicaps*. Upper Saddle River, NJ: Merrill/Prentice Hall.

Rosenfield, S. A. (1987). *Instructional consultation*. Hillsdale, NJ: Erlbaum.

Rosenshine, B., & Stevens, R. (1986). Teaching functions. In M. C. Wittock (Ed.), *Handbook of research on teaching* (pp. 376–391). Upper Saddle River, NJ: Merrill/Prentice Hall.

Sabornie, E. J., & deBettencourt, L. U. (1997). *Teaching students with mild disabilities at the secondary level*. Upper Saddle River, NJ: Merrill/Prentice Hall.

Salend, S. J. (1998). *Effective mainstreaming* (3rd ed.). Upper Saddle River, NJ: Merrill/Prentice Hall.

Salend, S. J., & Gordon, B. (1987). A group-oriented timeout ribbon procedure. *Behavioral Disorders*, 12, 131–137.

Schmuck, R. A., & Runkel, P. J. (1985). *The handbook of organization development in schools* (3rd ed.). Palo Alto, CA: Mayfield Publishing.

Schultz, T. (1974). Development of the appreciation of riddles. *Child Development*, 45, 100–105.

Schumaker, J. B., Denton, R. H., & Deshler, D. D. (1984). The paraphrasing strategy (learning strategies curriculum). Lawrence, KS: University of Kansas.

Schumaker, J. B., Deshler, D. D., Alley, G. R., & Denton, P. H. (1982). Multipass: A learning strategy for improving reading comprehension. *Learning Disability Quarterly*, 5, 295–304.

Schumaker, J. B., Nolan, S. M., & Deshler, D. D. (1985). *The error monitoring strategy*. Lawrence, KS: University of Kansas

Scott, J., & Smith, S. C. (1988). *From isolation to collaboration: Improving the work environment of teaching*. Elmhurst: IL: North Central Regional Educational Laboratory.

Scruggs, T. E., & Mastropieri, M. A. (1988). Are learning-disabled students "test-wise?": A review of recent research. *Learning Disabilities Focus*, 3, 87–97.

Semmel, M. I., Abernathy, T. V., Butera, G., & Lesar, S. (1991). Teacher perceptions of the regular education initiative. *Exceptional Children*, 58, 9–25.

Shanker, J. L., & Ekwall, E. E. (1998). *Locating and correcting reading difficulties* (7th ed.). Upper Saddle River, NJ: Merrill/Prentice Hall.

Silverman, R., Zigmond, N., & Sansone, J. (1981). Teaching coping skills: A school survival skills curriculum for adolescents with learning disabilities. *Focus on Exceptional Children*, 13(6), 1–20.

Silverman, R., Zigmond, N., Zimmerman, J., & Vallecorsa, A. (1981). Improving written expression in learning disabled students. *Topics in Language Disorders*, 1, 91–99.

Slavin, R. E. (1984). Team–assisted individualization: Cooperative learning and individualized instruction in the mainstreamed classroom. *Remedial and Special Education*, 5(6), 33–42.

Slavin, R. E. (1988). *Student team learning: An overview and practical guide* (2nd ed.). Washington, DC: National Education Association.

Smith, T. E. C., & Dowdy, C. A. (1989). The role of study skills in the secondary curriculum. *Academic Therapy, 24*, 479–490.

Smith, T. E. C., Polloway, E. A., Patton, J. R., & Dowdy, C. A. (1995). *Teaching students with special needs in inclusive settings*. Boston: Allyn & Bacon.

Smith, T. E. C., Polloway, E. A., Patton, J. R., & Dowdy, C. A. (1998). *Teaching students with special needs in inclusive settings*. (2nd ed.). Boston: Allyn & Bacon.

Spache, G. D. (1981). *Diagnostic Reading Scales*. Monterey, CA: CTB Macmillan/McGraw Hill.

Special education costs about twice the price of regular education. (1988). *Education of the Handicapped, 14*, 1–4.

Stainback, W., & Stainback, S. (1984). A rationale for the merger of special and regular education. *Exceptional Children, 51*, 102–111.

Stake, R. E. (1978). The case study method of social inquiry. *Educational Research, 2*, 5–8.

Stanovitch, K. E. (1991). Word recognition: Changing perspectives. In R. Barr, M. L. Kamil, P. B. Mosenthal, & P. D. Pearson (Eds.), *Handbook of reading research* (Vol. 2, pp. 418–452). New York: Longman.

Stanovich, K. E. (1992). Speculations on the causes and consequences of individual assumptions and their implications for reading instruction. In P. B. Gough, L. C. Ehri, & R. Treiman (Eds.), *Reading acquisition* (pp. 307–342). Hillsdale, NJ: Erlbaum.

Stevens, R., & Slavin, R. (1991). When cooperative learning improves the achievement of students with mild disabilities: A response to Tateyama–Sniezek. *Exceptional Children, 57*, 276–280.

Stodolsky, S. S. (1984). *The subject matters*. Chicago: University of Chicago Press.

Strichart, S. S., & Mangrum, C. T. III (1993). *Teaching study strategies to students with learning disabilities*. Boston: Allyn & Bacon.

Strichart, S. S., Mangrum, C. T. III, & Iannuzzi, P. (1998). *Teaching study skills and strategies to students with learning disabilities, attention deficit disorders, or special needs* (2nd ed.). Boston: Allyn & Bacon.

Sugai, G. M., & Tindal, G. A. (1993). *Effective school consultation: An interactive approach*. Pacific Grove, CA: Brooks/Cole.

Suritsky, S. K., & Hughes, C. A. (1997). Note-taking strategy instruction. In D. D. Deshler, E. S. Ellis, & B. K. Lenz (Eds.)., *Teaching adolescents with learning disabilities* (2nd ed., pp. 267–312). Denver: Love Publishing.

Tangel, D. M., & Blackman, B. A. (1992). Effect of phoneme awareness instruction on kindergarten children's invented spelling. *Journal of Reading Behavior, 24*, 233–261.

Tateyama–Sniezek, K. M. (1990). Cooperative learning: Does it improve the academic achievement of students with handicaps? *Exceptional Children, 56*, 426–437.

Todd, J. (1967). The Ohio program for neurologically handicapped children. In J. I. Arena (Ed.), *Management of the child with learning disabilities: An interdisciplinary challenge* (pp. 109–112). Pittsburgh: Association for Children with Learning Disabilities.

Torgesen, J. K. (1985). Memory process in reading disabled children. *Journal of Learning Disabilities, 18*, 350–357.

Turnbull, A. P., & Turnbull, H. R. III. (1997). *Families, professionals, and exceptionality: A special partnership*. Upper Saddle River, NJ: Merrill/Prentice Hall.

Turnbull, H. R., & Turnbull, A. P. (1998). *Free appropriate public education: The law and children with disabilities* (5th ed.), Denver: Love Publishing.

U. S. Department of Education. (n.d.). *America 2000: An educational strategy*. Washington, DC: Author.

U. S. Department of Education. (1996). *Eighteenth annual report to Congress on the implementation of the Individuals with Disabilities Education Act*. Washington, DC: Author.

U. S. Department of Education (1997). Nineteenth annual report to Congress on the implementation of the Individuals with Disabilities Education Act, Washington, DC: Government Printing Office.

U. S. Department of Health, Education and Welfare. (1979). A *report to Congress on the implementation of Public Law 94-142: The Education of All Handicapped Children Act*, Washington, DC: Government Printing Office.

Vallecorsa, A., & deBettencourt, L. U. (1997). Using a mapping procedure to teach reading and writing skills to middle-grade students with learning disabilities. *Education and Treatment of Children*, 20, 173–188.

Vallecorsa, A., & Garriss, E. (1990). Story composition skills of middle-grade students with learning disabilities. *Exceptional Children*, 57, 48–56.

Vaughn, S., & Wilson, C. (1994). Mathematics assessment for students with learning disabilities. In G. R. Lyon (Ed.), *Frames of reference for the assessment of learning disabilities* (pp. 459–472). Baltimore: Paul Brookes.

Veit, D. T., & Scruggs, T. E. (1986). Can LD Students effectively use separate answer sheets? *Perceptual and Motor Skills*, 63, 155–160.

Voltz, D. L., Elliott, R. N. Jr., & Cobb, H. B. (1994). Collaborative teacher roles: Special and general educators. *Journal of Learning Disabilities*, 27, 527–535.

Wade, S. E. (1990). Using think alouds to assess comprehension. *Reading Teacher*, 43, 442–451.

Wade, S. E., Trathen, W., & Schraw, G. (1990). An analysis of spontaneous study strategies. *The Reading Research Quarterly*, 25, 149–166.

Walker, H. M., & Walker, J. E. (1991). *Coping with noncompliance in the classroom: A positive approach for teachers*. Austin, TX: PRO-ED.

Wallace, G., Larsen, S. C., & Elksnin, L. K. (1992). *Educational assessment of learning problems: Testing for teaching* (2nd ed.). Boston: Allyn & Bacon.

Welch, M., & Sheridan, S. M. (1995). *Educational partnerships: Serving students at risk*. Fort Worth: Harcourt Brace.

West, J. F., & Idol, L. (1990). Collaborative consultation in the education of mildly handicapped and at-risk students. *Remedial and Special Education*, 11(1), 22–31.

Will, M. C. (1986). Educating children with learning problems: A shared responsibility. *Exceptional Children*, 52, 411–415.

Wilson, S. (1977). The use of ethnographic techniques in educational research. *Review of Educational Research*, 47, 245–265.

Wittrock, M. C. (Ed.). (1986). *Handbook of research on teaching* (3rd ed.). Upper Saddle River, NJ: Merrill/Prentice Hall.

Wolery, M. R., Bailey, D. B. Jr., & Sugai, G. (1988). *Effective teaching: Principles and procedures of applied behavior analysis with exceptional students*. Boston: Allyn & Bacon.

Wolf, K. (1991, October). The schoolteacher's portfolio: Issues in design, implementation, and evaluation. *Phi Delta Kappan*, 129–136.

Wong, B. Y. L. (1987). Directions in future research on metacognition in learning disabilities. In H. L. Swanson (Ed.), *Memory and learning disabilities: Advances in learning and behavioral disabilities* (pp. 335–356). Greenwich, CT: JAI Press.

Wood, J. W. (1998). *Adapting instruction to accommodate students in inclusive settings*. Upper Saddle River, NJ: Merrill/Prentice Hall.

Yell, M. L. (1998). *The law and special education*. Upper Saddle River, NJ: Merrill/Prentice Hall.

Ysseldyke, J. E., & Algozzine, B. (1983). LD or not LD: That's not the question. *Journal of Learning Disabilities*, 16, 29–31.

Ysseldyke, J. E., & Algozzine, B. (1995). *Special education: A practical approach for teachers* (3rd ed.). Boston: Houghton Mifflin.

Ysseldyke, J. E., & Christenson, S. L. (1987). Evaluating students' instructional environments. *Remedial and Special Education*, 8(3), 17–24.

Ysseldyke, J. E., & Christenson, S. L. (1993). The instructional environment scale (TIES) (2nd ed.). Austin, TX: PRO-ED.

Zabrucky, K., & Ratner, H. H. (1992). Effects of passage type on comprehension monitoring and recall in good and poor readers. *Journal of Reading Behavior*, 24, 373–391.

Zigmond, N. (1978). A prototype of comprehensive services for secondary students with learning disabilities: A preliminary report. *Learning Disability Quarterly*, 1, 39–49.

Zigmond, N., & Baker, J. (Eds.). (1995). An exploration of the meaning and practice of special education in the context of full inclusion of students with learning disabilities [Special Issue] *The Journal of Special Education*, 29.

Zigmond, N., & Miller S. E. (1992). Improving high school programs for students with learning disabilities: A matter of substance as well as form. In F. Rusch, L. DeStefanc, J. Chadsey-Rusch, L. Phelps, & E. Szymanski (Eds.), *Transition from school to adult life* (pp. 17–33). Sycamore Publishing.

Zigmond, N., Vallecorsa, A., & Silverman, R. (1983). *Assessment for instructional planning in special education*. Upper Saddle River, NJ: Merrill/Prentice-Hall.

NAME INDEX

SUBJECT INDEX